THE MATRIX OF FAITH

The Matrix of Faith

RECLAIMING A CHRISTIAN VISION

JEFFREY C. PUGH

A Crossroad Book
The Crossroad Publishing Company
New York

The Crossroad Publishing Company
481 Eighth Avenue, New York, NY 10001

Chapter 3 is a revised version of "*Fides Quaerens Intellectum:* Anselm as Contemporary," published in *Theology Today* 55, no. 1 (April 1998).

Printed in the United States of America

Library of Congress Cataloging-in-Publication Data
Pugh, Jeffrey C., 1952–
    The matrix of faith : reclaiming a Christian vision / Jeffrey C. Pugh.
       p. cm.
    Includes bibliographical references.
    ISBN 0-8245-1898-5 (alk. paper)
    1. Theology, Doctrinal. I. Title.
    BT75.2 .P82 2000
    230 – dc21   00-011230

1 2 3 4 5 6 7 8 9 10   10 09 08 07 06 05 04 03 02 01

To Jan,
whose love and compassion
bring much healing to the world

Contents

Contents

Preface

W HEN I WAS TELLING a colleague about this project, his response was something along the lines of "Why are you wasting your time with dead white guys?" There was laughter, but the intent behind the remark is one of the reasons I wrote this book. My response was that the past informs the present, and we are never truly done with it. This book is not just about the past; it is also about the present and the future, specifically, whether or not Christianity has a future in our world. But, for better or worse, we have been shaped by the voices of the past, and many of us have no idea how strong that shaping has been.

The figures chosen in this book represent some of the most pivotal moments of that shaping. This is not to neglect those voices of men and women who have other ways of telling the story of Christian faith. Theologians and thinkers of many different communities are presently engaged in recovering some of the lost voices of the tradition through their discovery of the stories of those who were on the edges of the formation of the Christian tradition. They are also creating new and diverse streams of Christian tradition. Those perspectives inform and are found throughout the pages of this book. But we cannot neglect those whom we now critique, for we need to know where we come from.

The question of whether Christianity has a future is a serious one, and I am not sure it has an answer yet. One of the main themes in this book is that Christianity's future may well rest with its past, but a past that has been lost to us because it did not participate in the controlling of the institutional life of Christianity. The irony of this book is that it deals with people who did have a role in that formation. They are questioned as well for what they have brought to us.

But even in the midst of these questions I have asked about the ways in which they may have something of value for us to reflect on in the world in which we live. We may think that much harm was done by those like Aquinas or Augustine, but perhaps this is because we have failed to consider how we might understand them in a different way. This is true with all of the figures in this book. Because they are seen as the formers of tradition we can too easily overlook their contributions when we no longer see the need to adhere to the tradition they shaped.

This is the attitude of many in the Western world today. Christianity seems to have no visible impact on the world in which we live. It is a world of massive violence, inequity of wealth, over-consumption of resources, and environmental abuse. This world is marked by rapidly shifting cultures and technologies, causing us to constantly be aiming at a moving target. It is also a world of tremendous beauty and potential. The tensions we live within come from the fact that while we have used our abilities to construct a world of technological achievement and mastery, we have lost sight of our need for the spiritual resources to live in it humanely and justly.

It is this world I have tried to describe briefly in this book. In doing so I have used a term that is notorious for its fluidity: "postmodern." In fact this word probably means what anyone who is using it at the time wants it to mean, but I have tried to give it a contextual meaning by describing the world to which it belongs. If the reader wants a shorthand definition, then maybe "postmodern" means the time we are presently in. I hope that my use of this term will not be read in an ideological way; it is only meant to indicate that we live in a time of great change and flux.

This book is a great risk as well. I realize that many may be disappointed in the brevity with which the figures of this book are treated. Certainly no scholar of Augustine would be happy with the attempt to treat his thought in such a small space. But the purpose of this book is not to treat all these figures adequately as much as it is to take one small part of their thought and suggest that they still have something for us to consider today. In truth, if readers become intrigued enough with this tiny sliver, I hope they will seek out the whole pie.

This book is written for all those who wonder if Christianity has a place in the world and for those who believe they know what that place is. I believe there are many useful things that the present-day critique is bringing to us that we can use for thinking about faith, but I also believe that postmodernity, while a useful corrective, should never become normative. I have tried to indicate why in this book, but as a way of anticipating what is to come I would like to say that my treatment of the various theologians in this book is done with the belief that even in the midst of so much that is partial, fragmentary, and socially located, something shines through that seems to transcend all human constructs.

Sometimes it comes in the lives of people who mirror the best of humanity and call us to a brighter vision than the one we are presently captivated by. Sometimes it comes in the moments of realization that we have of our connectedness and responsibility to all that is and our sense that we truly are co-creators with God of a world that is constantly emerging before our eyes. And then there are those grace moments in life where love overcomes hate, forgiveness overcomes bitterness, peace overturns war. In those moments we are aware of something that subverts business as usual, and it is in those movements of God's spirit that we glimpse another way.

It can be a risky business to use the past to explore the present and the present to interpret the past, but I think the risk is worth it. I hope that future generations will not dismiss us as creatures of our own time, bound by the chains of historical location, for there is that about the human spirit that lives through all times and touches us all. We will impact those who come after us, but let us hope that we will do so with the wisdom gained from our struggles and not the foolishness that results when we seek only that which benefits ourselves and no others.

In all of life we owe great amounts of gratitude to those who have been agents of grace in our lives. I have more debts than I can repay, but I would like to get a start on them by expressing my gratitude for the many who read parts or all of this manuscript in its many manifestations. I especially am appreciative of Professors Stanley Hauerwas and Larry Rasmussen for their helpful remarks and encouragements. I am also grateful to my colleagues at Elon College who read parts of this manuscript, notably Professors James Pickens, Anthony Weston, L. D. Russell, John Sullivan, and his wife, Gregg. Thomas Tiemann, Paul Miller, and Steven Deloach have provided encouragement and support for this project almost daily. I also am deeply appreciative of my department and our chair, J. Christian Wilson, who read parts of this text and offered helpful suggestions. I also wish to express my appreciation to Elon College for the sabbatical semester in which this book first started coming into view.

Not only my colleagues at Elon, however, but my students were helpful in responding to this book. Special thanks go to Andrew Villwock, who read the entire work and commented on it. I also thank JoAnn Barbour, Tatiana Malatesta, Darice Fichter, and the students of my modern theology class in the spring of 1999.

Without the vision of Paul McMahon of Crossroad this book may never have seen the light of day. He has worked with patience and care to see that the book was done the way I had hoped, and I am thankful for his help. The work of John Eagleson was invaluable in helping me better to communicate my position.

Above all I am deeply grateful for the wisdom and grace that I have been granted in the presence of my wife, Jan Rivero. Her patience as I was struggling with this book, her comments about the book that caused me to rework the material, the faith she expresses in her work in campus ministry have all been inspirational to me as I have moved through this project. But most importantly it is in her ability to love this world that she most deeply influences this book. Her children, Kristen and Ryan, have enriched my life as well with their presence. Finally, this work is influenced by the questions and faith of my daughters, Joy and Miriam, and Miriam's family, Ben and Benjamin. They have moved into the world in ways that have brought grace to those they know and love, and I pray it will always be so for them, for they have graced my life tremendously.

Elon College
Advent 2000

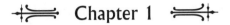

Chapter 1

Unplugging from the Matrix
Waking Up to the New World

> The tree which moves some to tears of joy is in the eyes of others
> Only a Green thing which stands in the way.
> — WILLIAM BLAKE, *Letter to Dr. Trusler*, 1799

I N THE SPRING OF 1999 a movie was released which became something of a sleeper hit that year. After much urging by my students I decided to go see *The Matrix*. As I watched the movie and reflected on my students' enthusiastic reception of it, I realized that whatever the term "postmodern" might mean, the world my students knew was a part of something far different from the world where I was located. They are on the edge of a new world, a world of virtual reality and computers, a world that would have seemed incomprehensible save in science fiction stories.

In the movie, the main character, Neo, is approached by a woman named Trinity. He is a computer programmer, hacker, and subterranean outlaw. She is an emissary from another figure, Morpheus, and has come to Neo in the hopes that he is the so-called "Chosen One." As the story proceeds, Neo discovers that his entire existence has been stimulated as part of a computer program plugged into his neural network. Machines built with artificial intelligence have taken over control of the world, and they are cultivating human life for an energy source. Neo's entire life has been spent in suspended animation while his world of experiences has been constructed by a computer program plugged into his cerebral cortex. He is in truth nothing more than a glorified battery. Only a few persons have escaped this storage facility and found another reality outside of the computer generated matrix that keeps people unaware of their true status.

Neo becomes enlightened, an "awakened one," when he accepts Morpheus's offer to become liberated. Morpheus and his crew are

1

able to plug into the matrix using their own equipment and operate both within and without the computer reality, but the matrix affects their bodies, and death in the matrix can mean death in the real world.

The conflict of the story emerges in the contest between the forces who created the matrix and those who have become aware of their true situation. Neo, as the supposed "Chosen One," is able to master the matrix in such a way that he is able at the end of the movie to establish the parameters of what is possible in the matrix, thereby wresting control of the matrix from its creators.

The movie plays off differing constructions of reality and leaves the viewer feeling slightly disoriented. Of course, one of the questions asked in the movie is whether it is better just to accept the matrix as your reality and enjoy it. Wine tastes wonderful, food is exquisite, sex feels good, and who really is in charge doesn't seem all that important. Who cares if you are lying in a cubicle of chemicals, waiting to be farmed for the purposes of being a living Duracell battery? After all, reality is relative, and one could just as easily be as valid and useful as other possible realities.

In some ways the movie can be seen as a parable of postmodernity. Reality isn't what it used to be, and probably isn't close to what it will be, because realities have become increasingly diverse in the world. Not only the realities, but the very way we understand them has changed. It used to be so simple. My worldview was what I structured my life around. It was a given; there were cherished communal assumptions that just were not questioned. The world is not so simple anymore. There are competing, conflicting realities to contend with, and how we adjudicate those perspectives is not as obvious as it used to be. Like Neo, we woke up to a new world, and nothing seems the same comfortable place we were used to.

The world we woke up to was far different, with the realization that human societies had no small role in constructing reality and legitimating its own perspective over and against other realities. It is this world which has been labeled by many the postmodern. However, this has been a notoriously difficult term to define with any precision. It usually means whatever the person using it wishes it to mean, reflective of the wish we have to control terms and discourse. "Postmodernity" is a term that is extremely fluid and hard to give any definitive understanding. This is only one of the reasons that the use of the word can be so frustrating. But it must be given its due because while the definitions differ according to who is doing the defining, there is a notion that we are sailing into uncharted waters today, and no one really has a compass or fix on where we are going.

It is a makeshift word, carrying the baggage of so many agendas. For many it can denote funny architecture, or perhaps the nonlinear framing of a movie like *Pulp Fiction*. Or it may raise images of obscure French philosophers with names like Derrida or Foucault, who write in impenetrable language and seem to have left common sense at the door to the bar. Maybe the postmodern in contemporary culture means anything that juxtaposes styles, cultures, traditions. It is Star Trek meets Star Wars.

In truth, academic fashions come and go, but the situation the term "postmodern" is trying to describe remains with us. The supposed "culture wars" described by James Davidson Hunter are only one battleground upon which this is being played out: the forces of orthodoxy, represented by those who see reality as a fairly simple grasping of what is there to be grasped, absolute ethics and morals, versus the forces of progressivism, where reality is a little harder to come by.[1] The camp of reality against the camp of reality as a construct are engaged in classrooms, media, and political structures to shape and influence our world.

In this emerging new world, all the things, the artifacts of human society that we create, are containers of meaning. Our art, architecture, music, systems of knowledge, beliefs, even our clothes, are the spaces where our creative powers fashion the world. We are seeing the birth of a global superculture which impacts us all with its values, beliefs, and commerce. Barely aware sometimes of its existence we find a world that exists without boundaries, identities, or accountability, save to the shareholders. This culture has no ties to state or nation, no loyalty to anything other than making profit. It is fed by mass media which continually create new realities for us to live by, packaging and marketing a brave new world for us to embrace. McWorld is a place where cultural distinctions are being blurred by the covert takeover of life by Disney and McDonald's.

In this world, opinion is something to be manipulated and politics loses depth as all becomes a carnival, a theater of the absurd where politicians seek to spin stories and lives to create a view of reality in the psyche of individuals and nations. In their desire to create worldviews some politicians even opt for totalitarian control. Premier or president, cleric or guru, all will create an identity for you to embrace if you will just fall lockstep into the reality they fashion. Others, more democratic in nature, will seek to establish official social codes that everybody with common sense realizes are true and will adhere to. Once you comply with these rules you can become an accepted member of society, and perhaps you will gain great reward.

In the midst of this ferment intelligent persons take a hard look and decide they will take the way of irony. The intentional distancing of the self from public forms of life has reached the level of an art form in American culture. Late night shows like *The Letterman Show* or popular shows like *Seinfeld* show persons never invested in anything like an authentic commitment. They parody life around them, wink at the audience, and float in a state of detached amusement through the world. No real blood and guts moral conflict here, just the ironic laughter at living in a confused world.

There is a vague feeling of discomfort among many now because it feels as if the boundaries are less distinct. Cultural identities, personal identities, familial identities all seem to be in play. The communal glues of social structures—democracy, community, even love—seem to be less real, not as solid as they used to be. We increasingly meet different realities to consider. We used to know how to sort this out, but that doesn't seem to be the case anymore. What type of world are we living in?

In the movie *The Mission*, the story is told of a group of priests who established a mission to the Guarani Indians in the jungle region on the borders of Argentina and Paraguay in South America. Because of political considerations in Europe, the Roman Catholic Church, in the figure of a papal emissary, decides to allow the state to assume control of the mission territories. This decision in effect dooms the priests and the Indians to certain death. After a horrendous slaughter and destruction of tribal life the representatives of the church and state confront one another. The papal emissary questions the necessity of the violence and asks if it was all necessary. The politician answers that it was indeed necessary. The reason he gives is that "we live in the world, the world is thus." To which the emissary answers, "No, thus have we made the world, thus have I made it."

It is this notion of world shaping which drives the postmodern spirit to wander the present age looking closely at the world we have created and asking how we got here and where we are going. And perhaps, more importantly, asking what type of world we created that has brought us to this point of cloning, artificial intelligence, global warming, and technology growing so fast we do not have the spiritual ability to deal with it. Any examination of the contemporary world must begin with a view to the one being replaced. So, let us see how we built the world of modernity and then proceed to examine why it is that this world is apparently being replaced by something else.

Getting Here from There

Let us begin with a story. In the years of 1639–40 in the small Dutch town of Sontpoort, a young Frenchman was thinking, reflecting, and writing his reflections down on paper. He had fought in the Thirty Years' War and had watched the turmoil and suffering generated by the forces of religion and politics, always a deadly cocktail to imbibe. He was seeking a way for humankind to live unafflicted by the emotion, superstition, and destruction engendered by religion, politics, and other destructive habits of the human race. He was also concerned about other matters. His only child, an illegitimate daughter named Francine, died of fever at the age of five in 1640.

Since the Renaissance, a new understanding of humanity had been moving across the horizon of Europe, one that spoke of the autonomy of human beings. Rather than locating the self in the midst of social and institutional structures such as Christendom, the self was moving to the center of its own domain. Humankind possessed its own power, and fields of discovery lay in front of it.

In the emergence of the autonomous person knowledge was seen as the primary category for the reconceptualization of human existence. What René Descartes was concerned with sitting in the Dutch countryside was what the reliance upon external authorities had produced in the world. These authorities had authorized death and destruction on a massive scale. Not only that, these authorities, in the form of the Inquisition, had threatened the Italian Galileo with instruments of torture six years earlier because of his support of Copernican astronomy and then placed him under house arrest. He couldn't get his scientific masterpiece, *Dialogues on Two New Sciences,* published in Italy; it had to be smuggled to Holland. Descartes realized that another way for knowledge had to be found that did not rely on the whims of religious leaders and political rulers.

The new scientific theories were challenging believed assumptions about the world and were creating new ways of understanding life. Suspicion of external authorities was giving way to the self-authenticating power of critical reason and rigorous rationality. Whether conceived of by rationalists or empiricists, the power of the mind to offer certain knowledge was a central feature of the beginnings of the story of modernity.

René Descartes was struggling with his own intellectual chaos, having seen so much suffering and pain. He wanted a foundation, something secure, anchored to the real, the true bedrock of existence. Surely, he thought, there must be some Archimedean point that was fixed enough in the world that no one could dispute it. In fact, Descartes had articulated that center when he wrote that we must take everything we believe and subject it to doubt. The only thing he found that he could not doubt was that he was a thinking self doing the doubting. The progenitor of modernity had been created when he gave us the formula *cogito, ergo sum,* "I think, therefore I am." The human being was a thinking subject, a center of autonomous and rational power.

The consequences of this pivotal moment in the story we are telling are numerous and with us still. All that wasn't about the thinking subject was matter, and a dualism emerged which would shape the Western world. Matter was the domain of nature and the sciences were capable of exploring, experimenting with, discovering, and mastering that domain. No appeal to tradition, no external authority other than microscope or telescope need be consulted in order to understand the world.

In the world of the mind the empiricists, believing all knowledge was sensory, and the rationalists, believing truth resided in logically defensible and secure first truths (for instance, mathematics), staked out territory that would bring about the modern world. These approaches would lay out the directions for science that could incorporate both empiricism and rationalism in its ongoing quest for knowledge.

As the story progressed the names of Bacon, Copernicus, Galileo, Newton, and countless others would mark the narrative of courageous thinkers seeking to become unshackled from the superstitions and oppressions of religion. As these thinkers explored the world, they conceived of causal relations in a certain way. Mathematical formulations seemed to offer a great deal of pragmatic knowledge about the way the heavenly bodies moved. Sir Isaac Newton would take these principles and portray the cosmos as a mechanism, operating under laws that could be apprehended by the use of reason.

In this story of human enlightenment, thinkers became convinced that reality was objective and discoverable. Knowledge could be found that was universal and certain. Language, as a tool of discovery, was directly representational of reality and could be trusted to correspond with the ways that things really are. And so we created, through the power of our reason, a way of viewing the world that seemed so commonsense plausible it could not possibly be questioned by sane people.

Reality, like the truth in the television show *X-Files,* was "out there" and all we had to do was discover it. This world was graspable by language, observation, and experimentation. Any representation of the world that came through language or science was accurate and direct to such an extent that the world and words we used to describe it were connected.

As this picture of the material world was being painted by the inheritors of Descartes, another view of reality was being explored. While the external world was coming into focus, the internal world was also being examined. In the realm of the mind the rise of "critical" thought made its impact upon the surfaces of the landscape. Perhaps no greater crater was fashioned than the one by Immanuel Kant (1724–1804). Never straying far from his world of Königsberg, Germany, he was also interested in discovering how knowledge could be put on firm footing, but he was more interested in exploring the mines of rationalism.

One of the main questions that thinkers had been asking since Descartes (and even before him) was how the mind as a nonmaterial entity conformed itself to the objects in the world, which were material objects. Kant took another path to the resolution of this issue by asking how the world conformed itself to the mind. In his writings he rigorously examined human reason and showed that the mind was not merely a passive recipient of knowing, but was active in the process of knowing. While the senses may give us some of the data we need to know a thing, the mind categorizes, sorts, and organizes the data in such a way as to make sense of disconnected information.

So empirical knowledge was a product of the interaction of the senses with the organizing processes of the mind. But there were also other things that humans thought were real, but which were outside our empirical knowing and classification. These things existed apart from direct observation, where no sensory experience was possible. We might think of such things as the universe as a causal whole, or the human being as a free agent, or even something like the aesthetic experience of beauty, or the existence of morality transcendent to human creation. These are not empirically verifiable, but that does not necessarily preclude their existence.

Kant believed that while we have no direct path to knowledge of what he called noumenal things, we can use our rationality to make inferences about reality. Take the notion of human moral agency, for instance. While we have no direct knowledge of a freely acting self, I do see Janice Smith making moral decisions in her life. If this is observed in most of human life it must be a rational assumption to see human beings as moral agents. Kant even appealed to what he saw as the universal moral experience—that humans have this notion of what they ought to do. They have a sense that it is better to save life than to destroy it.

Kant was working in a particular cultural climate not too far removed from that of Descartes and Galileo. He was looking for the foundations upon which he could universalize a moral reasoning that could stand apart from the political and religious conflicts of Europe. Kant had no intention of banishing God from his system, but he said it was necessary to deny a certain understanding of knowledge to make room for faith. But this faith was not universal, whereas his categorical imperative (all actions should be judged on whether we want them to be applicable to all people at all times) was.

These years between Descartes and Kant were time spent rewriting a new story, a new narrative of how the world is. This story would leave an indelible mark on humankind, right down to the present age. One dimension of this mark was the enduring legacy of dualism on all forms of intellectual and cultural life. Dividing the world into realms of pure and practical reason, knowledge and faith, empirical reality and ethical action, science and religion, we have started schools of thought and cultural movements which take these divisions as their guiding principles. But perhaps more importantly we created a worldview that, once constructed, assumed the form of a given and true picture of reality to the minds of modernity.

The work of Descartes, Kant, and others who participated in the building of what has been called the "Enlightenment project" resulted in an illusion about how we understand the world. Even though Kant himself spoke of a boundary of understanding which rests outside our grasp, the die was cast. The creation of a supposedly universal human nature meant that such factors as social location, cultural limitation, and self-interests could be transcended in order to attain the supremely rational and universally reasonable precepts by which we should live. In this illusion it was one of humankind's most cherished beliefs that all people would know how to live and what to do if they would just follow those principles built on universal foundations, applicable to all people at all times. It is this world, this story, that is being replaced with something at once more unsettled, and yet more promising. We turn now to the questioning of the narrative bequeathed to us by the Enlightenment and the story which many feel is trying to take its place.

Reality Isn't What It Used to Be

Walter Truett Anderson, in his book *Reality Isn't What It Used to Be,* tells the joke of three umpires talking shop after one of their games. One says, "There's balls and there's strikes and I call them the way they are." Another responds, "There's balls and there's strikes and I call 'em the way I see 'em." The third umpire says, "There's balls and there's strikes and they ain't nothin' until I call 'em."[2]

Of course, anyone who has ever attended a baseball game can tell you that depending on whom you root for may cause you to see the issue of balls and strikes differently, but at this point let us consider the first umpire. He might be considered a classic realist. He believes that human knowing is a matter of seeking direct correspondence between the external world and our epistemological judgments. This is the worldview I have been describing. We believe we have a fairly accurate view of reality. Things are the way they are, and I can apprehend and describe them. There is a wall, here is a desk, the apple is red, and all is right with the world. We believe that most people share our view of the world and our perspective of reality should be the same.

What is harder to grasp is that this very understanding of the world is itself a construct, created by ideas like those of Descartes and Kant, not to mention three centuries of science. That reality is objective and discoverable with one true authentic meaning, that knowledge can be found which is universal and certain, that language is directly representational of reality and can be trusted to correspond with the way things really are, all this is a fiction, a device of our own creation. This is the critique of the postmoderns.

But surely, you respond, the apple is truly red. You cannot tell me that the thing I comprehend with my senses is not there? Of course, postmodernists would not deny the existence of reality, but it is a reality we are embedded within. Even the way we process color is the complex interaction of biology and physics. Our eyes, for instance, convert the energy of light into color through our retinal cones and neural transmitters. Because of the molecular structure of a certain thing all the particular spectrum in light energy becomes absorbed into an object with the exception of what gets reflected back to us. If we were to change this process we would find things much different. If my biology worked differently from yours, say I were colorblind, then my world would not be the same as yours. My mind would be manufacturing a different reality for me to comprehend. Or, to put it another way, the grass is not green, the sky is not blue, and the flowers before me are not varying shades of purple. I am manufacturing the experience through my bodily ability to process the information it takes in and interacts with. Even so basic a reality as color is in no small measure a product of my mind. I am constructing the reality that is constructing me.

We are, all of us, in a world that we are constantly interpreting, to ourselves and one another. But to think this makes those who are part of the classic realist perspective very uncomfortable. Who cares about any of this? we ask. The apple is red and it tastes good, and all this other stuff you are saying is so much nonsense. A ball is a ball, and a strike is a strike; everybody knows that. Actually this is precisely what is being called into question by the contemporary understanding of postmodernity.

It is psychologically much easier to live in the story written by the Enlightenment. It is more comfortable to see the human being as privileged and imbued with vast powers of reason. Indeed, if universal principles were accessible to human knowing then in some ways the human becomes godlike, transcendent of time and space. We believe we have abilities that grant us special powers.

The roots of modernity were planted in a soil that assumes that knowledge is objective, testable, and if sought correctly, explainable. If we live in this story we stride through our world supremely confident that we can assess, judge, and distinguish with certainty reality and how to test it. And, in point of fact, have we not done many wonderful things with our technological prowess? Have we not conquered many diseases and other dangers of the natural world by acts of heroic effort? Have we not extended ourselves into space? Have we not overcome social bondage and entered into the new age of prosperity?

We have even managed to explain scientifically those nonempirical dimensions of human life that perplexed Kant. We can discover the right genetic code or the neural processes that influence human behavior. We can explain religion and the manifestations of religious life or the aesthetic dimension of existence by appeal to psychological or cultural factors.

The goal of our intellectual quest to unlock the world of nature, to peer behind the veil, was to serve humankind, not to dominate it or nature. We would create a better world, one not built on sectarian strife, religious wars, and power politics, where human beings served as the unwilling pawns of larger forces. This world would be a better place where science and technology would be employed to bring us more wealth, health, and freedom. And, I suppose, there are some who could interpret the world just so. However benign the narrative we repeated to ourselves in the last three centuries, the reality has proven to be far more malignant as the destructive powers of science and technology made themselves felt in a distinctly horrific way in the twentieth century.

There are a host of voices which have been questioning this paradise we would fashion with our knowing selves. These are the voices which question whether our morality, our choices, are based on a detached and neutral rationality. They question why we seek to impose our reality on theirs as if our reality were the only viable reality for the world. They point to our grand illusions of egocentricity, ethnocentricity, and aristocentrism and call us down from our tower of supposed transcendence to view life from the perspective of the other, the ones who are not heard in the backwash of our technological mastery and scientific control.

They take many identities and wear many faces. They span all times and cultures. They are the workers in coal shafts who lose years of their lives to feed the need for energy. They are the children sent to factories of despair in developing countries, or workers in offshore plants earning pennies a day as corporations pursue ever more profit at the expense of their employees.

These are the voices that question the reality we have built on the assumptions of modernity. The citizens of Nagasaki and Hiroshima, of Auschwitz and Buchenwald, of Iraq and the Balkans question whether the atom or the microchip have been such great servants of humankind, or whether perhaps the grand narratives that shaped us need to be critiqued and rewritten. These are the inhabitants of postmodernity, the dissenting report which calls into question all pretensions of human society to universal claims of neutrality, detached rationality, and political altruism. These stories were there from the beginning of modernity, but they are making themselves felt more today. It may, however, be informative to briefly touch on some of the earliest dissenters of modernity before we proceed.

Voices of Suspicion

One place to begin tracing the negation of modernity and its Enlightenment roots is with a philosopher called the "patron saint of postmodernity," Friedrich Nietzsche.[3] Born in 1844 into a very religious family, Nietzsche followed a different path. He rejected his religious heritage and became a professor. Brilliant, but troubled, he was plagued by physical and mental disorders, dying in August of 1900.

In his life he launched a protest against all forms of Enlightenment thinking that claimed the status of received truths. We do not have access to a storehouse of ideas, available to all right thinking persons; rather we generate our own truths, specific to each time and location, he argued. Human knowledge is not apprehension of some eternally existing reality, but is a reality we ourselves create. Truths are created by our metaphorical employment of language, our constituting these linguistic constructions with illusions of reality, and then canonizing them as codes which we must believe in order to truly apprehend the world. Unfortunately, this is all our illusion, Nietzsche believed. Rather than this, he maintained that we fashion the lies by which we live in order to create the world that serves our needs. We are not discovering the world in any real sense; we are more exercising our power to shape it for our devices. All attempts at establishing a transcendent truth should be unmasked for what they are, our will to power, to have control over things and people.

This "will to power" constitutes one of the primary forces of human behavior. It is a manifestation of our desire to show our strength. Our very thought systems are part of this desire. Art, language, values, all these share in the human desire to display our ability. All things serve to advance us in the world, whether individually or corporately. Religion as well is a part of this process. Rather than acknowledge that morality is a product of localized cultures, religion argues that it is universal and related to a transcendent object. This is bad enough because it creates localized tribes, each believing that it has an inside track on the one true God. But it gets worse. Religion makes people docile and timid in the face of suffering and oppression. The rulers are those who use the humility and self-debasement that much of religion exalts as

ideals to gain power over persons who are too afraid to live life
on their own terms.

In *Thus Spoke Zarathustra,* Nietzsche used powerful imagery
to announce the death of God and the coming of the Superman.
Christianity had lost its ability to shape the lives of men and
women. The mythological world of retributive justice no longer
held sway over the masses as science had come to replace the outmoded and outdated myths. But the death of God was not to be
mourned; it was to be celebrated, for now humankind could loosen
the shackles of oppression. A new "transvaluation of values" could
emerge which would make for more authentic and realistic human
existence.

From the ashes of a decayed and corrupt civilization, new stories
would exercise their power on humankind. These stories, "myths"
in the words of Nietzsche, would provide the structure which
would cause creative responses to the world. Language would be
a vehicle that carried the myths and opened the doors to us that
were closed. Whatever truth there could be for us is constructed
by language.

These construals carry their own truth. They do not appeal to
universal foundations; they do not make a connection between
word and world an assumption. The new stories and myths, according to Nietzsche, are truthful by the language, the images, and
the content of their narrative. As he tells his story of Zarathustra he does not appeal to categorical imperatives; he merely has
Zarathustra speak his truth and the rest of the world can either
accept or reject the truths he bears. If we accept them, we can be
freed from those illusions that will keep us enslaved by politics,
religion, and philosophy. If we reject them, then we will continue
on in our blindness, unable to see that what we consider to be
objective reality is but the fragmentary and relative construction
of those determined to fashion a world in their image and stamp
it with the imprint of their supposed transcendent reality.

Nietzsche called into question the whole Enlightenment enterprise of finding universal foundations for thought and challenged
religion's claim that it was responding to a reality not of its own
design. While we will hear more from him in our chapter on Bonhoeffer, he was one of the architects of the house of suspicion. He
was, however, not the only builder.

Another voice which would make itself heard in the world was that of Ludwig Feuerbach (1804–72). A critic of Hegel and his system, Feuerbach wrote a book entitled *The Essence of Christianity*. Like Nietzsche, he believed we invest the world with a profound sense of meaning, and that ultimately this meaning is traceable to notions of a Deity or supreme being. He thought that the ideas about God we have tell us as much about ourselves as they do about the thing itself. God loves us, cares for us, forgives us, seeks our health, empowers us to accomplish good on God's behalf, and even rescues us from the abyss of nothingness with the promise of eternal life. In other words, God exists only as the product of our construction, a symbol of our interior world. The God who meets us in Feuerbach is the one we ourselves create to reflect our deepest wishes and desires of what we hope for, especially the hope that life goes on after we die.

Because these wishes or desires are so fundamental to the construction of human societies and cultures, Feuerbach believed that we could discern within the symbolic structures, rituals, and logic of religious doctrines aspects of human life which were hidden from our consciousness. If we applied critical reflection to the elements of religious life we could find in the human psyche the reasons for the origin of religion and the images of God. Not only was religion a projection of human desires, but his theory would be a tool for an alternative reading of the Christian symbolic structure.

And Feuerbach was not the only one making this point. Sigmund Freud would carry these views into the world of psychoanalysis with his writings. One of the best known was his small book *The Future of an Illusion*. In this text, Freud paints a portrait of a humanity beset by the elemental power of nature. Devising ways to traffic with these powers through naming them or using anthropomorphisms, we created the great storehouse of religious imagery and symbol through which we objectify our deepest psychological needs, fears, and desires. We projected this objectification into the cosmos and named it God, calling society to worship it and give it ultimate allegiance.

Freud critiques the allegiance that humanity gives to the world of religious doctrine and beliefs, saying that that which calls for our ultimate commitments is that which we allow to be questioned and held up to scrutiny the least. At one point he writes:

> We say to ourselves: It would be very nice if there were a God, who was both Creator of the world and a benevolent providence, if there were a moral world order and a future life, but at the same time it is very odd that this is all just as we should wish it ourselves. And it would be still odder if our poor, ignorant, enslaved ancestors had succeeded in solving all these difficult riddles of the universe.[4]

These, of course, are only a few of the persons who fashioned the culture of critique arising from the heritage of the Enlightenment. There would be many others who would raise issues with the story of modernity. Karl Marx would check in with his critique of religion as a social structure for class oppression; Søren Kierkegaard would question the assumed connection of culture and Christianity; Bertrand Russell would also tell the world why he could not accept the tenets of religion. Common to all these voices was a strong sense that the quest for certainty and indisputable truths begun by the legacy of Descartes and Kant too easily slips into an agenda which marginalizes dissent and nonacceptance of the purported truths presented by rationality and science.

What may have been intended as serving us has ended up as the tool by which most of us were brought into the service of the elites who, after all, have the power to construct what a society believes to be true. We should regard with suspicion any view which trumpets "The Truth," or even any economic system which promises freedom. Likewise, any state which calls for our allegiance, even unto death, should be regarded with careful scrutiny. We should wake up to the fact of our enslavement. Like Neo in the matrix, we should unplug from our reality, or at least get enough distance on it to see it for what it is. Modernity gave us a narrative to live in, that we should "boldly go where no man has ever gone before." But what is the terrain of modernity we see around us now?

Modernity's end has been a landscape littered with mass death and destruction, and human misery on an unprecedented scale. Religion, according to this critique, has been an ally in our entrapment to those forces that enslave and oppress. This is the position from which the present critique of postmodernity proclaims the dying of the former age and the beginning of a new one. Let us then turn to the present and ask the question why this has importance for Christians and how the tradition of such an ancient faith can engage and address postmodern humanity.

Knowing in the Postmodern World

When the spirit of critique moved across the waters of modernity, it found a dynamic present that plays itself out globally. Put simply, all societies created a reality that structured their worldview, that placed them in the world, that gave them identity. As you read these words, you do so with certain assumptions and beliefs about yourself and the world you live in. If you are a Serb, you might interpret this book differently than an American. If you are African-American you see a very different reality than an Asian or Caucasian. Likewise, if you are a woman instead of a man, your interpretation of the world may be very different.

These differing perspectives, or worldviews, are the result of the many cultural and social forces which shape us. According to social scientists like Peter Berger, we accept certain plausibility structures as being an authentic way of looking at the world.[5] These structures constitute our beliefs about the world and those things that we hold true about those beliefs. If a majority of a culture or a society believe something to be true (whether or not it should be is an entirely different matter), then for that culture it is true. Or, if I say it's a strike, it's a strike.

This is the social construction of reality at work. These constitute our descriptions of the way the world is, and, in our awareness of them, we find another idea that causes us concern. What features of these constructions will serve as norms or criteria for truth or goodness, for moral behavior, for social life, or cultural expression? Philosopher Richard Rorty argues that any criterion for judging is itself a human construction and carries its own agenda of human motives. There is "no standard of rationality that is not an appeal to such a criterion, no rigorous argumentation that is not obedience to our own conventions."[6]

We are caught then in a wheel that is ever turning but never going anywhere. My beliefs are a product of my cultural location with all the attendant baggage that entails. If I try to break free from my ethnocentric predicament, I do not find objective criteria by which to judge critically. I find, at best, agreement among inquirers, who are themselves constituted by particular languages, histories, and stories which I may or may not share.

As I look around me, I see those constructions of reality at work, and I realize that usually someone's view is dominant, or controls all dissent. As Berger relates, there may be cognitive minorities, those who have a minority report to share, but they are usually marginalized, or, in liberal societies, tolerated. But seldom in a dominant view of reality are dissenting voices allowed a place at the table, a position from which their perspective may emerge as the new paradigm for how persons should live. And so, naturally, the postmodern asks the question: "Why is your view of things the one to which I should offer my obedience?"

This question brings us to the door of one of the most important aspects of our contemporary age, called by various names but usually recognized as the "other." If many see in postmodernity the negation of modernity, the erasure of all known signposts along the way of existence, the reason for this may be concern for those faces and voices that do not share in the making of the world. This is the space occupied by the category of the "other." Resistance may be futile, as the Borg of *Star Trek: The Next Generation* thought, but resistance must be maintained on behalf of the individual against the collective. Theologian David Tracy contends that it is this turn to the other that constitutes the intellectual and ethical motivation for postmodernity.[7]

Those worldviews, beliefs, and cultures that have silenced dissent must be carefully explored and critiqued. Indeed, the constructions must be deconstructed in order to overcome the hegemony of the dominant. Only as we explore what is believed to be present in our systems of supposed truths (beauty, order, reality, morals) will we find that what we believed to be given truths, accessible to all rational and right thinking persons, are illusions. This illusion says that our language and thought directly represent reality as it truly exists. Thus, our description of things is an accurate representation of the way things are.

Previously we used the experience of color to talk about the classic realist position. If even something so supposedly "given" to us is absent, what basis exists for us to argue that language and thought deliver to us anything other than what we have created? We believe we live in a world of things not fashioned by us, but upon closer inspection we find that even such things as facts of nature, cosmic laws, and manifestations of divine will are products of human activity that do not intrinsically participate in reality.

Think, for instance, of every time someone says: "Well, it's a fact that...." What usually follows is some self-generated opinion about the world or people, or even nature. Scientists are very careful about attributing facticity to objects because that assessment may change according to the evidence. In another manner, if you lived in South Africa in the 1970s and 1980s, your "facts" about relations between ethnic groups and access to resources would have been very different depending on where you stood on the color line in that country.

The point of all this is that the process of deconstruction was initiated in the hopes that our agendas could be unmasked and our pretensions to objectivity could be exposed in order to let other voices offer us perspectives that should be considered and respected. If we believe our view of things is the right or correct view, we will engage in systemic destruction of the other in order to maintain our world. If it is God's will that Europeans dominate the "heathen," then the "heathen" must be dominated. Who are we to stand in the way of "manifest destiny"?

The marginal and different form the subject matter of postmodernity. The invisible ones function as the central intellectual category of the new world. What was before a plausibility structure which ordered our world has now become one reading of human history, residing with all the others for a voice and place at the table. The other has returned with a story of her own to tell. The boundaries we have established with such care, the gated communities of our unconscious indifference are being transgressed by truths both unsettling and liberating. They come to us as stories in the midst of our story, as a counternarrative to our accepted narratives, as the face that says: "Do not kill me."

Did You Hear the One About...?
Narratives and Their Constructions

Once upon a time that was before all time, God created the cosmos and everything in it. Among all the diversity of the world, God chose my particular group for special favor. Indeed, creation

was meant entirely for me. Everything I did with my life was ordered along the lines of honoring the one who gave me and mine
life. Unfortunately, not everyone was so blessed and thus, being
jealous, they envied my gift. They became my enemy, not because
I disliked them, but because they sought to take what was mine.
Therefore, I had to make sure I kept close tabs on them and knew
what they were up to all the time so I could ensure they did not
take what God had rightfully given me. In fact, if they had what
was rightfully mine, then I was justified in taking it back for me
and mine. My justification comes from the will of God, who has
ordered the world in such a way that we must be obedient to the
structures of authority and government, even if they call for the
destruction of other cultures.

This story can function as a grid upon which many other stories
can be placed. It has been the template upon which other cultures
are constructed. In truth, there are countless stories of human existence that we can point to as examples of how we are placed and
located in the world, and many of them are variations of the above
story. What was the story Columbus believed when he sailed for
the new world, or the one that the conquistadors listened to when
they conquered the Americas? What story provided the foundation for Europeans to take North America from its inhabitants
or enslave millions of differently colored persons in the name of
God? What worldview allows Germans, British, Slavs, Japanese,
Chinese, or anyone else on the face of the planet to see themselves
as the chosen ones, privileged by God, and justified in all their
actions because it is divine will?

Jean-François Lyotard addresses the problem of what happens
to the other in his treatment of what he calls "metanarratives."
These metanarratives, whether intentionally constructed or accepted as a communal assumption, function to structure worldviews and legitimate the practices of a given community. There
have been controlling narratives from the time humans could tell
stories, and almost all the world's religions have metanarratives
which place cultures in the world in a particular way. Often how
culture is placed in the structure of a metanarrative will exclude
the humanity of others who do not participate in the telling of
the story.

Postmodern thinkers tend to be suspicious about the role

of metanarratives to shape and inform worldviews without the possibility of internal critique. These stories can be as vast as Christianity (or any other world religion), or as localized as a tribal story of Amazon rain basin Indians. It can be as old as Judaism, or as recent as the myth of progress, which still holds many in its power. The suspicion can be summed up in Lyotard's statement: "Simplifying in the extreme, I define postmodernity as incredulity toward metanarratives."[8]

Whether one can accept this particular definition of postmodernity as an accurate one is open to question; however, one thing is certain, stories exercise enormous influence on us. We can see their power in our family stories, in our national stories, in our religious stories. But the suspicion emerges when we realize that the stories themselves are human construals of life, written from a particular place and time, offering their own view of reality and interpretation.

When one of these localized stories claims an overarching legitimation for all cultures, we have a problem. Does this narrative claim more for itself than it can legitimately claim? Your version of the truth of things can be cloaked with universality, and maybe even divine will, but it is blind to its own projections and human-oriented construction. Metanarratives claim a totality that simply cannot include the entire world.

In the construction of these overarching stories religion plays a significant role. For Peter Berger religion functions as a sacred canopy, a covering we place over culture or society in order to legitimate our particular perspective. This canopy functions in different ways. In some cultures, the metanarrative answers the ultimate concerns of human life: Who am I? Where am I going? What should I do? Why is there suffering?

These questions might be answered by the laws of karma, samsara, and reincarnation. If you suffer, you were bad in a previous life. The suffering are paying their karmic debt. Or these questions might be answered by the notion of retributive justice. God will reward the righteous and punish the wicked. Regardless, religion has played a role in shaping the perspective of many through its propensity to tell stories.

This one idea is a prime example of how a concept, given to us by a metanarrative, can function to unconsciously shape, and even control, us. I sometimes tell students the story of a friend of mine who had a baby born with congenital heart defects. He would have many heart operations in his first two years and be deaf and mute his entire life. It was a devastating time for the family. One morning their pastor came to visit, and the first words out of his mouth were, "What sin did you commit that God gave you this baby?"

The initial reaction to this story is one of horror and revulsion. How could anyone be that cruel or unfeeling to say such a thing? But then I go on to ask my hearers what was the first thought that went through their mind when they had some misfortune visit them. Usually with a surprised look, they answer, "Why is this happening to me?" or, "What did I do to deserve this?" That pastor was articulating something which many people unconsciously believe: that God rewards the righteous and punishes the wicked. Actually the whole tradition of classical theism stands behind these types of beliefs, and this tradition is being rethought in circles from evangelical Christianity to process thinkers. This is a metanarrative, and it exercises its greatest power when we just assume its truth without questioning why we believe it to be so.

Or to take another example, one of the foundational metanarratives of modernity runs something like this: Humankind has entered a new age with the exercise of our autonomous human reason. We are the product of an evolutionary process which moves from simpler to ever more complex forms of life. Our role in this has been one of unending progress and advancement. Our science tells us more and more about the world, and our technology enables us more and more to master it. Since we are no longer lost, ignorant, and slaves to the world, we can control our environment. We will be able to eradicate disease, stop hunger, and serve all human life. Our wealth will grow as we master the economic forces which lead to ever increasing development. We can create a McWorld where all are united by prosperity and play in the fields of Disney.

This myth is losing force among us. At first it may have been the madman in the street crying to those who would hear, but now it is a chorus of voices that have been oppressed and marginalized by the narratives of progress. The totalizing dimension of the metanarrative has served the technological and intellectual elites, but now the appeal to a universal story is met with cries of *jihad,* a hundred different holy wars of resistance against the empire built upon the reality structure of money, technology, and power.

In the world toward which we are moving, no grand narrative exists whereby all will be guided toward the *telos,* or goal, of the story. Those master narratives carried the dark side of servant narratives where morality was construed in such a way that all must fit, or be regarded with fear and oppression. In the war on totality, launched by postmodernity, all pretense to universality is unmasked and the order we try to impose upon the life of the world is revealed for the hegemonic power grab it truly is. And, as we come face to face with this destablizing and horrific knowledge, what of us? If my story is taken away, where do I find myself anymore? From the corporate to the individual we now turn.

What Is the Story We Are Writing?

As I survey the landscape of the present world and I see the stories that shaped me receding into the background, I ask myself, who am I then? What is a self in the new world but a series of temporary identities, tried on like new clothes and then discarded for something prettier down the line? What defines me in the bricolage of postmodernity? Maybe the Buddhists are right and there is no self, no solid and secure center of the universe that I can point to and say, "That is what I am!"

In the wake of the collapse of so much that I thought was given and true, what can I trust anymore? I was placed, defined, and identified by the stories that are becoming whispers, ever harder to hear. I used to feel optimistic about life and culture. I could trust my reason, my language, my thoughts, my culture, my nation, but now these have undergone serious critique and I am left with suspicion. For a time I could have gone back to Descartes, and while doubting everything, still be left with *cogito ergo sum.* But now, I am not so sure.

It may have begun with the turn toward the heliocentric reality offered by Galileo (actually offered by others before him, but according to the narrative he occupies the central position). Earth was no longer the center of the universe, and humankind no longer seemed the center of existence. As time moved on, we discovered other odd things.

We built a view of ourselves on the basis of autonomy and power, on confidence in reason and rationality. We would control the world, but now we realize it is we who are being controlled. If we build an artifact and the artifact becomes employed by us (everything is included from hammer to computer chip), it will end up defining who we are. As one example, take the computer. I am constantly amazed at how people's patience is shaped by the computer. Fifteen years ago, I was impressed that my computer could process words; now I become impatient if I can't get information from the web instantaneously. Things that frustrate me were not even a part of my reality just a short time ago.

And this is true in the most comprehensive sense. Everything we create ends up defining us as individuals. None of us are untouched by this dynamic. More than this, when I truly grasp the reality that our tools or technology define us, I am brought closer to a realization that cuts to the bone. I may not be constituted by consciousness or moral agency or free choice. I may not have freely chosen the self I believe I am. I may, in fact, be a social construction of reality, defined by my historicity and social location. The meaning systems and structures of discourse I participate in structure how I understand myself. In the terms of postmodernity, I have become decentered.

The unitary I has become dissolved into the constructs of a thousand different realities. If I define myself by the transitory realities of history, ethnicity, and culture, I must question exactly who is doing the thinking and choosing, the willing and doing. Is it the I or the not I? Kenneth Gergen probes these issues, making connections between the loss of self in postmodernity and the multiplicity of forces, each seeking to make us in its image. He writes:

> Under postmodern conditions persons exist in a state of continuous construction and reconstruction; it is a world where anything goes that can be negotiated. Each reality of the self gives way to reflexive questioning, irony, and ultimately the playful probing of yet another reality. The center fails to hold.[9]

We are at the mercy of our world, and we don't even know it. In the religion of consumerism, we are told by the high priests of advertising how to live, what to be or not be, how to have life and that more abundantly. This car is you, these clothes are you, this thing is you. You are malleable in the plastic world and unknowingly you are being defined to conform to whatever demographic group an advertiser desires. Just give us that magnetic strip and we will give you an identity, tax included. To paraphrase the Memorex commercial: Is it real, or virtual reality?

Does Christianity Have a Future?

These cultural, intellectual, and social forces constitute enormous challenges for Christian faith. To put it baldly, how can I put my trust in a faith that was born in another time, another place, another world? Of what relevance is Christianity in the face of such a critique? I feel the critique's power in the core of my being because one would have to be blind not to acknowledge the manipulation of Christianity in the guise of truth. How many times has destruction been unleashed upon human and more-than-human life in the name of Christianity (as well as all other religious structures)?

The discomfort becomes particularly acute when we approach the beliefs of Christianity. I now understand that doctrines may have been the products of social forces and even power plays. Can I believe in a doctrine formulated under the direct supervision of the emperor Constantine at Nicea? In what way can I look at the relativities and contingencies of history and see anything that is significant for my age and culture? Do I form communities of withdrawal, cognitive minorities that construct faith in such a way that it is only accessible to my sect? Paul Lakeland asks some salient questions for theology in the postmodern era when he writes:

> First, how, if at all, is God to be considered personal any longer if the anthropomorphic and the anthropocentric are to be eschewed? Second, what are the tasks of Christian community in an age marked by pluralism and suspicions of metanarrative? Finally, can the christocentricity of Christian theology be retained only at the price of a psychological reduction of salvation, if the church is not simply to revert to cult status? Putting it even more briefly and bluntly, is

there a place any longer in postmodern Christianity for God, Christ, and the church? And, if not, is there really a place for Christianity?[10]

These are the questions that will be explored in the following chapters. While I believe that the contemporary critique is one that needs to be heeded and entered into, I also believe that the distance between the premodern, the modern, and the postmodern is shorter than we may imagine. We may no longer live in the world of the three-tiered universe, or the world that the Bible inhabits, but in some way we live in the text which confronts us, calls us to something other than our own delusions and projections, and meets us as the Other.

In the following treatments of Augustine, Anselm, Aquinas, Luther, Schleiermacher, Bonhoeffer, and Barth, I explore distinct parts of their theologies that serve to illuminate our quest for understanding and wisdom in the postmodern era. Each theologian will serve as a case study to question postmodernity and interrogate the present. One mark of the postmodern can be the privileging of the present over the past, and it is just these voices that can grow so dim over the years. There are ample and powerful critiques in present theology that are thoughtful and come from many other quarters of the theological world. While I believe these are a necessary part of ongoing tradition, the past has its own story to tell us.

Augustine on the self, or Anselm on rationality and theological thinking, or even Barth on the role of tradition in theological reflection can offer us some perspective that fills out and enlarges our world of understanding. It may well be the case that they still offer us fruitful avenues of exploration even given their historical and cultural distance from our age. These treatments can only serve as hints and clues of ways that tradition still speaks across the ages, cultures, and positions of humankind. The plenitude of books and articles concerning these thinkers are ample testimony to the realization that within all our epistemological limitations we are cognizant that these voices still address us in our context with issues which span time and culture.

But the hearing of these voices cannot be done under the weight of a naive position, the position of the first umpire. The very word

"God" has come under suspicion as the product of human generation and self-projection, and the symbolic furniture in our houses which carried this name will have to be rearranged. All talk of this symbol must be carefully sorted through in order that we might discern whatever validity exists there.

Karl Barth, in a play on Ludwig Feuerbach's name, once wrote that Christianity would have to pass through the "fiery brook" of Feuerbach's critique in order to address the world with integrity. In a nod to deconstruction, I would agree that we must be very zen when we come to the art of interpreting tradition and Christian faith. It is said that when you begin zen training, a mountain is a mountain; during zen, the mountain is no longer a mountain; and after zen, a mountain is a mountain.

The point, of course, is that when we engage in the process of deconstructing our cherished realities, nothing seems the same anymore. This leads to fear and consternation because we do not know what to believe. The solid, settled, and secure is no longer thus. The mountain is no longer a mountain. When we embrace the critical deconstruction of our naive world constructions, when we see the mountain for what it truly is, it ceases to be obscured by our naivete. In the move to postcritical reconstruction, however, we have a new mountain, a different mountain, but a mountain nonetheless. As Christian faith takes its journey up the mountains of postmodernity, it will also find a new faith, one vastly different, but the same nevertheless.

 Chapter 2

Searching for Myself
Augustine and Postmodern Identity

To thine own self be true, and it must follow, as the night the day,
Thou canst not then be false to any man.
— POLONIUS TO LAERTES, *Hamlet,* SCENE I, ACT III

There will be time, there will be time
To prepare a face to meet the faces that you meet.
— T. S. ELIOT, *The Love Song of J. Alfred Prufrock*

I N THE GREEK MYTHS there is the story of Proteus, son of Neptune. Proteus was a figure able to change himself by shifting into certain forms. He could go from wild boar to lion, to dragon, and even sound like flood and fire. What Proteus found difficult and would not do unless seized and chained was to commit himself to a single form, a form most like his own from which he would carry out his function of prophecy. One wonders what this ancient story, explored by many others today, might tell us about ourselves.

All over the world people sit in front of computer screens and tap out identities that they create with a few keystrokes and some imagination. Unburdened by the constraints of physical community they weave these identities in chat rooms, user groups, and other venues where they have the freedom to construct whomever they want to be. They are free to relate to, interact with, and exist in a cyberworld composed of nothing more solid than light and binary code. These are the protean selves of the postmodern landscape.

In a recent *Newsweek* the cover story concerned the rise of plastic surgery and how it is increasingly being employed as a consumer choice for people who are insecure about their identities in the world. People being interviewed wanted someone else's body, to be sculpted to their ideal of perfection. The article quoted pa-

28

tients who said they were judged on what they looked like and how they dressed. The most alarming part of the article dealt with how much younger the patients were becoming, many of them teenagers. One of the young women said she wanted to be "thin, but healthy in a toned sort of way, kind of like Madonna." Proteus lives on among us today.

I am sitting in a small town in America; a short distance away are some Kosovar refugees. Or I am in London at a coffee shop in Bayswater, drinking Italian coffee, eating French pastry, being served by a Turkish waiter, and watching Muslims preparing for evening prayers. Tonight I will see these same people attempting to make connections with American college students. We live in this world of social saturation, created in no small part by our technologies. In this whirl of activity we have created what Kenneth Gergen calls the multiphrenic self. This term is meant to describe the fragmentations of self and its conceptions that whirl at us from so many directions we lose all sense of what an authentic self might look like, indeed whether such a thing even exists.

We are experiencing a saturation of messages flowing into us from the cultures we are becoming. The mobility of people, symbols, and narratives that constitute the world we live in entail a landscape of fast-moving boundaries which are psychological, physical, and conceptual. In this world the points so familiar to us are getting harder to fix. "Who are we?" we ask ourselves, and a number of different answers emerge from the midst.

I am the four selves on my computer screen, all maintaining different conversations, one of which may depict me as the opposite gender. Or maybe I am the chemical transformation of myself through Prozac or Zoloft, and my real self is my pharmacological one. After all, didn't I read the other day where I am the sum total of the chemical processes that are my body? If I change the chemicals, I'll become more of what I am meant to be.

Or perhaps I can take another antidote for multiphrenia and embrace fundamentalism as a way to anchor myself and understand my identity. A young soldier in the army of the Taliban says, "I am a soldier of Allah." No identity crisis here. Perhaps I surround myself with my own cultural cloak and condition myself on the basis of what is presently popular among American conservative Christians. What would Jesus do? What Jesus would do usually sounds suspiciously like what a middle-class participant in a capitalist society would do.

Maybe I become *homo economicus* and define myself in relation to my job. The only problem is that the economic world acts much differently than it used to. A number of decades ago our fathers read a book called *The Organization Man*, but now what would we read to get a fix on how corporations use their work force, *The Changes-Jobs-Often Person?* With increasing mobility and exploding information systems we find no settled place to define ourselves in relation to our work. In this new world we are more often defined by our stock options than by our roles at our jobs.

Another variant of *homo economicus* is *homo consumerus*. We see all around us the symbolic manipulation of desires, where advertisers and corporations gather detailed information on our desires, preferences, and choices. We are targeted very carefully by these purveyors of purchase because they realize that people construct their identities by their consumption and present themselves to the world by their possessions. I am my American Express magnetic strip worn thin by countless swipes with the laser.

We create these economic icons, like the "swoosh" symbol of Nike, or the names on the clothes we wear, and then we work to manipulate cultural, historical, or sexual identity through images and iconic representation. I can really "be like Mike" if I buy the right shoes, or even use the right cologne, or the telephone service that features the cute cartoon characters. As I move through the world I am seeing the collisions of a hundred different realities and in each collision new fusions of reality are emerging which define me, and over which I seemingly have no control. I find myself populated with the character of others, even as I colonize them and their electronic or flesh-and-blood representations. The social ghosts of a multiphrenic world haunt me with whispers I don't wish to hear. Who are you really? Is there even a real self there? Aren't you really who we say you are and will be? How can you be this, if you are that?

Living in the Material World

In his book *A Rumor of Angels,* the sociologist Peter Berger tells the story of a magical train station in France. It seems that at this particular station a large percentage of persons going to Paris would misplace their Catholicism. Somehow or the other it just seemed to drop off persons entering Paris at this station. Of course, they somehow always found it going back home, right where they left it.

The point of the story is that social institutions and commitments go a long way to forming who we are. This also goes to the heart of what we discussed in the first chapter. There is a growing awareness that society as we know it is in many respects the product of earlier understandings, assumptions, and inventions. A society or culture forms along the lines of what went previously, and changes will come when the structures of plausibility are overturned in favor of new ones.

However we place or see ourselves, the cultural context we grow up in is also a significant factor in forming our identities. The profound impact of cultural formation and identity shape us in fundamental ways. If we grow up in India we are likely to reflect the narratives and constructs of that setting. We will internalize those structures of life that are significant to us. If a particular segment of Indian culture does not promote the notion of romantic love but sees the value of arranged marriages, then we will grow up thinking that we are not to marry the person we love; we are to love the person we marry.

In all cases of the social construction of reality there are dynamics at work which seek to shape our subjectivity. Media, politics, religion, and the ever ubiquitous advertiser all seek to make us in their image. All these forces are keenly interested in structuring beliefs and using them to manipulate us into allegiance. If I grow up happy to have marriage arranged, but then I become influenced by television, movies, advertising, or a computer friend to seek an ideal of romantic love (itself a cultural construct), then in what sense am I making a decision and not being manipulated into one?

The connection between national identity and personal identity is even more profound, and even more fragile. I can live one mile from you, even less, but there is a border, invisible to us but there nonetheless, that determines our lives. It will shape us to hate one another, do violence to one another, to be less human to one another, even to destroy one another, and ourselves in the process. All this in the name of ethnic identity and national pride. We are willing to commit the ultimate sacrifices or commit the ultimate atrocity, all over a line created by historical accident, the origins of which we cannot even recall.

What, then, can we say about the self, about our personal identity, that we are so ephemeral, so fragile, as to be so carelessly defined by state or national boundary? We are so easily defined by invisible lines drawn in the dust and sands of the will to power, or carried about on electrons that bring us images of who we are, that we become fleeting shadows, malleable to the whim of those who wish us to serve their turn. When the deepest feelings of persons can be defined by transitory artifacts of culture, in what sense can we even talk about having a self? We are worse off than Proteus because we have no fundamental shape to shift into.

At first glance we might find all this somewhat threatening. After all, didn't we grow up with the notion that we are self-made persons, freely choosing and acting in the world? Hasn't everyone everywhere seen what appears to be so plain to common sense? We have self-help groups, self-defense classes, self-actualization therapies. This is such a given reality. Self is what I am, what we are. This concept of something solid and sure, this concept of a self is what we have constructed an entire global world on. Psychology and psychotherapy are based on the premise that something like the self exists. Our systems of justice and morals and ethics are based on the notion that we make free choices. We put people to death on the grounds that they are able to make decisions. We even convict people whose lives have changed and do not represent a danger to anyone because we believe in the sanctity of personal responsibility.

We carry forth the work of another Greek god, Prometheus, who brings wisdom, political and moral order, and re-forms humanity. We have the power of the gods, to choose, decide, and act. We will finish the job God started by the exercise of our creativity. In the modern world, constructed from the Renaissance and Enlightenment ideals, we become the focal point of the story. Who is like unto us, able to harness the power of the atom?

Probably as far back as Plato, Aristotle, and Socrates we saw the modern self being born. We were body and mind, struggling with the interior and exterior worlds. And we did so from a position of self-consciousness. Perhaps the point that demarcates the modern subject was Descartes, who could not doubt the existence of a reflective consciousness. I think, therefore I am. My reason exists outside the bounds of illusion, for I can use it to doubt everything but its own existence.

Whatever vast and powerful social forces were at work in the flow of history they were moving in the same direction with the rise of the Western world. As we previously saw, reality was conceived as something "out there" that I from "within here" experience, perceive, and respond to with a Reason that is a neutral, value-free tool with which to discover reality. And not only discover, but master.

We are like Pico della Mirandola's Adam in his 1487 work, *Oration on the Dignity of Man*. In Pico's renarrating of the creation accounts God gives humankind unlimited powers to make itself what it will in a world of which humanity is the pinnacle. God tells Adam: "The nature of all other creatures is defined and restricted within laws which We have laid down; you, by contrast, impeded by no such restrictions, may, by your own free will, to whose custody We have assigned you, trace for yourself the lineaments of your own nature."[11] So this is how we contoured identity and the self. Independent, autonomous, self-reliant, we have moved through the world, taking in the "facts" and choosing what has meaning and what doesn't. The human subject was the disinterested arbiter of truth, and the human ego was the self-centered locus of meaning.

Identity building was done in the context of social institutions that undergirded this view of ourselves. The state, church, guild, or family were all powerful forces in shaping identity. These institutions had the solidity to encompass a host of differing life projects. Why, even democracy can tolerate a little dissent as long as most people believe that we have the powers of rational judgment and the desire for the common good. The autonomous self also supports the structures which gave it birth.

And like all good stories, the myth of the rational, self-actualizing, autonomous self had its shadow tensions. One of the reasons the modern self was born emerged from the chaos of religious violence in Europe. It is no accident that Descartes and Galileo are working during the Thirty Years' War. If we can find the locus of identity that will allow us a rationality and perspective not formed by superstition and ignorance, we will be able to stop this senseless bloodshed. Or so they hoped.

But even when modern humanity formed as the self-centered, integrated ego, it carried with it the shadow. For mastery of the world became power over it, or at least parts of it. Whether it was other ethnicities or nature itself, the modern self soon revealed it was self-deceived. It may have been "reasonable" to enslave others for economic reason, or conquer them and take their land in the name of manifest destiny, but whose reason was being applied? Promethean humanity wanted subjects all right, but not those who would authenticate themselves when the slavers came.

We have carried this quest for the self and its identity into the modern world. One of the most significant paradigms embraced in the Western world was the Freudian paradigm. It was the concept of the integrated and permanent self that was the ideal. Freud believed that in order to have the most fully integrated self a person could have, the role of the unconscious was crucial to the emergence of self-understanding. Freud also knew there were a multiplicity of factors that were at work in the human psyche. In his tracing out the model of the id, ego, and superego, Freud gave us an internal world not unlike one populated with the Homeric gods, different forces that must be given some attention.

Walter Truett Anderson makes the point that Freud's map of the self and the various internal constituencies of human being helped pave the way for the appearance of the postmodern self. The ego is not centered in a world of security and solidity, captain of its own fate. Why the ego was really not even master of its own house. The single-agent image of human persons was seeing its reality called into question, and the mood became anxious.[12]

As the disciplines of human knowledge began to train their attention toward the reality of the self, we realized that we might be in for something of a shock. First of all, there were the scientific investigations like Robert Ornstein's work on consciousness and the dual hemisphere structure of the brain.[13] This became popularized and seeped into the cultural context as a truism. The left side of the brain was the arena of rationality, the right side, the province of the artistic side of us. Even though this is not the assumption of cognitive scientists, it is still seen as a given about human life.

Another model of human agency and existence emerged with

the path of materialism. The mind-body problem is carved up into a series of processes whereby the isolating of certain functions of human identity like emotions and feeling could be targeted and, if malfunctioning, treated with chemicals. We are chemically determined. The notion that emotion, reason, and character are solid components of a self gives way to the realization that I am only the fragments of my DNA.

One of the television characters on the *The Muppet Show* used to tout the theme, "better living through chemicals." Though said tongue in cheek, an entire generation took that to heart and created more work for the psychiatrists. Why, if we could have gotten some Prozac for Dostoyevsky or Valium for Kafka they wouldn't have had to be so gloomy all the time.

And while this materialist assault on the self was proceeding, another challenge to the image of Mirandola's Adam was launched. From the direction of the sociologists we heard that a self, or human identity, was a product of social construction. As much as fundamental beliefs, or social plausibility structures, the self was also a product of larger forces, influenced by the cultural context within which it lived, moved, and had its being. The very deepest part of me is a product of language and is formed by the cultural and social arrangements that shape my life. Every culture creates its own version of the self, and I am my culture's picture.

This reversed, of course, the Enlightenment's belief that language was a tool to mediate reality to us, for in the postmodern world language also has the capacity to create new realities. Language structures meaning for us; it can even function to produce subjectivity as intricate as feelings and emotions. Ludwig Wittgenstein, who gets a lot of postmodern press, said that "the limits of language…mean the limits of my world."[14] Our experience is limited by our linguistic structures. Other cultures have been known to have other emotional experiences in some part because they have a language that is able to create unique emotions for that particular culture.

This does not mean that language is a passive medium that creates the world; rather, the ways in which we use language create the meaning and value that surround us. We use the tools at hand to understand and assign meaning and value, and the tool often used is language. We are born into a world that has made a certain connection between language, meaning, and reality. We create the world, and then we inhabit it, assuming the truth of our own constructions.

These languages, we saw previously, create narrative structures or frames out of which we live and experience the world. I am born into an environment that makes a connection between the words I use and the world I see before me. Thus I order the world according to my words. My understanding of self and identity is formed in my interaction with this world. I am defined by my linguistic world, but I interact with that world to devise the sense of it. In what sense am I not creating a self at the same time?

So, we are shaped, you and I, in a world where many voices are vying for legitimation and the social structures themselves are seemingly less institutional and more provisionary. If I existed in the social structure of the divine right of kings, I suppose my view of myself would carry a rather different perspective. The languages available to me might speak to my social, familial, or ecclesial communities and how those communities relate to the reigning power. But this is not the age in which my self is being defined, so I look for those other forces which seek the power to define me.

Since the postmodern critique is especially keen to search for the dynamics of power and its abuses, we might think about one of the most powerful shapers of the self in this society. Psychology determines for many how we shall view ourselves and our relative mental health. The conceptions of the self, identity, and language that emerge from there are highly influential in contemporary life. We saw earlier that the concept of the self lies at the heart of most human endeavors. Psychology and psychotherapy are based on the premise that something like the self exists. In many corners the idea of the integrated and permanent self remains an ideal. The modern self is assumed to be both descriptive of human consciousness and a model of mental health, although some might think the notion of integration is outdated.

But, as Michel Foucault was to point out, psychology is an agent of social order and control. If the goal is creating integrated and unitary selves that are able to function and contribute to culture, what better way to ensure this than that we will have a ready model of what is considered "normal"? What happens to those, however, who do not mirror the linguistic category of "normal"?

What of those who look at the world and perceive it as itself locked into a type of collective insanity?

Well, one place to sort it out is in the DSM-IV (*Diagnostic and Statistical Manual of Mental Disorders, 4th ed.*), one of the standard manuals for psychological disorders. This manual lists the behaviors of certain disorders and outlines possible lines of treatment. Does this manual report objective, ontological disorders, or does it create realities that thirty or forty years ago did not exist in the human self? The terms in the manual are predicated on the model of an integrative and healthy self. They are definitions of disorder, of disease, according to the latest prevailing knowledge in the realm of psychology. As the mental health profession tries to explain undesirable behavior, it creates a language to describe it, and then this vocabulary finds its way into the public arena. Persons in society begin to see themselves as people suffering from "borderline personality disorders" or some other affliction, and they begin to respond to people on the basis of these definitions.

What may be approached more carefully by professionals in the field who do employ other measures of health to accurately assess a person's well-being gets treated somewhat carelessly in the public arena. As a result persons define themselves and give power to others to define themselves on the basis of these categories. But these categories are changeable and over time they do change significantly. In the worst possible case you have the profession become the state's tool to define mental health, as was the case in the Soviet Union with dissidents.

Thus the profession is maintained by its power to connote, through language, what the well-adjusted self looks like. And at first glance, this would seem to be the correct way of assessing mental health. Yet, consider for a moment that behaviors classified by the American Psychiatric Association as disorders three decades ago are now "off the list," and behaviors not even classified years ago are now used to define someone's identity and assimilation into society.

Carrying this suspicion a little further, we might ask why two decades ago a religious commitment to a community such as the Hare Krishnas was seen as inherently pathological (as was a number of other communities that did not fit into the mainstream). The devotee was seen as a prime candidate for deprogramming, which was the forcible removal of the adherent from his or her community and subsequent psychological coercion by both trained and untrained persons. Why was adherence to a religion outside the mainstream considered problematic by some psychologists such as Robert Jay Lifton? Could it have been that some psychologists reserved the right to make the distinction between what was or was not a healthy religious affiliation? Was a person truly disordered by joining a new religious movement? Who defines this in our society says something about the power of defining a self.

So who are we? Am I my biological self? Am I an accidental dance of the molecular and genetic coding? If so, then what am I doing when I sell my body fluids to doctors or various blood, sperm, or egg banks? Am I less my self when I do so? Am I my body? Like those who seek plastic surgery to feel better about themselves, do I locate my identity in the shape of my nose or the curve of my hip? Am I my political self? Am I susceptible to propaganda and malleable by the societal pressures around me, defined by political party or racist creed? Am I one person in the city of Paris, another in the countryside?

More than the individual "I," who are we, as human beings? Surrounded by so much in the way of fast-moving cultures, we are locked in a global identity crisis of monumental proportions. The communications age seizes and manipulates the dissembling of cultures and identities (a Japanese boy to his mother as he gets off the plane in Los Angeles for his first trip to America: "Look, Mommy, they have McDonald's in America too!). The reason for our identity crisis is that we have always defined ourselves by the narrative frame that constructed our culture. Different cultures had differing narratives about radically different worlds from the one we live in today. Yet it was precisely these myths, metaphors, and stories which placed us, located us within a larger system of meaning, gave us our maps for navigating the world.

But those communities are being viewed differently now. Truth is understood to share the vagaries of self- and communal construction. All former beliefs are being challenged, or at least questioned. The technologies of social saturation are moving us to the point where we are content to live in a world of virtual reality, where we create images and identities from our deepest projections and broadcast them to the world. I am the imaginary other you see on your active matrix screen, and you are the object of my projections.

In this world our identity seems less inner directed and more outer directed. The gravity of cultural conformity keeps us in mad pursuit of the artifacts of popular culture as our things define us. There is some vague anxiety about having to keep up, but it passes temporarily with the newest acquisition from the Home Shopping Network. Culture is becoming fragmented, the narratives of life are multiplying, and the plurality of possible identities is exploding. Kenneth Gergen's multiphrenia appears more threatening than promising as endless options of self-conceptions spin us away from the center and any sense of what an authentic self might look like.

In this setting of a self, decentered from the traditional harbors, what does it really mean to say we have a self-identity? If we change according to the cultural ethos around us, if identity is at the heart of the narratives of politics, class, status, and religion, what now defines us? So much seems manipulated, transient, and superficial. We seemingly live in the land of the hungry ghosts, wandering around looking for sustenance that will feed us and make us solid.

Actually, these problems are not unique to our age, or our lives. Since Heraclitus or the Buddha these issues have been wrestled with. And since Christianity has been a part of the cultural narrative, it too has been concerned with the self and its complexities. The apostle Paul was certainly no stranger to wondering about the forces at work inside of his psyche. When he writes to the church at Rome about his struggles to define his self-identity, he can sound like the rest of us as we try to figure out the forces that compel us. At one point he writes, "For the good that I would, I do not; but the evil which I would not, that I do. Now if I do that I would not, it is no more I that do it, but sin that dwells in me" (Rom. 7:19–20). This notion may strike us as somewhat quaint, but Paul at least knew that defining a self was a struggle.

Besides Paul though, no figure, has cast a greater shadow on the tradition of Christianity and thus the Western world than Augustine, bishop of Hippo. His influence extends down to the present age in any number of ways, but it was his self-reflections in the *Confessions* that became a part of the Western world's understanding of itself. In the hope of gaining some perspective on our dilemma with identity formation and the self, let us examine Augustine for some possible avenues of thinking about this issue and perhaps some wisdom for the postmodern self.

Augustine and the Search for the Self

Probably one of the greatest framers of the narrative of the Western world was St. Augustine of Hippo. While at first blush this seems like an incredible and unrealistic claim, upon closer inspection we can see that this statement has some merit. Ask any person in the culture of Christianity about their understanding of God, evil, sin, even sex, and that person will most often answer with the categories and language that Augustine fashioned. Augustine's conception of God and humankind's fall away from this God became a narrative of such power that it is widely believed to be not just one person's theology, but the truth of God itself. Augustine's theology achieved the position of being an unquestioned assumption that "everybody knew was true."

His understanding of human nature has been used by politicians and political theorists to think about the role and purpose of political systems, both benign and malignant. His formulation of the just war doctrine, originally formulated as a justification for defending the powerless, has become the accepted currency in legitimating the political order's maintenance of the status quo among powerful nations. The notion that the state is maintained for the restraint of evil has been a primary justification for totalitarian states and democracies since the Roman empire.

In the area of sexuality, Augustine is being blamed for many of the problems we have about the exercise of human sexuality. Given the excessive amount of attention we pay to Augustine's struggles with this dimension of human existence, it would appear that he has taken an unfair burden of the blame for our inability to gain perspective on this part of human life. In fact, he is seen by many moderns as being the root of the problem, and we are well rid of him.

But for good or ill, Augustine arranged the furniture upon the stage of the Western world's drama. The irony is that most people don't even recognize it. It is the mark of the social construction of reality that we are rarely conscious of where we are getting our ideas from. And this narrative Augustine formed has exercised its hold on us, even to the ones who reject its framing.

Augustine's story begins with the omnipotent God, sole creator and ruler of the universe. God has total control of all events and is totally independent. This perfectly good God is also perfect in knowledge and all other virtues and powers. This God created a setting that was good in its own right, but with the appearance of humanity something went wrong. This creation, above all others, had the powerful gift of free choice, able to choose between good and evil. Under the command to love God, human beings disobey their creator by taking that which was forbidden. They are judged guilty by this good God (who, after all, cannot be unfair), and punished with exile from paradise. We are thus doomed to have the memory of paradise, but never able to return to it.

If the story ended there, we might have no other response than despair. But, according to Augustine's interpretation of Scripture, God is graceful, and even though we share the primal sin of the first humans, God becomes embodied in Jesus of Nazareth to pay the penalty for our disobedience and bridge the gap between the human and the divine. This omnipotent God knows who will and who won't be saved, but even though some won't accept the mercy, all are judged correctly.

In its barest story form, this is one of the founding narratives of our culture. It is nothing close to the complexity of Augustine's thinking, but it is part of the outline of what became known as "Augustinianism." It is this that many persons reject when the mythology of Christianity no longer holds any sense of credibility. This is what many of my students have rejected as part of the outmoded mythology of religion. We will return shortly to this story and its implications, but before we do, perhaps a look at the outline of Augustine's life can shed some light on the origins of his theology.

Augustine was born in the town of Thagaste, in North Africa, then part of the Roman empire. By the year 354, Augustine's birth date, it had been an area that had seen much conflict between the Catholics and the Donatists. Named for their leader, Donatus, this group would figure prominently in Augustine's life. They had undergone severe persecution and valued the constancy and purity of those who did not lapse under Diocletian's harsh punishment of Christians.

His childhood was fairly normal. He was raised by a Christian mother, Monica, and a father who does not figure prominently in his story (a fact of which much is made in some treatments of Augustine). He had a comfortable enough life. He was schooled in the cities of Carthage and Madaura. There he read some of the Latin classics of Virgil and Cicero, from which he gained some of his ideas about love and life. He won high praise for his rhetorical skills, which were highly prized in the culture.

While he was a student in Carthage he exercised his feelings of love by taking a concubine and fathering a son, Adeodatus ("gift of God"). This relationship would be a significant one in Augustine's life and lead to much speculation among Augustine's commentators. In his recounting of his relationship with this woman, Augustine says that he was faithful to her for fifteen years. But when he began to climb the ladder of Roman society he was willing to put her away in order to marry someone else in an arranged marriage.

His life at this time was very conflicted. He found himself in studies, but he also liked to hang around with a group of boys who aspired to be tough. So, in Carthage, he was a graduate student with an unwanted baby and a sexual partner. There were financial and familial strains which made him yearn for the escape of hanging around with the subversives.

At Carthage Augustine had a conversionary moment when he was reading Cicero's *Hortensius*. He was converted to philosophy and explored more earnestly the philosophy of the Manichees. He also heard the siren song of asceticism as he came to believe that if the body could be tamed the quality of life would be enhanced. It was at this time that Augustine's involvement with the Manicheans deepened. Their founder, Mani, preached a cosmology that was very dualistic. They believed that they contained exiled God-particles in them that had to be wrestled free from the gravity of evil. This battle between light and dark was not just cosmic; it was individual as well and gave Augustine one of his earliest models of self-understanding.

After his studies and his return to Thagaste, Augustine began his career as a teacher. He sought to convert others to his new religion, one of whom was his closest friend. When Amicus converted back to Christianity and then died, Augustine was disconsolate and returned to Carthage, where he recalled in his *Confessions,* "I was restrained within my own unhappy territory, unable to live there or to get out."[15] This inescapable desert of the heart would be his home for quite some time.

Back in Carthage, Augustine began to reflect more critically on the Manichean philosophy and began to question some of the Manichean mythology. After one of their sages was unable to answer some of Augustine's questions, he moved even further away from the mythos, in no small part because he went to Rome. No longer the center of the empire and diminished by a certain shallowness of power, Rome still possessed enough allure for an ambitious, intelligent teacher.

While no longer enamored of the Manichean philosophy, Augustine still benefited from that community when he was appointed to a position in Milan. This position was rather prominent and raised Augustine's social stature considerably. He had his own entourage, including his concubine and son, as well as his mother and assorted secretaries, stenographers, and servants. It was in Milan that his concubine was sent away and his marriage to a wealthy and well-connected heiress was arranged.

It was also in Milan that Augustine encountered the bishop of the city, Ambrose, but he was not to be as influential on Augustine as was a group of Christian neoplatonists. The ideas he encountered here began to answer many of his questions. In both the philosophical communities of which Augustine had been a part the intellectual elite all saw their souls bound to a realm of turmoil and conflict. In exile from the world of perfect light, beauty, and being, they could only catch fragmentary glimpses of the far shore through attentiveness to the spiritual dimension. By meditation and discipline they could escape the imprisonment of an earthly existence and move toward their true home.

If the Manicheans found hope in the shards of light embedded in their souls, the elite of Rome and Milan clung to the platonic wisdom of the ideal world of unitary being from which we are exiled and toward which we can move. These ideas were very attractive to Augustine, but he still realized that an inner conflict raged in him that was a gaping wound. He wrote of the day in the garden of Milan when he was wracked with indecision and conflicted of will about his religious and personal life:

> Within the house of my spirit the violent conflict raged on, the quarrel with my soul that I so powerfully provoked in our secret dwelling, my heart, and at the height of it I rushed into Alypius with my mental anguish plain upon my face … and then in my frenzy I tore away from him, while he regarded me in silent bewilderment. Unusual, certainly, was my speech, but my brow, cheeks, and eyes, my flushed countenance and the cadences of my voice expressed my mind more fully than the words I uttered.
>
> If I tore out my hair, battered my forehead, entwined my fingers and clasped them around my knee, I did so because I wanted to. I might have wanted to but found myself unable, if my limbs had not been mobile to obey. So then, there were plenty of actions that I performed where willing was not the same thing as being able, yet I was not doing the one thing that was incomparably more desirable to me, the thing that I would be able to do as soon as I willed it, because as soon as I willed—why I would by willing it!
>
> How did this bizarre situation arise, how develop? The mind commands the body and is instantly obeyed; the mind commands itself, and meets with resistance.[16]

Caught in this conflict of self-control Augustine goes deeper on an interior journey of exploring the will. His inner dialogue with the past as he approaches another conversion is rendered in striking language. He speaks of the fragmenting of the self and the plurality of voices that he struggled with: "Moreover, if we were to take the number of conflicting urges to signify the number of natures present to us, we should have to assume that there are not two, but many."[17] In this multiplicity of voices we see Augustine preceding Freud in his understanding of human life. Old mistresses of habit and inclination were "plucking softly at my garment of flesh and murmuring in my ear, 'Do you mean to get rid of us? Shall we never be your companions again after that moment … never … never again?' "[18] The one who had so entertained these voices was on his way to another land, and the old habits were resisting his journey.

In that garden Augustine heard a young voice compelling him to read the Scripture, and he read the words of Paul, "Not in rioting or drunkenness, not in clamoring and wantonness, not in strife and envying, but put on the Lord Jesus Christ, and make no provision for the flesh to fulfill the lusts thereof." This settled the matter for Augustine and his friend Alypius. They were converted to Christianity and immediately went to tell Monica.

After his conversion he would begin catechetical instruction and start writing down his thoughts about his newfound faith. He was baptized in the spring of 387 and turned toward the shores of North Africa. His journey was delayed as war had broken out, and while they were stranded at Ostia, Monica died. Since his journey to Africa looked impossible at this point, he went back to Rome until he could return to Thagaste in spring of 388.

His original intention had been to set up a monastery, but he had acquired a reputation as a Christian apologist, and when he went to Hippo Regius he was immediately enlisted by the resident bishop to teach and preach. While there he became bishop of the city and spent the rest of his life writing, arguing, and creating the legacy that would ensure his influence to the present time.

It was in the circumstances of his debates with the Donatists and later Julian, a young bishop, and Pelagius, a British monk, that Augustine's reputation would solidify into something like what we know today. The portrait of "Augustinianism" in contemporary times is the picture of a man haunted by sexual memory and harsh doctrine, so concerned about sin and self-introspection that he distorted Christianity. Many times those who painted the picture did not take care to truly understand the world Augustine lived in. The basic ideology upon which his beliefs rested have been replaced by new ones, and one of the problems we face is that Augustine's system of understanding Christian faith has become identified with Christianity itself.

As Augustine's life developed in his struggles with his opponents, he would remember himself as the creature of an omnipotent God, lost in sin and carnality, needing to throw himself on the mercy of this God. More than as a philosophical construct, he saw the human journey as the struggle of the pilgrim soul not in a reasoned or mystical contemplation, but captured by sin and totally unable to work itself out of this dilemma.

While we may think we are far removed from Augustine's world, we must acknowledge that when he turns his insightful eye on the power that humans wield when they are able to grasp at absolute freedom of choice he sounds amazingly contemporary. We moderns may believe that with the right education and the right social conditions the moral behavior of humans would improve, but Augustine was far wiser. All we have to do is look where the earthly city took us in the last twenty centuries. Besides the continuing indifference of the wealthy and the powerful to the poor and dispossessed, the oppression of millions by political rulers, the continuing exploitation of humans as little more than chattel in the fields and mines of the earth, we have the specter that haunts us still. Between two world wars and beyond we created ever more efficient torture chambers, poison gas, sinister biological weapons of destruction, and two holocausts, one the old-fashioned way, one atomic. Jews and Japanese alike raise their voices and confront us with the ways in which we lust for power. The notion of Augustine's *libido dominandi* reveals itself in the destruction and death we have wrought on an unprecedented scale.

While Augustine's particular formulation of the origins of the human condition may not convince many of us in the contemporary setting, his observations on human life are consistent with the facts. G. K. Chesterton's remark that the reality of original sin can be observed at that point on a lovely summer afternoon when bored children start torturing the cat points to something Augustine knew—humans don't seem to work the way they should. If we want to dismiss Augustine we will have to ignore the voices of the homeless, the dispossessed, the tortured, mutilated, and the dead who ask us (and God) "Why?" Original sin is a concept that needs a lot of rethinking, but it is, in the minds of some, the only empirical doctrine of Christianity we have. Does Augustine have anything to add in our quest for understanding ourselves? The issue of what constitutes a self and how we respond to that is before us.

We Are Spirits, Living in the Material World

When we began this chapter, we looked at the situation of how persons are defining themselves and their identities in the world.

We saw a landscape of fragmentation and dissociation that is creating the conditions where many are arguing that no such thing as the self really exists, save as the result of social and psychological cultural constructions. There are selves that are decentered, but we have lost the ability to place self in the postmodern world. We are lost.

We are also creating, through the manipulation of images, a shadow world where fact and fiction, reality and identity have become blurred. Evidences of this abound in such cultural artifacts as *The Blair Witch Project,* purportedly a movie about three people out in the woods looking for a legend and leaving behind supposed footage of their ordeal and disappearance. Clever in itself, this movie was hyped to iconic status by the use of the Internet and stories of misinformation placed in several different media outlets and Internet web sites. These stories gave the illusion of reality that caused many people to argue for the "truth" of the Blair Witch tapes. A blurring of the lines created the reality that people wanted to happen in order to sell more tickets.

Another example of this is a new technology called *Avatarme Ltd.* You step into the *AvatarBooth* and follow the list of instructions as cameras take pictures of you from different angles. The result is that a computer character based on your image appears on screen within moments. It has your face, build, and clothes and can run, jump, and interact with other avatars. The possible applications are numerous, but one is struck by the fact that now we will digitally project ourselves into the entity of the Internet and become the thing we project. How will our technology define our sense of self? Are we becoming a people of surfaces alone, without the texture of depth? Are new entities being created which will populate the world while we stand always behind the curtains, like Oz's wizard?

This is where the look back at Augustine might serve as a corrective for us, because he struggled with the notions of self and identity in a way that is lost to us today. His views were complex and intricate, and we cannot do them full justice, but I want to at least touch upon the contours of his thinking. He has a few concepts that might cause us to reflect about our notion of a self and could even offer us some guidance in the postmodern wilderness.

Besides his most obvious observation that something is fundamentally distorted about human life, Augustine was astute in his observations about the ways in which we see, interpret, and participate in life. He believed we need to be attentive to the way in which we move through the world because we carry the seeds of our own destruction within us, and if we do not truly know ourselves, the power of pride, ambition, power, even love, will create havoc in our lives. Any passing glance at a movie or a television soap opera provides be ample evidence of this particular observation.

Augustine writes in the tenth chapter of the *Confessions* that human beings are a great mystery. We are caught up in the tension of knowing much about our individual selves, but we do not know ourselves and we cannot even trust our own reports about ourselves. Whether because of his neoplatonism or his exegesis of Scripture, Augustine believed that we are not only ourselves, but also the whole of humanity. We have a dual identity. In one sense we are individuals, but we have an identity that makes us one with the corporate life of all human beings. Our individual identities are mysteriously unique, governed as they are by the memories of personal histories, experiences in body and time, freedom of will to choose, and the intellect to reflect on choices.

Unfortunately, we are also marked by the profound wound of something primal and destructive. This wound causes a certain self-incurving that brings us to turn into ourselves and remain forgetful of that identity that is rooted in commonality and solidarity with humankind and God. In this place we are unable to comprehend the abyss in our own hearts, and we have lost the sense, the reality, of our unique and individual being before God. Personal identity is lost to us as we become a bundle of competing selves.

The irony of our predicament is that the deepest identity of ourselves is the image of God which is within us and constitutes the end toward which we should be moving. The self-incurving which we do as humans is toward the wrong goal. The truth of the self is within us, but not in the space that most of us occupy. The way to God, Augustine argues, is through an encounter with those false selves we build that keep us from authentic self-knowledge about our true status. But, and here is the rub for many, we cannot even begin this journey to authenticity until we are enabled to do so by the grace of God.

The several selves that seek voice within us conflict with one another and lead to struggle between competing forces in human life. Augustine speaks to the dispersed and scattered elements of our lives when he writes, "Now my years waste away amid groaning.... But I have leapt down into the flux of time where all is a confusion to me. In the most intimate depths of my soul my thoughts are torn to fragments by tempestuous changes."[19] It is this fragmentation that leads Augustine to ask those perennial questions about identity, "Who am I, and what am I?"[20] He sums up the paradox of both his and our life when, in talking about moral decisions and why he chooses the way he does, he writes, "It is I who willed it, and I who did not—the same I."[21]

We are all aware of these tensions in our lives. The various interior conversations that each of us has can be shown in many instances. We may appear on one hand to be self-making, self-creating creatures, but we also seem to be fragmented and weakened, caught in compulsions we do not understand. We may find Augustine's reflections on sexuality distorted in modernity, but he was dead on target when he said sex made people behave out of a false sense of self and perform absurd acts. We have ample cultural models of how the complex of forces that are involved with our sexual lives compel even world leaders to behave unwisely, out of control, and not in touch with an authentic and unitary self.

Because of these compulsions we forget our true identity, that which rests deepest within ourselves. We have lost understanding of ourselves, and we do not know who or what we are. We can only glimpse that which we have lost and what we might have been. In our entrapment to our self-incurvature we have lost a crucial freedom to be able to understand ourselves. We do not possess the freedom to tell the truth about ourselves and our self-absorbing obsessions. The incoherent selves that compete within us render us incapable of a liberating self-knowledge. We actually imprison ourselves because we will not give up the meager pleasures that come from self-deception. If we can manipulate the world around us to the service of those other selves, the ones so abundant in the postmodern circus, then we need not truly confront the helpless and needy fragmented selves we truly are.

It is a difficult if not impossible task to free ourselves, in no small part because our past is very much alive in our present. In his writing *On the Trinity*, Augustine argues that we are a psycho-

logical image of the trinitarian image of God. Our lives are formed
by self-memory, self-understanding, and self-willing. While these
exist in perfection in God, in us they are imperfect and create the
conditions for our dis-ease.

When Augustine writes that there is an area of ourselves which
not even our spirit knows, he believes that none of us can suf-
ficiently search our own heart because of the sheer size of the
interior world. This can be a source of anxiety much more than
comfort. In our choices we might choose an action, the memory
of which causes us to keep choosing it. If we are choosing from
the place of fragmentation we may choose those acts which, while
pleasurable, are self-destructive and harmful. This is especially the
case if the acts produce approval from those around us, because
one of the marks of our self-distortion is that we are like actors
in a play, seeking to present a particular role to the audience.
If we fail to recognize this, these choices become habits which
sow the seeds of our self-destruction, because then we become enslaved to the habits which become compulsions. Once again, we
are fragmented.

These compulsions need not be such obvious choices as alcohol,
drugs, or promiscuity. These choices can be very subtle. Ambition
is one such choice. At first we do not think much of how this
influences us. We want to succeed or be the best we can be at
something, and this seems rather helpful to our movement in the
world. But, left to our own devices, we may find ambition has
created the conditions in us for betrayal of colleagues, neglect of
our family and friends, and fear of not reaching our full potential
or the irrationality of trying to stay on top.

Augustine knew there was a danger in our thinking we know
what we are really like, because we do not know, cannot know,
and without grace will not know. Self-knowledge is distorted about
the ways in which we think about ourselves and our relationships
with the world around us. Our actions are motivated more often
by self-regard than self-authenticity.

We construct self-images from a storehouse of memories and the
stimulations we receive around us. Maybe we use the postmodern
carnival to choose the identities we will wear, like masks to cloak
ourselves with roles we wish to play, but ultimately all images of
ourselves are corrupted by our projections of what we secretly

wish or desire. The fragmented selves seek their own pleasures. Even our religious identities are not immune from the gravity of such profound deception. Freud was quite right when he argued that our images of God could be constructed of the same material as a transitory and false identity. Without a true reading about ourselves we are deceived about the God we would follow. Think for a minute about how many people's images of God suit their will to power or their culture's agendas. And think how tragic it is that many images of God are fashioned by fear and despair and other images of an inauthentic self.

We form these false selves and selves-in-relation and then mistake this image for what we really are. Yet we are obscured from seeing ourselves as we truly are because we live in a type of exile from ourselves. We have forgotten, failed, or refused to see that our ultimate identity is in the God within us, the image we neglect. At first glance this may seem like the worst form of hubris. Who are we to think we share the divine life? Is this not another illusion? The creature claiming equality with the Creator? However, we still have this notion we cannot shake that we do live an impoverished existence. And in our best moments we act and live as if something greater defines us. The gulf between what we were intended to be and what we have become is so vast a wasteland we cannot even negotiate the terrain. The multiplicity of our lives has left us bereft of a center, and not just in this postmodern world. According to Augustine, we have been decentered all along.

If we want to know ourselves, or to grasp some authentic sense of identity, Augustine suggests that we must first see ourselves in God. Contrary to pride and hubris, this vision may result in some unwanted and unhoped for exposures to something other than that image we desire to project to the world, the role we wanted others to see us play. We may begin to see our frustrated souls as part of our fractured selves. We may gain the knowledge that the emptiness of our lives cannot be filled with more excitement in the postmodern party room, but from the realization that we are loved.

This is difficult for us because love has become so distorted among us. Because of our self-incurvature, love of our own power becomes love of one's own power over others. How many relationships are built in the world which revolve around this dynamic?

And how many lives are shattered because love, power, and control are fashioned from the storehouse of our own self-regarding wills and desires? These desires and the will formed of them motivate us to act in ways that become habits and distort all our attempts at love, because we cannot tell the truth about ourselves to ourselves. Living in self-deception about our true situation, Augustine argues, leaves us unable to recognize our own tendencies to destruction of self and others.

Because these motivations are present within us, cloaked by our belief that we really want the truth, we are afraid of God's love because we are afraid of being destroyed. The truth is, Augustine says, we will be destroyed, but the selves that deconstruct were not our deepest being. That which is destroyed lived an impoverished existence in the prisons of pride, ambition, self-pity, and forgetfulness. We can journey to something better, but we need to be resolute in our journey: "There is some light in persons, but let them walk fast, walk fast, lest the shadows come."[22]

The shadows are always present; Augustine was aware of this. But if we are not attentive we will create a world of nothing but shadows. Augustine himself has been used to create shadows with the invocation of the just war to justify any political conflict, as witnessed by President Bush's use of it before the National Religious Broadcasters meeting during the Iraq conflict. Augustine's insights into human being in the world have been used by totalitarian systems to try to control their citizens in the name of "restraining fallen persons."

Were he among us today he might well have pointed to and critiqued the distortions of his thinking. He would have pointed to the necessity to consider the historical circumstances that gave rise to his writing. One core notion that he probably wouldn't have jettisoned was the absolute supremacy of God and the accompanying absolute helplessness of humankind, as well as the soul's dependency on the grace of God. It is just this which so many react to in Augustine. It is a difficult thing to accept the fact that we need to be saved from ourselves, even more, that we are incapable of saving ourselves. The unmasking of hidden impulses, the courage to take off the masks we wear before the world, the willingness to deconstruct the fragmented and false selves that speak and command us is not a job we are able to do alone. And it is just that disability that is so disturbing, for we see ourselves as autonomous, free, and constructing the world. Surely world-constructing entities are not enslaved to some ancient story about estrangement from God?

But on some deeper level the estrangement is from ourselves. For in the depths of ourselves there rests a true identity, not the one constructed from the ephemeral world of postmodernity. In this shadow world of nebulous entities, existing in streams of light and digital images, we find our culture surfacing and staying there. We are cast about by the blender of multiphrenia. We are riding a roller-coaster that twists, turns, does stomach-turning maneuvers, but has no destination in sight. We are constantly moving in and out of identities, never able to rest, lest the world realize that all is image and no substance exists under the surface textures of the postmodern carnival. Augustine speaks to us still in this context when he writes: "For you, O God, have made us for yourself, and our hearts are restless until we find our rest in you."[23]

In a world populated with protean selves we shape-shift to meet the necessity of the moment. But these shapes carry the shadow of deception, the actors we become for one another in order that we might maintain our illusions. Nietzsche and Freud saw this when they realized that the performative aspects of humankind lead to all manner of deception. Augustine had in mind a more radical deconstruction, one which influenced the course of the Western world. For all his failings perhaps he leaves us with some things we need to face. In the postmodern world the soul has become a self, and a self not in touch with its true situation is precarious, as changeable as Proteus. Once we find our most fundamental shape, however, we will be able to offer words of truth and prophecy to a world in love with its own destruction.

⊹══ Chapter 3 ══⊹

Thinking about the Unthinkable

Anselm and the Quest for God

Fides quaerens intellectum,
faith seeking understanding

I N THE NOVEL *Roger's Version,* by John Updike, a seminary professor is beset by a young computer whiz who is seeking the
ultimate mystery about God by using his computer to unlock the
code that will make everything clear. The student tells the professor that it is all in the numbers, and if he can figure it out he
will have a clear and distinct revelation of God. Throughout the
rest of the book the professor and student argue the case as to
how, exactly, God is known to us. The notion that God can be
found by the efforts of a computer program depresses the professor, who believes the search for God is far messier and unsettling
than decoding the right message from heaven.

Similarly, the seldom seen and very unsettling independent
movie *Pi* tells the story of another erstwhile genius and seeker
who is also crunching the numbers on his array of computers in
a grimy little apartment in New York. He is hard at work on decoding the mysteries of the universe by using numbers. There are
others who are also interested in this pursuit. It seems that some
Jewish Kaballists are interested in his discoveries, as well as Wall
Street types who believe the patterns he is working on may reveal
the mystery of economic forces and will be very valuable in the
pursuit of profit. So in this movie both the profane and the sacred
are in their own way after the knowledge they believe rests "out
there" somewhere waiting to be revealed.

Not only in the movies, but also on National Public Radio there
is a segment that comes on occasional Saturdays which features
someone known as "the math guy." The math guy is Keith Devlin,

a professor from California, who has the wonderful gift of being able to take a subject that confounds many people and to make it extraordinarily interesting. One of the most interesting things he talks about is something called the Fibonacci numbers. This sequence of numbers occurs within many of the phenomena of the natural world. From flower petals to the stripes of the leopard, it seems that there really is a correspondence between our understanding of mathematics and the external world.

Since Pythagoras we have examples of persons who seek the clue for the meaning of the universe in such processes of the mind like mathematics. Certainly this is one of the foundations of science and is not limited to those who seek some religious secret in understanding the world. The impetus for this comes from the fact that we are embedded within a reality we are constantly seeking to interpret and make sense of. The main idea is that reality is somehow out there waiting for us to read it correctly. We have seen how this notion of the world has undergone scrutiny in modern times and how our capacity for interpreting the world has been pointed out to be a distinctive activity of human life. This also has had implications for how we do theology.

In this chapter I want to suggest that Anselm of Canterbury gives us an intriguing perspective on the way we intuit the reality of God. He shares something with the previously mentioned examples because he does believe that the existence of God is present to our minds, but it is an existence discovered by faith.

In our day, it may seem difficult to imagine Anselm of Canterbury (1033–1109) as having much to contribute to the struggles of contemporary theology. The notions of partiality, relativism, and contextuality that mark our age do not allow us easy assent to Anselm's certainty concerning theological ideas. The confidence in reason he possessed seems foreign to an age in which the recognition of the historical character of human existence is often said to entail the abandonment of theological projects rooted in the past.

We live in a time in which reason is seen as contextually analytical. Most do not see reason or rationality existing outside the limitations of the culture and history within which it emerges. Thus understood, the methodology of reflection, analysis, construction, and criticism is to be seen as circular reiteration of reason's historically conditioned background beliefs. Reason does inform human knowing, but always as a project rooted in a contextually particular location. For many the issue is how any connection with the past can inform the contemporary discussion at all.

Epistemological issues have replaced metaphysical ones as being of primary importance for us. With the breakdown or erosion of foundational certainty and the recognition that reality can be both generated and interpreted according to who is doing the reasoning about it, theology struggles with the increasing multiplicity of contemporary perspectives. The debate over the lack of foundations for knowledge and meaning produces anxiety since we realize that the historical and experiential bases of faith and theology are themselves interpretive endeavors.

This raises a host of questions about reason's employment in theological thinking. Put bluntly, if Anselm formulates a doctrine of salvation like substitutionary atonement on the model of a medieval legal construct, how much credence should we give this in our age? Or, to use another example, if a contemporary theologian formulates an idea of salvation that draws from the worlds of scientific inquiry or current cultural ideas, how can this be seen as normative if fifty years from now our understandings of the world have changed? Given the critique of those like Ludwig Feuerbach or Sigmund Freud, who argue that in talking about God we are merely projecting ourselves out into the world, how do we accept theology as anything other than a human construct?

These are the questions that exercise us. The choices we make in the face of these questions and uncertainties reflect judgments about our agendas and interests. If I construe a notion of God's causal activity in the world, on what basis can I argue that this may really approximate God's interaction with the world? Or is the construal a very clever attempt to domesticate God for my use? In the midst of indeterminacy of meaning, conflicts of interpretation, shifts in understanding, are there any paths reflective of something other than a culturally and historically conditioned perspective which will be swept away by the sands of time?

And following what we have said earlier, what role does human reason play in any of this? Are there only specific, localized rationalities; or does reason transcend in some way our social and cultural locations? If we accept the fact that no secure foundations exist for the universal agreement or acceptance of reasoning, can we still maintain that something about our thinking does touch the transcendent?

In what follows, I would like to suggest that Anselm offers us something to think about. While his approach can be highly problematic, his concerns were remarkably similar to ours. I will examine one piece of his legacy, the ontological argument for God, called the *Proslogion,* in order to show that he offers us insight into theological method which may enable us to think through some of our most perplexing issues.

Anselm's Journey

According to Anselm's biographer, Eadmer, Anselm was attending to a very ill king when he was suddenly named the new archbishop of Canterbury. Depending on the veracity we can grant to these accounts, Anselm fiercely resisted this office with tears of protests, bleeding noses, and clenched fists. Reportedly, the king could not press the pastoral staff into Anselm's clenched hands, and finally the assembled bishops forced open his hands and closed his fingers around the staff. He was then carried into church to shouts of acclamation, while he himself protested against the assignment. The day ended in no small confusion; however, Anselm still held the crozier.

Whether we can take all this on face value depends on how much credence we are willing to offer the sincerity of Anselm. Other reports indicate this was the hoped for result of Anselm's own machinations revolving around an extended visit to England from his home monastery in Bec, France. Thus, while he may have protested fiercely in the beginning, as the subsequent proceedings took place, he did not object when he could have stopped the process at any point. How had Anselm's life come to this? He was at one moment a monk, a thinker, alone in contemplation on the mystery of God, and the next he was the archbishop of Canterbury embroiled in the public life of the church.

Anselm was born in 1033 in the Alpine town of Aosta, an ancient Roman town on the Italian-French border. In about 1056, he moved to the north, crossing the Alps and living in different areas of the Rhône valley and France. Eventually he ended up in Bec, where he was taught by Lanfranc, the prior of Bec.

Lanfranc had a reputation as an able administrator and advisor to the powerful. He had acquired some fame as a teacher, but his commitment as a monk had made a significant difference on the life of the monastery at Bec; and by the time of Anselm's arrival, the monastery itself stood in a position of importance for the church.

Anselm himself felt very pulled in two different directions—one was the desire for intellectual fame and the other was a longing for monastic order in his life. He committed himself to the life of a monk and was diligent in following the demands of the Rule of St. Benedict. But he was also acquiring grammatical and philosophical skills that would serve him for the rest of his life. His education at Bec, under the tutelage of Lanfranc, would lay the groundwork for the rest of Anselm's life.

In his earliest works, Anselm was very much interested in the issues of how logic and linguistics operate. He was intrigued by the acts of speech and language which are the basis for logic. He thought he could penetrate the surface of words and appearances to reach the reality to which they refer. This was very much what Anselm was exploring in one of his first works, *De Grammatico*.

Yet, the other aspect of Anselm's life was being cultivated as well, for his dedication to the interior life was intensifying at Bec. He was writing his *Prayers* and *Meditations*, which were more along the lines of spiritual guides and advice than of philosophical treatises. He brought this strong sense of meditation to his theological work and biblical grounding.

He was also becoming immersed in the thought of Augustine. He claimed Augustine as the one who provided the seeds that were to flower under Anselm's care. He absorbed Augustine, finding there fresh perspectives, new insights, and a way to approach theological reflection. Under the influence of Augustine Anselm not only felt the need for a more intense personal devotion; he gave it a more profound intellectual expression.

In this intellectual endeavor, Anselm followed a process that embraced the pursuit of knowledge that came both from the senses and also from the mind's introspective knowledge of itself. Yet, for him, all knowledge ultimately leads one to the knowledge of God. Empirical observation is coupled with spiritual introspection in such a way that one ascends beyond the corruptible and worldly things toward the incorruptible and heavenly things.

While Anselm shared Augustine's passion for the intellectual explorations of faith, his journey would focus on the introspective aspects of the monastery. He would not share Augustine's living so deeply in the turbulence of the world, nor his strong sense of historical development. This was evident in some of his earliest writings, such as *Prayers* and *Meditations.*

These writings were to put the distinct stamp of Anselm upon the development of medieval spirituality. One of these primary changes was in the soul's movement from a corporate, anonymous environment, to the individual standing alone before God, engaged in deep introspection and seeking God's remedy for the effect of sin on the individual's life. This strong inward turn was accompanied by a disciplined and high degree of mental exertion for realizing abstract states of being. Five years later in the *Monologion* and *Proslogion,* introspection had become the first step to the knowledge of God.

Much intellectual ferment was taking place around Anselm. The rise of the secular schools meant that disputes and debates became an accepted means of clarifying thought. Localized and particular understandings, based on reading, were brought into systematically contrived juxtapositions in order that new knowledge might emerge. This was a reversal of Anselm's method. Sharpness of understanding rather than prolonged meditation became a prime requirement for the execution of reason.

But something else was important about Anselm's employment of reason. He was developing a method of reasoning that did not necessarily make appeal to external authorities, a fact Anselm's mentor, Lanfranc, thought was misguided. The authorities had always been the proper guides. Though beneath the surface the Bible and Augustine may have been presupposed, no overt appeal to either is made in Anselm's reasoning process.

Questions are raised, using this method, about the relationship of introspective reasoning and authoritative statements on Christian faith. Indeed, Anselm's own orthodoxy was questioned because he wouldn't employ outside authors or appeal to biblical authority. But Anselm felt very strongly the need to ascend beyond the gravity of sin and self-interest present in human life.

This exerted a profound pull on reason, and for Anselm meant that spiritual discipline was crucial to the free exercise of reason.

Even in Anselm's day, many thought his position difficult to maintain because he tried to achieve a theology based on reason to the extent that anyone who gave serious thought to Christian doctrine could not fail to be orthodox. Anselm carried an overwhelming sense that the glory of God is inaccessible to human understanding. Yet, it is this very inaccessibility which ought to cause us to stretch our minds in search of God.

Between 1076 and 1078, two pieces of writing came from Anselm's pen which were to employ this use of reason. The most famous of these, the *Proslogion,* would forever seal Anselm's fame within the Western intellectual heritage. This argument is the only general philosophical argument discovered in the Middle Ages which has survived to still exercise the interests of philosophers.

Revisiting the Argument

This interest has shown up in the numerous books and articles that have recently been published about Anselm's argument for the existence of God from philosophers and theologians like Charles Hartshorne, John Hick, and G. R. Evans.[24] Its fascination can be seen in the story of the English philosopher Bertrand Russell, no great friend of theism, who was walking in London one day when he remembers:

> The precise moment, one day in 1894, as I was walking along Trinity Lane, when I saw in a flash (or thought I saw) that the ontological argument is valid. I had gone out to buy a tin of tobacco; on my way back, I suddenly threw it up in the air, and exclaimed as I caught it: "Great Scott, the ontological argument is sound."[25]

In the argument Anselm connects the word "God" to a specific definition, "a greater than which cannot be conceived." While Anselm is wondering why humans have conceived of "a greater than which cannot be conceived," he formulates a series of thoughts which lead him to God's existence. While our purpose in this chapter is not to extensively treat the argument, the general lines of it run in a particular direction.

Even the Fool who is described by the Psalmist as one who says in his heart there is no God will answer, if questioned about what God is, that God is that than which nothing greater can be conceived. If he understands the meaning of the words, then even the Fool will admit that we have this conception in our minds. The "greater than which cannot be conceived" exists in our understanding. If this existed in our understanding alone, it could be surpassed by something greater, that which existed in reality as well as the understanding. Therefore, God exists in reality as well as the understanding. There were, of course, numerous objections to this form of the argument which led Anselm to a second form of the argument. In response to the monk Guanilo, who raised the issue of how humans can imagine the most perfect islands, but that doesn't necessitate their existence, Anselm moves his argument to another line of thought.

The greatest possible being, a "greater than which cannot be conceived" still exists in our understanding. But here the argument diverges. This being either can or cannot exist, or has contingent existence. But this being could be surpassed by a being that must exist, a being whose nonexistence is inconceivable. The greatest possible being has necessary existence, because to even conceive of nonexistence means something greater can be thought, a being whose nonexistence is impossible. Therefore, God cannot be thought of as nonexistent without self-contradiction.

Historically, this argument came to be known as the ontological argument for God's existence, but the irony is that the term "ontological" may be a misnomer. The term was given by the German philosopher, Immanuel Kant, and suggests that the argument amounted to an attempt to derive being (*ontos*) from reasoning (*logos*). From the conceptual notion of "that than which nothing greater can be conceived" Anselm, so Kant believed and interpreted, argued to the existence of God so that no contradiction emerges between thought and being. However, the question is whether the argument can be seen in such a way that it should not be defined by the concept "ontology" as defined by metaphysics.

For Kant, the fallacy of the argument rests precisely in the notion that being cannot be generated from the process of reasoning itself. Even more than this, when Kant critiqued the supposed ontology of Anselm's argument, Descartes's later formulation of the argument entered the picture, muddying the waters and leading some to argue that it is Descartes's formulation of the argument that Kant actually critiques.[26] This informed Kant's notion that "existence is not a predicate," and the ensuing dismissal of the argument occurs on the basis of a purely logical relationship between subjects and predicates and whether or not a correspondence between knowing and being coinheres.

The issue seemed buried with Kant, but such is the intriguing pull of the argument that it emerged again in the 1960s with the works of various philosophers such as Norman Malcolm and Charles Hartshorne, and theologians such as John Hick. In these later evaluations some have argued that the supposed ontological nature of the argument has been wrongly interpreted.

Earlier than this, Karl Barth recognized that there was a second dimension in Anselm's reasoning, but, more importantly, Barth found in Anselm a way of theological reasoning. More specifically, Barth called attention to the fact that the starting point of the argument was faith, not conceptual obviousness. The motto *fides quaerens intellectum,* which inaugurates the *Proslogion,* indicates that faith does not merely provide reason with neutral data; rather faith leads reason and rationality all along the speculative way. But in this instance to where does it lead? A linguistic-logical analysis, or an ambiguity in human experience that issues in an intuitive sense of the divine?

Perhaps we can say a little of both. Anselm's biographer, Eadmer, speaks of an illumination concerning this argument that Anselm had during Matins, yet he had been living with the issue for quite awhile and was certainly using the conceptual world available to him at the time. There does appear to be the sense that "intelligence proceeds from faith because rationality consists mainly in recognizing in faith the permanent and radical condition of the possibility of thinking."[27] Rationality takes place most accurately and completely within the dimensions of faith, particularly when rationality is bestowed by the object of faith's reasoning, God. In this way theology moves according to a prior determination of its object from faith to knowledge. Reason has to believe in order to understand.

For Anselm the determination of faith establishes the beginning as well as the end of faith given by God. It marks as well the boundary lines for theological thought. We cannot think of God because God lies at the limit of our understanding. Because God is the very thought which does lie at the limit of our understanding, reason detached from faith cannot achieve understanding. In other words, faith is the first condition of speculation and the last horizon of understanding.

This does add an interesting notion to Anselm's supposed ontological argument. The fact that God dwells in what Anselm terms the unreachable light is not only the beginning; it is also the end of the argument. Knowledge would never abolish faith or God's inaccessibility; rather it makes us discern God's inaccessibility as a definite feature of God.

This paradoxical feature of Anselm's being suspended between the presuppositions of faith and divine hiddenness allows for a reading of Anselm that does not lend itself to the interpretation that Kant and others have given it. To ask the question why humans have conceived of a thing a greater than which cannot be conceived seems to be starting along the path of intrinsically connecting knowing and being. Faith leads us to the notion that God can be thought of only as something we cannot conceive:

> The only evidence that thought might really deal with the question of God and his supposed essence consists in this: it can transcend all conceived concepts, and, more, it can experience the limits of its conceiving power.... As long as our thought can still think in concepts, no God appears; God appears only as soon as thought cannot go further: God begins exactly where and when the concept falls short.[28]

The overwhelming sense that the glory of God is inaccessible to human understanding and a belief that it is this very inaccessibility which ought to cause us to stretch our minds upward in search of God informed Anselm's approach in the *Proslogion*. The idea of God is not derived by human ingenuity or effort; rather Anselm starts with the principle of meditation, clearing away the clutter of everyday concerns to find how God structures reason. Without this meditative discipline of prayer and the foundation of faith, no argument such as this would emerge.[29]

Barth's Interpretation of Anselm

While others may have been concerned and exercised by the Kantian legacy of the supposed ontological dimensions of the *Proslogion,* it was Karl Barth who, by investigating the *Proslogion,* would call attention to Anselm as a contemporary source for theological reflection.[30] Rejecting the ontological interpretation, which he felt was foreign to the argument, Barth centered on the issue of rationality and theological method. He knew that the intellect which concerned Anselm was not knowledge in the abstract, but knowledge informed by faith. The intelligence of faith consists in a meditation on the object of theology, God, as the proper object.

It is not theology's place as faithful understanding to seek to establish this object; rather God establishes the limits and parameters within which theological investigation takes place. God bestows, in grace, any ability to think rightly. Such a theology finds its goal in the conditions of prayer. Done in prayer then, even at the boundary line, there is a connection to be made.

This connection is not one of a constituent ordering between being and thought. Rather the connection is between the general awareness of thought and words, and the knowing that comes from the rationality determined by God. And what is this rationality that is so determined? It is not an inherent capacity of human reasoning, a universal ability of all human beings. There does exist a natural rationality which allows us to deal with experience, form conceptions, and make judgments, but this is not the rationality grounded in faith.

Human thinking, guided by and under obedience to faith, allows for a fuller understanding of the rationality of faith. This allows for the conditions of true knowing. But another ground of understanding is present as well. For in addition to knowing, there is the reality of the Word and action of God in revelation, or the proper object of faith. This higher ground functions as the goal of human understanding, resulting in a relationship between the knower and the known, between humankind and God.

However, the relationship between human knowing and the being of God is based on and rooted in a third and ultimate order, the source of all truth, which is God. Barth says this ground of knowing is identical with the totality of all orders of knowledge. It is on the basis of God as the ultimate truth that any correspondence occurs between our knowledge and the reality of God.

The truth of an object's existence and nature is dependent upon God as the source of all truth. Epistemologically speaking, faithful knowledge and understanding is connected to the source and ground of that very knowing. This is not given to us as an immanent nexus of the relationship between the human and divine, because it is not recognized by us in a way which makes the correspondences a constituent part of human epistemology. God is the master of all means of knowing, so in the event of knowing, it is God who orders the coherences between knower and the known such that true perception occurs.

In Barth's reading, any interpretation of Anselm that assumes Anselm posits an intrinsic link between thought and reality to ground his argument does not consider the epistemological order of an understanding formed by faithfulness. If truth is to be obtained, it is on the basis of God's gracious decision. This is the basis for Anselm's prayerful meditation at the beginning of the argument.

Given that God is inaccessible to us in our own inherent reasoning, God must order the correspondence so that in the act of understanding the believer's reason conforms to the reason proper to the object of investigation. Or put another way, if the rational knowledge of God is ultimately derived from God as Truth and from God's will, there does exist a correspondence between being and knowing, which takes place under the gracious and free action of God.

Barth saw Anselm as always standing on his own ground of *fides quaerens intellectum,* not accepting criteria such as universal human reasoning or religious self-consciousness as the guiding force in theological revelation. Anselm did not see an inherent and necessary connection between thought and reality any more than our age does. However, if we perceive reality to be fragmentary, deconstructed, and contingent, Anselm would argue that we see it this way because we attempt to rationalize the world on the basis of a natural reason or rationality not informed by the being of God.

This will always be the case when we make metaphysical

assumptions about the world on the basis of an epistemology un-
informed by the source of all truth. In theological discussion the
object of faith exists in such a way that it is impossible for it not to
exist, and impossible for it to exist differently, because it is given
in revelation and is certain in faith. Anselm's starting point is not
to seek what can be, but to seek what is, or better still, what cannot fail to be. He finds the way to knowledge on the basis and
confidence of faith that there might be a valid use of the human
capacity to form concepts and judgments.

Toward what "proof" then was Anselm pointing? What was
his aim with the *Proslogion?* Barth also takes up this issue and
points out that Anselm's thinking is done in relation to the One
whom he is to address and who stands over against the human.
Thus we understand immediately that theology is relational and
that the human position in that relationship is one of prayer and
obedience. Thought is not an autonomous process whereby we
storm the gates of reason.

The truth inherent in the articles of the Christian Credo forms
the basis of discussion. The objective reality found within the texts
of Holy Scripture and the Creeds is not open to question. Anselm
is not going to vacate his intellectual cathedra, even temporarily,
because it is on the basis of faithful knowing, the acceptance of
the truth of revelation, that the discussion proceeds.

In the *Proslogion* Anselm may have something to say to the
unbeliever; however, he does not do this in a strictly apologetic
sense. His primary audience was the Benedictine monks and theologians of his day. He is not walking hand in hand with the
unbeliever seeking to reconstruct God's necessary existence by the
force of logical necessity. He is not conceding an epistemic rationality without its being conditioned by God's gracious decision,
and ultimately by the totality of truth.

The argument is not played out on the grounds of unbelief
because the nonbeliever does not have the power of intellectual
self-redemption to go from a natural rationality to a faith-ordered
reason. Given what was said earlier about Anselm's inferring God's
existing from the very impossibility of producing any concept of
God on the basis of a critical examination of the limits of human
thinking, a God demonstrable by us through the universal human
reason or even religious self-consciousness would be idolatrous.

Nevertheless, it is important to realize that some common ground exists upon which to engage in discourse with the unbeliever. What both are meaning and seeking in their questions is the same. The believer cannot force the unbeliever into a position of knowing ordered by faith, but that does not preclude a movement where the unbeliever moves to the position of faith. Barth puts it this way:

> Anselm's Proof works on the assumption that there is a solidarity between the theologian and the worldling which has not come about because the theologian has become one of the crowd, or one voice in a universal debating chamber, but because he is determined to address the worldling as one with whom he has at least this in common—theology.[31]

Anselm's Vision for Us

We may not be able to follow Anselm completely along the path, but the issues he raises find contemporary relevance. The recognition of our historicity leads to an understanding of humans as people of tradition, shaped through languages, belief systems, and rituals of distinctive historical positions. Yet this same awareness sometimes paralyzes our ability to constitute priorities or paradigms in the face of conflict and changes in context.

We struggle with the issue of how Christian claims can be regarded as authoritative, yet contextually particular. How can the reasoning which stands behind these claims be separated from the context from which these claims emerge? Reasoning itself is contextually particular, tied to systems of meaning devised from within each context. This has often led those who interrogate religion and Christian theology to argue that a particular concept or even experience of God, and a certain way of seeing God's relationship to the world, are bound together and expressed in a particular metaphysical and historically conditional form. These concepts, derived from an experience of the world, were often absolutized and projected into the beyond.

The resulting critique has not come solely from those who have no religious commitment, but from the various dissenting theologies which question whether class, gender, or race interests can be transcended in the search for any possible universal human experience of God.

Anselm echoes our questions when he asks how it is possible for us to say anything about God. He realizes that reasoning does stand within that framework of beliefs and practices in which it emerges. There is no extracontextual alternative for this. Yet religious commitment is an important context for reasoning. One cannot divorce thinking about the object of faith from faith itself. Theology has always conceived its task as faith seeking understanding and in doing so has a commitment to an authority that supersedes any foundations on contextually based reason. John Thiel writes, "Within theology's own context of meaning faith seeking understanding well expresses the priority of contextual meaning expected by nonfoundational criticism of any exercise of reason."[32]

Because Anselm's *Proslogion* has all too often been read in the light of Kant's critique and all that subsequently followed, his distinctive theological reasoning has been neglected and overlooked. In his book on Anselm, Barth paid particular attention to his theological method and concluded that the usual critiques of Anselm were misplaced.

Loyalty to Christian identity remained for Anselm the first responsibility of theological interpretation and the only authentic basis for theological reasoning. Anselm would not have shared the belief that a progressive and sure epistemological foundation was at hand, immanently accessible, to which he could lead the unbeliever and from which they could share common assumptions.

Rather, Anselm appears to proceed on the basis that theological inference should defer in its logic to the meaningful context of Christian belief. Ironically, a wealth of articles have been published about Anselm's argument, and centuries of philosophers, theologians, and other interested parties have mulled over the *Proslogion*. If the abiding interest in his argument is any indication, it would appear that Anselm's theological reasoning is not restricted solely to the contextual world of the medieval Benedictine monastery, but transcends time and place to the extent that we still wrestle with the puzzle Anselm poses.

His argument does allow us at least a glimpse of how the relative and fragmentary character of reason and theology as seen from our perspective is only part of the story. At least in this instance Anselm's argument does indicate that reason can have some connection to a reality that we ourselves do not construct. This is one of the reasons that mathematics has the appeal that it does for many; the notion that the math we seem to intuit and reason about does have some correspondence with the world external to us. The continuing discussion concerning the *Proslogion* allows us to reflect upon the tensions inherent in all human reasoning and realize that while contextuality is crucial to an understanding of reason, it is not absolute.

Beyond this Anselm offers us other perspectives to consider. He is a theologian who moves within the context of a narrative authority. His subjective belief has the tradition of the church as its point of reference. This tradition includes, among other things, the Bible as well as the creeds of the early church. But it is a tradition that Anselm is ready to reinterpret for his time as shown in his understanding of Jesus and his work found in his treatise *Cur Deus Homo?*

It is this tradition that sets the conditions and possibilities for theology. Anselm shows all throughout his thinking that he is compelled by a truth expressed by very concrete particulars. In the quest for understanding, the message of the gospel is affirmed in faith as universal. No matter the contextuality and limited nature of theological reflection, faith does not need universal justification to be meaningful for all times.

When theology abandons this ground in its desire to address the world, it may find itself with nothing to say. Seeking to justify itself within its cultural context, it runs the risk of connecting its theology so strongly to that culture that its construals of God will diminish when the cultural forms it arose within pass into yet other forms. Even Anselm is not immune from the force of social location. We can see in our time where theology has become a functional matter. We formulate a conception of the world, an idea of God in relation to that world, and the recognition of the world as experienced in the light of that idea. God becomes a religious symbol or concept, useful for employment in a variety of means and agendas. By theology's domestication of God, it has made itself more vulnerable to Feuerbach's critique than ever. The question for us is how we will respond to those who question whether theology has any relevance or voice if it merely mirrors our projective identification of self, tribe, and nation.

The great paradox in Anselm is that his commitment to the narrative authority of Scripture and creed allowed him the awareness that it is impossible completely to comprehend the word for God, because God would then be within the grasp of created beings and would be less than God. The notion that God stands as the limitation of our thinking permits Anselm to claim that the universality of Christianity is found in its expression of belief and not the expectation of an inherent, constituent rationality, common to all persons.

Even as Anselm offered us a realization of the relational and narrative character of theology, he offered another contribution to the contemporary context. His theology was rooted in a spiritual discipline and community. His theological method was based on an introspective meditation, and he worked hard to prepare his readers' minds through a homily, or an account of how prayerful a state his mind was in before he engaged them. This was especially true of the *Proslogion*. The authority of Augustine stands in the background of the *Monologion,* but in the *Proslogion,* a meditation arising from prayer addressed to God, Anselm stands on unique ground, prepared by his earlier writings and spiritual exercises.

In *Prayers* and *Meditations* some of Anselm's struggles find their first form. Theology begins as introspection, and for Anselm this introspection may lead to a profound sense of self-abasement. This is not an abuse of the self, but rather a recognition of how little we achieve under our own steam. This allows for a searching of the mind and heart to ensure that corruption does not hinder thinking and meditative reflection from working toward the same goal—the knowledge of God.

Disciplined consideration of our own being and Divine Being moves theology into the realm of contemplation. The sustained mental effort required in this effort serves to guard against the self-illusions that can taint reason. Indeed, we should even reflect on the notion of theology as a spiritual discipline in the contemporary context.

In this sense theology would require more of us than our academic preparation, or even our native abilities (or cleverness). It would require unrelenting honesty about our motives, our will to power, even our desires. I always find it ironic when we are confronted with theologies which argue that they are the authentic perspective for postmodernity, but also want to argue that all perspectives are provisional, save theirs. Whose interests are being served in contemporary theology? From where do such theologies emerge? What allegiances do they ask of us? Relentless searching of our theologies would be extraordinarily revealing.

One of the areas we should give greater thought to is the context of the community of faith for theological reflection. In the present situation where do we see theology emerging from communities where a rigorous spiritual discipline shapes the life and thought of the community? When the temptations to power and self- and corporate illusions are so strong we need the resources of those who are engaged in the necessary disciplines of spiritual formation to keep us honest.

It may be argued that seminaries and theological schools perform that function. However, we are experiencing the same reversal that emerged in Anselm's day. When the spiritual discipline that informed Anselm's *Proslogion* was neglected, the results were the schools, where sharpness of understanding was more important than prolonged meditation, thus reversing Anselm's path. Which model seems to inform contemporary theological education more? While there is movement in this area, I suspect Anselm's model of spiritual discipline could offer us some wisdom.

Theology today should pay attention to this aspect of Anselm. Engaging in the disciplines of prayer and meditation we may find in our theology something other than a projective identification of human and cultural constructs. We may find that reason can touch those places that reside in inaccessible light and transcend in some small way all contextuality. Communities that embody the joining of intellect and a spiritually disciplined intuition can offer truths that will intrigue and spiritually inform those who follow us. This would be a fine legacy for us to leave the future, to show that Anselm is contemporary with all ages in his search for God at the boundaries.

Chapter 4

Creation Calling

Thomas Aquinas and Ecological Cosmology

The earth should not be injured! The earth must not be destroyed. As often as the elements of the world are violated by ill-treatment, so God will cleanse them. God will cleanse them through the sufferings and hardships of humankind. — Hildegard of Bingen, *Meditations*

To a man with a hammer, everything looks like a nail.
  — Neil Postman, *Technopoly: The Surrender of Culture to Technology*

W HEN HILDEGARD WROTE the words above she could scarcely have imagined that her part of the world would have suffered the way it did in the twentieth century: the wounds of two world wars, suffering on a scale almost impossible to contemplate. And her particular part of the world has suffered even more from ecological disaster. It was not enough that the radium rain from Chernobyl drifted westward out of the Ukraine to make eating vegetables an uncertain experience, but her beloved Rhine Valley experienced the suffering of human folly. A Swiss government official reports that "the Rhine is now dead. The whole ecosystem is destroyed due to this accident."[33]

The river valley where two of the greatest mystics of Christianity, Meister Eckhart and Hildegard of Bingen, probed the mysteries of a world of interdependence and connectedness is dying from thousands of tons of chemicals and eight tons of mercury alone being poured into its lifeblood, the Rhine River. Further on, the Mediterranean Sea is yielding fish that are poisoned, and the specter of ecological disaster haunts the European landscape, especially in those countries where decades of neglect and pollution have released toxins into soil, water, and air.

Not just Europe, but the rest of the planet suffers from the same disease. We are familiar with the names. Bhopal, Love

Canal, Three Mile Island, and Chernobyl are only some of the most famous instances where human greed and shortsightedness has carried tremendous cost and suffering. There are more, of course, but these suffice to portray the myriad ways we are affecting the ecosystem in which we live, breathe, and have our being. Hildegard was right; we will suffer the consequences of our thoughtlessness.

At Love Canal, seemingly so long ago, but still very much a part of our consciousness, there were eighteen pregnancies. Out of the eighteen there were three stillborn fetuses, four spontaneous abortions, nine birth defects, including incomplete skull closures, multiple rows of teeth, cleft palate, congenital heart defects, and genetic damage. There were two normal births. All men living at Love Canal had the DNA in their sperm cells poisoned, and we have no known way of healing this.[34]

The very day I write these words the United States president is in the Ukraine, and the announcement is made that Chernobyl will be shut down fourteen years after the world's worst nuclear power plant accident sent plumes of radioactivity over Europe. Spewing two hundred times as much radioactivity as the atomic bombs that were dropped on Hiroshima and Nagasaki, Chernobyl took an estimated 8,000 lives, including 31 killed immediately, at least 4,365 workers who took part in the cleanup, and others who died of cancer and other radiation-related illnesses.

These deaths are not the only suffering from this event. Currently 400,000 adults and 1.1 million children are entitled to state aid for Chernobyl-related health problems, and massive unemployment affects the region. The cleanup and containment costs are staggering. The suffering from this abuse of the earth will be felt for generations, and Hildegard's warning acquires a contemporary urgency.[35]

Would that this were an isolated incident, but numerous books have been written which detail the growing ecological disaster that awaits us if we do not find ways to live on this planet in some harmony with earth the way it is. As we survey the state of the world, we see topsoil, necessary for food, being eroded. Demands for living space, shopping malls, and parking lots create the conditions where we are choking ourselves to death. The very sustenance of our lives is being swept away. In addition to these concerns there is the growing crisis of potable water. In the United States alone we dump eighty billion pounds of toxic waste into our water annually. Half of our water comes from underground aquifers, and yet reports are coming in from many areas that indicate we are poisoning these sources of life. Once they are poisoned we cannot clean up these sites, which means that the fifty thousand toxic waste sites that infect our environment are slowly poisoning the environment.

We have not even mentioned the ozone layer and the holes that appear within it. The increase of skin cancer worldwide points to the reality that we are protected from the sun's radiation by a layer of ozone, which if compressed would be about an eighth of an inch thick. This is all that stands between us and unimaginable health risks. And yet we are continually creating the conditions for the erosion of this protection. We are suffering from our inability to see the interconnectedness of all things.

This lack of sight results in another self-inflicted wound we deal ourselves. We are the species that channels a massive amount of resources and wealth (1.8 million dollars a minute) into the design and production of weapons aimed at destroying and killing ourselves and other life on this planet in the name of protection. Given the underground nuclear testing that takes place, we still unleash vast amounts of destructive energy into the very fabric of the planet.

This has just been a quick sketch of some of the concerns that stretch our ability and imagination for solutions presently. Everywhere we turn we are faced with the consequences of our short-sightedness and foolishness. Apparently we lack enough wisdom or courage to understand or envision the world in a way that would not cause continual destruction of it. Given the number of books that have been written detailing the destruction we are unleashing upon our environment, this comes as no surprise, but the question remains as to how we will respond to it.

I want to suggest that we got here on a particular path, and this was connected to a certain way of looking at the world. Indeed, I want to suggest that a certain metaphysical way of understanding the world has been our guiding factor in our abuse of it. In thinking through this I agree with the postmodern critique that questions a metaphysics that assumes a connection between its formulations and the way reality really is. I then want to think about the way Thomas Aquinas looked at the world and suggest that he has a perspective that could help us correct some of our problems today.

At first glance this may seem like an odd idea. A medieval theologian best known perhaps for those famous "proofs" for the existence of God with which students have had to struggle considered as a potential antidote for the dis-ease that afflicts us sounds like quite a stretch. But Aquinas may offer us something that we desperately need—a world perspective that contains wisdom, no matter how culturally situated it is. It is the wisdom that sees a relationship of the whole to the part and asks us to consider that when we don't perceive any goals or ends in things themselves, we will use any means necessary to accomplish our own ends. In some profound way we have arrived at the point of corporate suicide through a path of pieces and fragments, a process that began with the rise of modern science.

Moving God to the Margins

As we saw in the first chapter, when Galileo and Newton among others started recording their observations of the world, things became known to us differently than before. With the new focus on mathematical precision and verifiable results in testing, the world became known to us in quantifiable categories. In some respects because we were learning things we had not known before we came to trust the knowledge of the world that was opening before us. We could understand the laws that governed the universe and work out the relationships between things based on the work of math and physics. By this perspective we could examine the parts of things to understand how they worked.

Each particle of a thing carried within it its own reason for being, its own nature. By breaking down nature into autonomous particles we came to an understanding of the world as something like a machine, with each part contributing to the overall functioning of the machine itself. There was a connection between the way we saw the world and the technologies that developed around it. The formation of certain technologies was one response to the world we were exploring, but there were other consequences to this perspective as well.

With the development of science, models and images of Deity were proposed that sought to correlate what human beings were learning about the world. The most recognized image was the one of God as the great watchmaker, suggested by William Paley. In this model God was envisioned as the great watchmaker who fashioned the world as carefully as the finest watch. Every piece in the watch, intricately constructed and well designed, had a role to play in keeping the timepiece functioning properly. God, the designer of the world, was employed by many to interpret what they saw science giving them.

One effect of this was that persons who interpreted the world in a more organic way were largely eclipsed by the scientific worldview which saw nature as self-explanatory. In fact, the more science came to discover, uncover, and reveal about the world on its own terms, the less need there was to postulate a divine designer at all. God was used as a symbol to explain the gaps in scientific knowledge, pushed out with increasing regularity to the margins of human concern, save in the sense of individual salvation.

Science commanded near universal respect, scientists became our new priesthood, and science emerged in modernity as that way of knowing which could provide us with concrete universal answers about the way the world really is. As our reliance on the explanatory powers of science grew, our need for any other unifying hypotheses about life and meaning faded into the shadows of what was assumed to be medieval superstition. Modernity would reflect upon such ideas of the medieval period as the three-tiered structure of the universe, with heaven above, hell below, and earth poised between—and let out a quiet chuckle over sherry and cigars. Good riddance to all that ridiculous nonsense. And who could blame them?

But with the abolition of the medieval world something else was tossed out which may need rethinking. Medieval science, following Thomas Aquinas's intellectual mentor Aristotle, focused on "natural principles." This is to say, it viewed the world in such a way that saw every object or thing in the world as following its own goal or end (*telos*). All things have an inner purpose or natural tendency to follow their own nature toward the end to which they were being directed. Acorns become oaks, babies become adults, potentialities become actualities. This notion, that deeper purposes may lie within the processes of nature, was replaced by a mechanistic view of the world that saw things not in terms of final causes but in terms of material causes.

This movement has had profound consequences for our world because ideas have impact. As science compartmentalized and reduced nature to bits and pieces, ignoring the interconnections of a larger whole, it gave birth to the attendant rise of technology and the notion that we could manage nature for the human good. The issue of control and power always emerges in human existence because it seems to be one of the defining characteristics of it. Francis Bacon said knowledge is power, and he meant the power to use nature as we humans wish to use it. The very powers of nature, whether in physics or biology, have come into our hands, and we mean to direct them to our own ends.

That this power came with limits and boundaries was ignored for so long we forgot to even ask the question of whether we should split the atom, or map out the genetic code for every permutation of DNA. Nature exists for us to tinker with and even improve. Essentially, what we have done is to objectify nature, assigning it value only as it serves us. This objectification of nature has allowed a certain blindness on our part to creep in. We have the ability to do something, so we do, seldom thinking through the long-term effects. The technological manipulation of nature has resulted in the loss of something vital about it, its sacred dimension. To even suggest such a thing in our world consigns such a voice to the realm of the marginal.

But the banishment of deeper cosmologies than the ones we now give allegiance to means that the overshadowing of divine life in deference to our mastering the world carries with it a certain anxiety. Look at the rising awareness of the ecological disaster we are constructing and you can see the level of anxiety increasing. Of course, in the face of our misuse of the earth there are always options to pursue. One such option is to increase our sense of rational and technical control of the world.

This is a point that Neil Postman makes in his book *Technopoly: The Surrender of Culture to Technology.* He raises the issue of how technology, while enhancing the quality of our lives, has actually emptied our culture of substance and wisdom. We have evacuated the world of all but technical meanings and reduced society and culture to the logic of technology. He labels this condition "technopoly," which he describes as follows:

> Technopoly is a state of culture. It is also a state of mind. It consists in the deification of technology, which means that the culture seeks its own authorization in technology, and takes its orders from technology. This requires the development of a new kind of social order, and of necessity leads to a rapid dissolution of much that is associated with traditional beliefs.[36]

Connecting the sinews of artifacts, technology, and culture, he shows that we have developed a way of being in the world that says if we have the ability to do something we should do it. Hence the comment that to a person with a hammer everything looks like a nail. Technology and its attendant desire for control leads to the structuring of society that locates all meaning and purpose in our abilities to control and fashion the world as we so desire. This has served the purpose of disconnecting us from the world of nature.

We abstract nature with our technology and lose sight of its powers and potential. This could be seen as starting with Descartes's separation of the human subject from the world of objects. But even if the genesis of this habit of the mind is hard to locate, the reality of our separation from the world of nature has emerged in a world where we take light, sound, and speech, and convert them to the binary code of virtual reality. Therefore, we can stay disconnected not only from the world of nature, but we can stay estranged from other persons as well.

There has been a cost for our technological mastery and power. The material benefits we have enjoyed, which are significant, have been purchased at a cost, a profoundly ecological one. From flurocarbons to chemical fertilizers to genetic engineering of plants and crops to cloning and its uncertain future, we are putting into play forces that we cannot predict. Though we may think we control these movements of technological prowess, we are in for some unpleasant surprises.

As mentioned previously, our ability to explain and control the world has gone a long way to emptying it of religious meaning. Any sense of coherence or meaning we need is to be found in the world itself. Science offers us a public criterion for evaluating the world of nature and insurance covers us from acts of God, so what need is there for religion in public life? No recourse to religious interpretation is needed, or in some quarters even wanted.

In some ways this is certainly understandable; we are seemingly justified in putting away a superstitious and outmoded view of the world. But the question can also be raised as to whether our desire to vacate the world of religious meaning comes from the realization that were we to acknowledge the presence of something other, our own power would be called into question. The world seen and known by us is a system of material causes and effects, with no need for God. Would another perspective help us in our quest to do justice to God's intention for the world and enable us to more effectively address the ecological crisis? I want to consider Thomas Aquinas as a possible source of reflection concerning these issues and then return to these questions again.

Thomas Aquinas and God's World

In the year 1244 a young novice of the Dominican order was on his way from the University of Naples to the city of Paris. The relatively new order of friars was regarded with less than overwhelming appreciation by many in society and certainly would not have been seen as offering many prospects for the career of well-born young men full of promise. This was especially true of a young man whose parents had desired that he would become abbot of the monastery at Monte Cassino. So distressed were this man's parents that they arranged to have him kidnapped by his brothers on his trip and imprisoned for over a year at the family residence in Roccasecca. This did not discourage Thomas Aquinas from his ultimate goal, which was to become a member of the Dominicans and work for the causes of God.

At first blush the medieval world that Aquinas inhabited would seem to have little to offer to our own. It was a different time with different concerns, and the gulf between times seems too large to contemplate. If we think of medieval metaphysicians claiming to attain certain and final knowledge of God and the world by means of metaphysical reflection, we see the antithesis of much that has been examined as marks of contemporary thinking and society. Most of us simply do not think in the terms that Aquinas used.

If one picks up the *Summa Theologica* today one would quickly understand that Thomas's interests do not seem to coincide with our own. He treats questions that almost resemble zen koans. Should Christ have been born in winter? Why do fat men produce little semen? These are not issues we care much about, nor should we. His views on women in the place of nature are embarrassing today for obvious reasons. No one in their right mind would entertain the belief that women were made for the purposes of procreation, and that they are a defect of the male sperm, which in its perfect form contained men.[37] And yet those and more observations are found in the writings of Aquinas that would indicate a large distance from our time.

There is also the fact that Thomas is one of the architects of the classical theist position which has defined God for countless numbers of individuals. The notion that God is defined as omnipotent, omniscient, and immutable among other ideas has served to cast God in a conceptual framework that has impressed itself upon the minds of generations. While this model has been comforting in some respects, in others it has had the effect of not allowing newer models and images of the divine to emerge that might help us understand the problems related to theodicy.

Thomas also comes to us through centuries of interpretation where various "Thomisms" have vied for supremacy, each with its own agendas and interests. Which Thomas would be a more accurate picture of the way things really were? The work in recovering his legacy for us today has extended from persons such as Karl Rahner to Matthew Fox. Still, the fact that many today are working on thinking with him about some of the issues that face us indicates that while the distance from the thirteenth century to our own is long one, it is a journey worth taking. If his views seem outdated and his precise way of formulating questions seems quaint, he was asking questions about issues that are perennial. What is the relationship between God and the world? Why is there something rather than nothing? How do we participate in the life of God? These are issues that draw the attention of those who take seriously their faith. If Thomas seems archaic to us, we can still draw upon him for wisdom.

Though there is some disagreement about the precise place of his birth, its date is generally considered to be about 1225. He was born as St. Francis was about to die and within five years of the death of the founder of his order, St. Dominic (1170–1221). Born in the kingdom of Naples into a rather well-connected family, at the age of five he was sent, as was the custom of the times, to the Abbey of Monte Cassino. His parents' aspirations may have been for him to become the abbot of the monastery, but it was the site of conflict between the emperor and pope, so he was removed to further his education at the University of Naples.

This was a place where the works of the Greek philosopher Aristotle were studied seriously, which was a source of concern in some Christian circles. The writings for which Aristotle is best known today became available under the auspices of the Islamic world in the second half of the twelfth and first part of the thirteenth century. These writings were met with disapproval in some powerful academic quarters. They were banished by the faculty of arts at the University of Paris in 1215. So the study of Aristotle was seen by some as being subversive.

Aquinas was introduced to "the Philosopher," as he called Aristotle, by Peter of Ireland amid his studies in Naples. He also met members of the Dominican order of friars, which had a profound impact on him. As mentioned previously, this was a relatively new order and joining it was probably met with the same enthusiasm as hearing that one's child had gone off to join the latest new religious movement in our time. Yet after he stood resolute through his imprisonment, he did eventually make his way to Paris, where he proceeded with his studies and moved up the chain of academic achievement to become one of the greatest theologians of the church. The entire time he taught he worked on an astonishing literary corpus, the apex of which was his two famous *Summas*, *Summa contra Gentiles* and *Summa Theologica*, his most famous work. The stories of his capacity for writing and thinking are legendary and sometimes amusing.

In the years of his life after 1256 Thomas would become occupied with a number of different issues, some of which were attacks on his use of Aristotle and attacks upon his order. These issues would send him back and forth between France, Germany, and Italy. During these times he was keeping up a tremendous workload and dealing with a host of concerns. The pivotal moment came after Mass on the feast of St. Nicholas in December of 1273, after which he put away his writing instruments and stopped dictating. According to the material we have, Thomas answered concerned inquiries about his health by saying, "I cannot go on.... All that I have written seems like so much straw compared to what I have seen and what has been revealed to me."

Whether Thomas had a mystical experience that led to this moment has been a question taken up by many scholars of Aquinas. James Weisheipl has argued that Thomas may have suffered a stroke or other physical ailment due to overwork and exhaustion. There is some indication that he was physically impaired after this event. Regardless of the reason that Aquinas put away his work, the fact is that by the following March, at fifty years of age, this extraordinary teacher, writer, philosopher, and, most importantly, theologian had passed from the world.

In the recent wave of scholarship on Thomas writers such as Thomas O'Meara, M. D. Chenu, Jean Pierre Torrell, and others have shown that Thomas was a man of irenic spirit and facile mind. He was not threatened by new ideas, but was motivated by discovering in the world the traces of God's presence. Moving from question to question, issue to issue, he always asked about the how and why of anything he observed. He was looking for that which connects the diversity of life. Underpinning everything was the notion that God is the beginning and end of all things.

At the start of the *Summa Theologica* he declares that he intends to set forth sacred doctrine by treating, first, of God, second, of the journey of God to reasoning creatures, and, third, of Christ, who as human is our road to God. In this movement he moves from metaphysics toward the complexity of the human person, with an emphasis upon the affective and intuitive, on graced virtue and intellectual gifts of the Holy Spirit. In doing so Thomas has a decidedly theological focus in mind, much more so than a philosophical one.

But in his theological construction Aquinas brings in Aristotle, Augustine, other theologians, traditions of the church, observation, Scripture, anything that would help him understand the being of God in relationship with the world. He was Aristotelian in that he observed things from a scientific point of view, wanting to understand causes, effects, and relationships between them. In his observing of the natural world he sought to let each thing in its turn reveal what it had to show him about its being in the world. One of the places where we need to be careful when we come to Aquinas is that he developed his distinctive way of interpreting nature from within his own cultural milieu. Nature has a particular mode of being because of the notions of causality that Thomas in part gets from Aristotle.

Not only do things have material, efficient, and other causalities; they also have final causalities. So Thomas seeks to explain how things act and develop to their own end, and how things not only have their own ends, but also serve as means for other things. Thomas tries to understand the working of nature in relationship to these processes. And in doing so he comes to the belief that everything exists to accomplish these goals and thus achieve their own nature.

Behind all this is his notion that an order exists in the universe which is rooted in grace. Ultimately everything that exists does so by God's good decision. God is the final cause of all things; "the divine goodness is the end of all things."[38] He believed the human mind was able to reach reality, even in all its diversity, when it could perceive that grace and the goodness of God undergirds it all.

Contrast this with what we have previously said of the postmodern mind, which tends to see things much differently. We would see a profound disconnection between the language we use and the world we observe. We create the world, postmoderns believe, through the various means we employ to interpret and understand it. Aquinas believes, however, that theology searches for truth that exists and infuses all existence. More importantly, this truth is the grace of God, the presence of God in all things.

Because God is the beginning and end of all things, the structure of the *Summa Theologica* reflects the presence of God in all moments. There is the estrangement and exile of humankind from its full destiny, but that destiny awaits, and it is the *telos*, the goal of the life of the Spirit. As much as a physics of being, or a psychology of the human being, the *Summa Theologica* is an account of salvation history and God's presence not only in nature, but in Jesus Christ and, through the Spirit, in us as well. Grace is the foundation that pervades the entirety of this work. One of Thomas's guiding principles is that "grace brings nature to completion."[39]

This sense of grace is what allows Thomas to make connections between creation and creator, nature and grace, and creates the sense of his holistic cosmology. There are rumors of glory in the created which God transcends, but these things still bear witness to the creation's goodness and the activity of God in the world as a sustaining presence. Faith and love of God open one to the completion of nature where God uses ordinary human experience to speak of what is most sublime. Therefore our knowing the world comes to completion through our participation in God. The causal movement of grace and nature permeating Aquinas's theology allows, through revelation, for a true knowing of nature and God.

Care must be taken here, of course, to quickly insert that the knowing of God is a little tricky. Thomas says in many places that the ultimate in human knowledge of God is to know that it knows nothing of God. To speak of God is to speak of something that cannot be known. And yet we must speak, even if it is to speak of what God is not. We can see some hints of this when we look at things around us in the empirical world. For Aquinas knowledge moves from the empirical world to the intellectual, from the material to the spiritual. The human mind has an active as well as a passive function, and he believed we made judgments in our knowledge that would take us only so far. In the process of knowing he moved analogically, which for him was grounded in the divine activity of the universe.

As the human being comes to know nature as the realm of grace, faith is affirmed as the means in which God exists in intelligent being. This faith allows us to discern God as the sovereign cause of everything. Nature is the matrix of God's causality within which humankind and all creation have their mode of being in the world and the manifestations of causes and effects. All of this glorifies God. But even more, Thomas says, "All things, by desiring their own perfection, desire God."[40] When a being is existing in its truest sense it is moving toward its desire, which is God.

For Aquinas all things exist as parts of a larger whole, which is arranged toward one end, to represent the glory of God. One thing to note here is that the beauty, power, and grace of God are not necessarily found in spectacular miracles or huge events, but are most properly found in the ordinariness of everyday life in which things fulfill their destiny. As beings experience their lives in all their diversity and plenitude they are able to participate in the life of God. The reign of God is that toward which things move both in the present and in the world to come. This sense of teleology is fundamental to Aquinas and completely antithetical to us. Thomas O'Meara writes:

> Aquinas' principles are not opposed to the views of as-trophysicists, paleontologists, or theologians who accept evolution in nature. Becoming does seem to dominate galaxies of gas and heat as well as biological life here on earth. Aquinas stressed being, but, although he had little inkling of a world shot through with development and evolution, his theology nevertheless entertains stages in human life and history. Precisely his understanding of causality would have led him to appreciate a mature but delicate Power permitting worlds to unfold out of their inner capabilities. God is more glorified by an independent world of finite beings intricately emerging in time than by a planet where beings enter fully dressed like characters ready to act out a play.[41]

The created world mirrors, however faintly, the being and activity of God in an analogous way, for God is the source of all things which have been willed and loved into existence. Aquinas states,

> God is the cause of things by his intellect and will just as the craftsman is cause of things made by his craft. Now the craftsman works through a word conceived in his mind and through the love of his will regarding some object. Hence also God the Father made the creature through his Word, which is the Son; and through his Love which is the Holy Ghost.[42]

These ideas which Thomas develops before his ideas on original sin show a world of profound interdependence and diversity. This suggests not only that such diversity is an avenue for humans to recognize the work of the Creator, but that diversity of life is the way in which creatures fulfill themselves as well. All creatures share in the "dignity of causality." He respected the "soul" in both animals and plants. God's goodness resulted in the creation of all things, and therefore all things will participate in that goodness despite the presence of sin: "Now a gift of grace does not proceed from the light of nature but is added thereto as perfecting it."[43]

Nature is capable of manifesting the mystery of God and was intended for harmony with God despite the divisions we have made. It is sacramental, because it is blessed.

This was driven home to me in a powerful way when I was in a western state talking to a Navajo man about religion. His grandfather had been an important influence in the Native American Church, which uses peyote to enhance vision quests. His grandson was Christian, and I asked him how his relatives could distinguish between the sacred and the profane, or even good and evil, under the influence of peyote. His answer was that they did not make this distinction. They believed that God uses everything to reveal the sacred, even that which we think is profane. Sometimes, he said, you can only see where you need to go, when you see you are lost. I thought about this and realized that some of the greatest insights I had had about God were in the context of darkness. I left his home with a new appreciation of sacrament and the earth as a vehicle of grace. I had divided the world, but God is found in all spaces of the world, because, as Aquinas states, it all emanates from the goodness of God.

This was a conversionary moment for me, along the lines of what Aquinas himself may have envisioned for the readers of his works. Conversion can be a movement from not understanding the world as the arena of God's grace to seeing that, even in the midst of much woundedness, creation is the locus where grace manifests itself in all that is. Aquinas wants to show in his theology that at a far deeper level than is readily apparent with our divisions and separations, we are in the midst of divine presence.

This presence works in all of life within cultures and lives, motivating human efforts, sometimes even when we are unaware of it. But most intensely, this presence is most manifest when we are aware of it and seek to be faithful to it. This awareness leads us to see the earth with new eyes and even leads us to an ethic of resistance when we see that which does not honor God's intentions for the world.

Unaware of our true destiny we construct habitations of darkness where dominance, control, fear, and anxiety take over. And yet, according to the implications of Aquinas's thought, the world is still incredibly graced with light. Some of these lights are seen in persons such as Aquinas, but they can also be manifest in persons such as Bartolomé de las Casas, Oscar Romero, Dorothy Day, or Mahatma Gandhi.

In Aquinas's thought God extends Godself into the psyche and history of creature and creation. Even as God takes care to maintain the distinction between creation and creature, because God is essential being we also participate in the divine life.[44] In fact, all of nature participates in this life. All being is holy, and the infinite is found within the finite. One of the most essential features of Aquinas's theology is the notion that divine grace is working through the finite causalities of existence.

When Thomas says that "God is in all things and innermostly,"[45] he is proposing a revolutionary way of viewing the world. God is present in every moment of our lives, never absent to us, sustaining all life, even when it does not honor the grace bestowed on it. The divine mind is manifested in galaxies, diversity of life, personalities of all things. In some ways you could understand this as the notion that all the finite quests of life are movements toward a larger fulfillment and purpose.

When Thomas says that we look for that fulfillment we speak of God with images, stories, parables, and metaphors that cannot capture the thing we are trying to see. Ultimately what we desire transcends our ability to speak of it. And precisely because we cannot speak of it, love may be the greatest means we have to grasp grace. The spaces in the story of human life where this love extends beyond the usual bonds of family, partner, lover, or nationality are also those places where we catch the glimpses of grace.

These graced moments of human existence enable us to realize that God does not just create a world, but is the sustaining Spirit through which the continuing life of creation continues. God is the spring of all life and the manifestation of all that protects and values life. The love made manifest in the world towards creation would have been well understood by Aquinas because his theology was world affirming, not world hating. In everything there is more than appears to be the case. There is more to the stones and trees, more to the flowers and animals, more to the actions of humankind than we can even imagine. The depth of God is revealed to us in the world of nature, and in some senses this reality should cause us to respect the world, instead of trying to control it.

Still the question must be asked, is this just the vision of someone

locked into metaphysical orientation and Aristotelian methodology? In what way can we see this vision as offering us ecological
consciousness today? Surely this is a construction of what Thomas
wished, not an accurate reflection of what actually is, no matter
how much he thought it was. We turn to these questions to cast
into relief our world in relation to the one Thomas perceived.

Does Creation Have a Voice?

When we started this chapter we dealt with the issue of ecological
disaster and the results of our abuse of our environment. I suggested that part of this approach to the world came from science
and its ability to function as a world-shaping enterprise. In this
sense the picture of humankind we get is not so much Proteus as it
is Prometheus. We are the ones with the power to change the very
course of nature. We are the ones who will use our technology
to improve on the world and create a better environment to live
in. We will bring down fire from the gods because we can. I also
suggested that the rise of technopolies meant a loss of soul about
our lives.

What may not have been made so clear at that time is that
the loss of cosmology has brought us to a certain instrumentalism
about how we employ the artifacts we create. Because we have
no overarching picture of the world and our place in it, we have
entered into using our knowledge as power to shape and fashion
the world according to our own desires, but the results have been
mixed, as the ecological disaster we are spawning has indicated.

I then moved to consider in briefest of forms the theology of
Thomas Aquinas. I sought to indicate that Aquinas's theology gave
us a view of the world that said being is good in all its manifestations and all things have intrinsic value. In the infinite variety of
life everything has its place in the cosmos due to the grace of God
and since all things participate in the life of God we should have
immense respect for all life, in whatever form it reveals itself to us.
What we have not yet considered is how we might respond to the
type of postmodern critique we have covered up to this point. I
wish to think about Aquinas then in this respect and see if we can
still maintain that a medieval theologian, trained in Aristotelian
thinking, has a word for us.

One of the problems of previous thinking according to the postmodern perspective is that it made too great a claim for its metaphysics. Jacques Derrida speaks of the "metaphysics of presence," and what he means by this term is that people like Thomas would assume that what is present in our conceptual frameworks is what is truly and really there, a reality we have adequately grasped. When we are doing our thinking the metaphysics of presence is a perspective that says we simply reflect the things that are actually there. Another term we used for this was naive realism (remember the story of the three umpires?).

We saw in the first chapter that the contemporary critique says we can never get beyond our linguistic or conceptual subjectivity to what is really there because it is not a given; the very notion of givenness is itself a construction of our minds. One of the reasons this was of such concern was that our supposed apprehension of such things as "facts of nature," "cosmic laws," or even manifestations of "divine will" are illusions and our own productive role in these things remains hidden.

Because our productive roles remain hidden we will use these supposedly fixed truths to dominate and oppress others who do not share our opinions or feelings about such things. Thus we will oppress other human beings and say we are doing it in the name of God. Or we will pollute the earth and when questioned about it we will respond much as a former secretary for the interior of the United States did by saying that we could cut down all the trees because Jesus is coming back soon and we won't need them then. Whatever it was we did, the metaphysics of presence gave us permission to do it because we could rest assured that this is the way the world is.

And to be honest we see this in Aquinas. He believed that observation of the world resulted in a sense of things the way they really are. And when he looked closely at the amazing partialities of the world, the differences between things, the multitude of life, he thought that exploration of the world meant to probe at the reality of unitary Being that lay beyond the partialities of history, particularity, and change. But in contrast to the postmodern perspective, Aquinas had a sense that the world is not present to us for our mastery of it, but is offered to us as gift. We are enfolded within it as gift and invited as an act of grace not to dominate it. We are called instead to participate and share in the world as covenant with God.

In Aquinas we see the workings of a cosmology that responds to our pretensions to live in the illusion that we are creators of meaning for the world. We see in him a worldview that calls for an end to our violence of the dispossessed of the earth. Because he sees the world as a good creation, capable of manifesting the grace of God in the ordinary, he sees the sacredness in all things. And the more grace is grace, the more nature is nature.

This is an unknown thought to many of us because we live within the metaphysics of terror. Derrida may be right in arguing that our metaphysics has led to a world where force is seen as the path for resolution of conflict, where technology controls and dominates our lives, and where creation is seen as something to be used, tamed, and dominated. Violence is the way we keep order in this world. We even have phrases for it, like "new world order." But behind the manifestations of this order we see the imposition of homogeneity upon diversity, the sense of homelessness on a huge scale, and the disenfranchisement of the poor and technologically unskilled. We should be at home in this world, but we feel homeless.

We mentioned previously that "technopolies" are defining our world. The political, economic, and technological elites are defining the world the way they wish it. The truly marginalized in this society are those who resist the pretensions of society and culture to control and speak of a different world. This different world has usually been defined by an alternative cosmology to the one we presently endure. This cosmology is one where power and dominance give way to covenant and grace.

The metaphysics of presence has always had its religious counterpart, of course. There has always been a certain domestication of the divine whereby God is enlisted for the purposes of our subjection or rejection of others. In fact Christian theology has been employed for just this purpose, as evidenced by the fact that every time a society or political structure wishes to go to war to protect its interests, it invokes Augustine and just war theory. The confusion of this domination of others with the Being of God has been linked to Aquinas's theology as well. This is one of the reasons that faith has been relegated to the private realms of human society.

I am suggesting that Aquinas's theology has the resources to reveal our forgetfulness that all we share and participate in, land, food, air, is a gift given equally to all and meant to be enjoyed, and not abused, by the emerging technopolies for profit and power. In truth the last few centuries have led us to see the world in terms of immediate payoffs. Peter Gay says that the technological habit of mind is anti-teleological.[46] The notions of final causality or ultimate purpose in the world of nature are ignored in the contemporary world.

One of the places where the postmodern critique has spoken the strongest to us is in the notion that we must make space for the other, the different, the invisible. But the truth is we live in a time when the ecological scarring of the earth has revealed to us that the earth is other. The creation has a voice that is prior to our own, and we do not hear it. Every piece of destruction we visit upon this planet with our bourgeois aspirations of entertainment and wealth brings a cry of pain that we simply cannot hear because we have gone deaf.

We will respond to the world the way we see it, and in our seeing, whether we acknowledge it or not, there will always be a metaphysics, or a cosmology. Our relationship to that which we live within will be shaped by factors such as we have mentioned. We will take the shaping power of our language, our social constructions, and create the world we want, but the question Aquinas addresses to us is whether an ultimacy exists toward which we are moving. Thomas was able to see in ways we cannot that things speak for themselves. Creation has an eloquence that speaks for itself if we will listen, and this voice is not contingent upon our constructions; it speaks out of its own reality. This was the whole point of Thomas's approach to the world.

This is precisely what is at stake in the world today, the refusal to listen to things as they present themselves to us. We are so bent on defining and then dominating being that we lose sight of the possibility something resides as the sustaining power of the universe. Lesslie Newbigin writes:

A missionary encounter with our culture must bring us face to face with the cultural citadel of our culture, which is the belief that is based on the immense achievements of the scientific method and, to an extent, embodied in our political, economic, and social practice—the belief that the real world, the reality with which we have to do, is a world understood in terms of efficient [i.e., mechanical] causes and not of final causes, a world that is not governed by intelligible purpose, and thus a world in which the answer to the question of what is good has to be left to the private opinion of each individual and cannot be included in any body of accepted facts that control public life.[47]

This notion of all things moving toward their proper end is one of the things that so impacts Thomas's understanding of the world.

Knowing is always laden with perspective, social location, and unconscious desires, but there are moments of truth in our knowing that profoundly impact our relationship to all that surrounds us. Aquinas offered his construction in his theology that he believed corresponded to the ways things really were. When we read the specifics of some of these things we might find his perspective quaint, or even offensive in parts. We may not be able to follow him all down the line, but that should not leave us with the idea that the only other option is a totalizing constructivism.

Whatever else we may say about Thomas's theology he does lay out for us the possibility that we can exist in a relational covenant with creation that respects reality for what it is, a gift of grace. He does offer clues to suggest that the hearing of the voice of the other should extend to the nonhuman other found in the reality of creation. Only when we allow things to speak to us of deeper purpose will we truly be able to respond to their cry.

This may sound like so much nonsense to a culture that sees things only in terms of self-explanatory causes or materialistic self-sufficiency, but Thomas attended to the world as it was given to him. All around us we see the suffering of the earth and every living thing upon it. Hildegard seems ever prophetic in her call to us not to harm the earth. In the face of the materialistic and non-teleological mastery of the earth engendered by our technological prowess, we are met with the possibility that we are not listening carefully enough to creation's cry. What we cannot discern as an act of grace we will not receive with gratitude.

Postmodernity is right in its critiques of habits of thoughts that masquerade as the cloak for domination of others. But we can never banish cosmologies or metaphysics from our thinking either. As long as there is something here for us to reflect upon we will continue to raise the question of meaning. Perhaps then the question becomes, who gets to have the power to construct our worldview, who gets to decide what home looks like?

It could be that those who now shape our thoughts and assumptions will continue to do so. We can continue along the path of power grabs, profit maximizations, and solitary and isolating individualism. Given the popularity of the television show *Survivor* in the summer of 2000, many would see this as the way of world. And this is where we have been brought by our obedience to the gods of power and security. We also see the suffering of the waters and lands of the earth, the cries of those species that become extinct not because of the way of the cosmos, but because of our willingness to destroy anything in our path.

Or perhaps we can take a second look and reflect with a thirteenth-century monk about the origin of all things and our place in the world. Maybe we will find that creation in all its diversity is seen as inherently good and is marked by relationship. This relationship is best realized in a society of beings where all is respected for what it is and seen on the deepest levels imaginable as interrelated to all that is. This in fact is the world that science is offering us as it probes the mysteries of order in chaos and understands the dynamics of life that carry tremendous vitality and a sense of ever becoming and changing. The dance of difference and diversity that characterizes our observations of our world continues to reveal to us that we ignore the voices of the nonhuman others at our own peril.

In our anxiety to control we have lost sight of the fundamental goodness of all creation. This is one place where Thomas Aquinas, for all his cultural context, offers us some things to consider. He was willing to listen to things as they were, even if his listening was partial and influenced by the worldviews of his age. While nothing can protect the theology of Aquinas from critique, the question can be raised of whether he just might have gotten it right.

Chapter 5

Living into Our Story
Luther and the Bible

But my friends, I ask you: Is God a story? Can we, each of us examining our own faith—I mean its pure center, not its consolations, not its habits, not its ritual sacraments—can we believe anymore in the heart of our faith that God is our story of Him?   — E. L. DOCTOROW, *The City of God*

A NUMBER OF YEARS AGO a book entitled *The Bible Code* hit the market and created some interest in the Bible. The major premise of the book was that the Bible was written in a code, and the author had the secret for unlocking the code of the Bible so that the deep mysteries of the book could be revealed to the world. The idea was that God's secret message was embedded in the words of the biblical text, but an alphanumerical system formed the true message of the text. In this manner the Bible functioned as a talismanic book of secret knowledge and only those with the right knowledge were able to decode it. The ancient system of gnosticism, where the path to God is found through secret knowledge, seemed to have found a space in the modern world. At least that is the way it seemed to those interested in having the right key to understanding the mysteries of the universe. Even though there were many skeptics, the book did well in sales. This is not, however, the only example of the Bible's influence in the modern world.

In the summer of 2000 the largest Protestant denomination in America, the Southern Baptist Church, met to engage once again in the "battle for the Bible." The result was yet another victory for those who saw themselves in the position of arguing for the full and complete authority of the Bible. This victory extended to the imposition of a particular interpretation of the Bible which proclaimed that women should submit to the male leadership in the household and women were not allowed to be pastors of local churches because this violated "the clear teachings of Scripture."

Those who were arguing this position had begun a number of years ago an effort to turn back the denomination to its biblical roots by instituting demands on all their institutions and schools that they support the doctrine of biblical inerrancy. This is the belief that the Bible is without error and literally true in matters not only of faith and practice, but history and science as well. For all times and in all places the Bible is a perfect book (in its original autographs) and no error can be admitted because God is perfect and doesn't make mistakes.

This issue was not open for discussion within the denomination because proponents of this view saw themselves as the last bastion of faith in a pluralistic and relativistic culture. We live in a situation where moral confusion and chaos have caused society to leave the great truths of the Bible and follow after the false gods of this culture. Their opponents, many of them deeply conservative from a theological point of view and holding to a high position of the authority of the Bible, argued that no one group should have the ability to decide how the Bible should be interpreted for the entire denomination.

It would seem that a meeting of the minds should not be too difficult because they share the same faith and basically the same beliefs about the major issues of the Christian faith. But to those involved in defending the doctrine of inerrancy of the Bible, it is a life and death struggle, defining the very truth of Christianity. If, they argue, you acknowledge that some part of the Bible may be culturally conditioned, or that Adam and Eve may be symbolic of humankind's creation and subsequent self-incurvature, you are standing on a slippery slope of relativism that will lead right to secular humanism and descent into the morass of moral chaos.

This is not the only example of how the Bible finds its way into contemporary consciousness. One of the largest scholarly groups in the world is the Society for Biblical Literature with thousands of members engaged in all forms of research on the Bible and issues surrounding it such as origin and social setting. Every few years the media picks up on the latest story of the Jesus Seminar. This group, many of whom are members of the SBL, are astute at finding their way into the media, and often release information that shocks the nonscholar. They meet to discuss the status of the gospel writings of the New Testament and the life of Jesus. Voting with colored beads, they offer the best perspectives they can muster on what the authentic words and sayings of Jesus were. Not universally accepted, they have managed to create controversy by the large number of gospel passages they believe are not authentic words and deeds of Jesus.

These are only some of the ways in which the Bible still impacts the modern world. For many people these are examples of how far humans have to go to relieve themselves of the visages of superstition and religious authority. Others wonder how they can find truth or wisdom for contemporary existence within the pages of a text written thousands of years ago and cultural light years removed from a world of science and reason. Such is the power of the Bible to endure in the minds of so many diverse settings. The question for many people is why.

In the first chapter of this book we briefly alluded to the power of stories and narratives to shape our existence. We saw there that narratives are a matter both of creation and suspicion. In what lies before us we will take a closer look at the ways that narratives shape us, specifically the narrative of the Bible. After thinking through some of the implications of this from a postmodern perspective we will consider the sixteenth-century reformer Martin Luther to see if he has anything to offer us in the way of responding to postmodernity. We will then finish with some constructive approaches to the issue of biblical authority in people's lives and the ways that Scripture shapes us.

When we first brought up the issue of narratives in the first chapter we said that one of postmodernity's most succinct responses came from Jean-François Lyotard, who summed up the postmodern attitude by saying that he defined postmodernism as incredulity toward metanarratives. The metanarrative is that story, or series of stories, that functions in several ways, one of which is that it performs a legitimating role for culture or society. Those who see themselves as standing in the line of the postmodern perspective argue that no one account of existence, or the ways things "really" are, can provide an absolute and universal position of superiority. This is as true for the master narrative of Reason as it is of Religion. We must not give allegiance to any master narrative, the postmodern argues, because master narratives usually entail servant narratives of those who must be conquered or subdued when they do not conform to our stories.

Religion especially deserves close scrutiny because it grounds its narratives in the ultimate symbol of power, God. We find in almost all human societies and cultures religious stories used to constitute the most fundamental realities of life. Concepts such as nation, family, ethnic and self-identity, even law, come under the umbrella of the stories we tell one another about all the relationships we exist within. These stories are internalized by us without questioning and embraced not only for the story, but for the meaning they entail.

Think for a minute about the stories you heard when you were growing up. Some of them were national stories like George Washington and the cherry tree, or the stories of how Columbus discovered the Americas. Some of them were stories of your family and how you were named, or what you were like as a child, or even stories about weird Aunt Joy who ended up somewhere in Thailand. These stories, individual and communal, shaped your view of the world.

In religious stories, whether from the Qur'an, the Torah, or the Bhagavad-Gita, a meaningful order is narrated that provides the structure of your very existence within the complexities of social life. You are shielded from the terror of meaninglessness (which still creeps in for the really thoughtful) by these stories. Peter Berger in *The Sacred Canopy* states that there is a sheltering quality to the religious narratives of culture. The stories of religion offer reasons and divine warrant for the cultures we build as human beings.

Religion has been one of the most widespread and effective means of legitimation in the world. It ties together the narratives and construals of culture with the reality of the ultimate answer. It answers the why, where, and what questions we seem to be so fond of asking. If you have gone through a particularly difficult rite of passage, for instance, and you question the elders of the community, they are likely to make reference to the story that leads right back to God as justification for you giving up part of your body to become an adult. If you question the orders of leaders to kill other human beings in the name of national pride, ethnic identity, or even freedom, you may be told the story of how God gave the ruler authority over you, or how the just war doctrine allows for you to defend others. Never mind that you may have other ideas about how that is to be done; you must follow the demands of the story, because that is just the way things are.

Thus religious stories offer not just local, but cosmic, legitimation for actions, and these stories supposedly transcend all locality and individuality. Entire institutions of society are structured around these stories with attendant rituals and more stories to bring the greatest possible force of legitimation to the structures of society. And what is more important, these stories will explain why you are suffering, why there are inequities in society, who is evil and who is not, who should be destroyed and why.

It is precisely here that the incredulity should be the strongest. When we internalize a particular narrative of religious authority that legitimates the suffering of others or ourselves in pursuit of societal power, or even ethnic and cultural purity, we see another form of the establishment of power that excludes those not a part of the story. In the face of this postmoderns are likely to start asking questions. Who am I in this story? Why am I being asked to inflict pain and suffering on others? What story is being left out of the ones I am being told? What other stories should I be exposed to?

When we cease to raise those questions, when we have been totally assimilated, the narratives of culture have constructed a worldview that makes anything possible. We must kill because the other is an infidel or an enemy. Everyone knows you cannot trust one of "them." When we are ready to kill in the name of God, whether due to the narratives of holy war or just war, we have become nothing other than a totally socialized self, manipulated by the forces of culture. The universal claims of religious narratives often preclude difference and otherness. Those who adhere most strongly to the narratives of exclusion are often the most vociferous in their opposition to those who threaten national or cultic purity. By such violence the fears of the heart are revealed.

One need only look at the daily papers to see the truth of how this plays out in the global culture. How many examples can you offer that speak to the exclusion of others in the name of the one

God? Catholic and Protestant in northern Ireland, Muslim, Jew, and Christian in the Middle East, as well as Hindu and Muslim in India are only some of the instances where we see the narratives of ultimacy fueling the destruction of life. It does not take a particularly observant person to look at the world and see how the stories of religion have created the conditions for oppression, violence, hatred, and racism.

The very narratives of the religious can justify the violence. From the conquest stories of ancient Israel, where God gives the command to take the land, to the Neo-Babylonian conquests, where the mythology of the Enuma Elish pictures Babylonian culture as the dwelling of the gods in the midst of the chaos of surrounding communities, we see the sacred canopy being pulled over a particular group to the exclusion of others. Christianity itself is not immune from the narratives of violence, as a reading of the book of Revelation will show. Anywhere the destruction of the infidel is called for the postmodern response rightly raises the question, "Who says?"

When the narratives of Christianity are employed as a totalizing club to beat others into submission to doctrinal purity or serve as the means of exclusion from the community of faith, we cannot help but wonder, in whose authority is such a thing being done? We should be very cautious about grounding and legitimating a supposed universal perspective that does not transcend cultural and personal limitations and interests.

So where do we see ourselves in the story as Christians? If there were ever a metanarrative Christianity is it. From the creation of the world to the consummation of history, this story purports to be the grand story of all of existence. It answers all the important questions about where we came from, where we are going, what we are supposed to do while we are here. Entire peoples have found the deepest part of their cultural, national, and personal identities within the scope of this story. Centuries of Christian doctrine and dogma, faith and practice have been built upon the pages of the Bible, and now we are confronted with the argument that Christianity is nothing more than a social construct of those who wanted to legitimize their power by appeal to God. The postmodern question of "Did God truly say?" becomes an echo of the snake in paradise tempting us away from the living God and the comfortable stories we are so secure in. If we are sent into exile from here, to where shall we go?

Do we take the way of Nietzsche, refusing to construct or participate in the narratives that seek to force an order onto the world? His refusal to engage in the worldviews that surrounded him led him to favor aphorism as a means of communicating. These aphorisms were a set of comments, random and not necessarily connected, which incorporated different forms of language, thoughts, and modes of expression and which sought to deconstruct the structure of thought. By a play of forces in language he hoped that ideas would emerge, but decisive conclusions could be avoided. As when we are confronted with a zen koan, we might be short-circuited in our prescribed ways of thinking to see a new truth, or have a moment of insight, but ultimately this would not come from a narrative, structured order, imposed by force of tradition or weight of authority. What is the sound of one thought thinking?

The other extreme, of course, is to take the road of fundamentalism in all its variants. We can look at a text not as a narrative or story, but as *the* word of God, not open for discussion or even textual study. We can hold to the belief that all these stories and words were given directly to the original writers by the voice of God, and we do not find any error or human legitimation of social structuring whatsoever in their pages. This way also leads to an aphorism I saw on a bumper sticker once: "God said it, I believe it, that settles it." But what happens when obedience to a doctrine of the text leads us to isolation from the one who inspires the text? Our ability to deceive ourselves about the ways in which we employ the Word of God to serve our communal and individual interests remains cloaked by adherence to an idea which shuts us off from difference.

Is there a path between these two extremes that the Christian in postmodern society can walk, a Christian who lives in the recognition that what has been asked by the postmodern has the integrity of an honest question and deserves an honest and thoughtful response? Is there a place for the Bible to have authority for Christian belief and practice, given the critique we have raised? Does God speak to humanity in the midst of these stories?

The issues raised by the current age are crucial and we must face them, but before we do so, let us look at the figure who some say helped lay the foundation of the modern world by his refusal of the church's authority and his appeal to the Bible and individual conscience, Martin Luther. We shall look at Luther to see if he has any clues to offer us as to how we might see the Scriptures as a narrative that brings life and not death.

Struggling for Grace—Luther and the Text

It would seem that Luther is an unlikely figure to offer much of anything to say to us. In fact the charge can be made that Luther unleashed not a little evil in the world with his rebellion against the Catholic Church. Even overlooking the chaos that resulted from the Protestant Reformation, there was his virulent anti-Semitism, which was later used by the National Socialist Party in Germany to construct one of the most heinous narratives of modern times. It could be argued that Luther is just one more sorry incident in a history of places where Christianity has oppressed Judaism in subtle and horrific ways. What possible use could this prime example of religion as totalizing exclusion be for thinking through the issue of biblical authority? Can this be the negative way of seeing how an anti-Jewish attitude is found in the very foundational documents of the New Testament itself?

And yet it was on the very issue of biblical authority that Luther unleashed the process of the Protestant Reformation. It began for the reason that Luther could not find the comfort of a gracious God within the institution and found it instead in the pages of the Bible. In the pages of Scripture he found the answers to his struggles of how to be able to rest secure in the knowledge that he was loved. How may this be of any help to us today? By way of anticipating the answer to this question perhaps we will understand ourselves differently by an encounter with the story that brought Luther to a different place in his understanding of God.

Martin Luther was born in the year 1486 to parents who were part of the growing middle class of Germany. He carried the burden of a superstitious age. In the environment he grew up in the devil and dark powers were never far from the door. They served as source of constant anxiety, concern, and conspiracy. An odd noise was not just the beams of the church going through the nat-

ural process of expansion and contraction; it was the devil seeking
to disrupt the worship of the people of God. Luther grew up in the
midst of such a world and carried a lifelong preoccupation with
such things.[48]

One of the results of growing up in such a world is that fear-
motivated piety was one of the most powerful forces in his life. He
grew up with an understanding of Jesus Christ as God's judge who
recorded and weighed our merits and dispensed divine justice. This
negative and punishing image of God profoundly shaped Luther,
but it also made him rebel all the more against the religious context
within which he found himself. Because he could not trust God's
judge to be of any comfort, what comfort could be found, he found
in the saints, particularly St. Anne. It was to her he called when
he was caught in a fierce thunderstorm that changed his life.

Luther was educated in strong schools, exposed to the nascent
humanism of the Brethren of the Common Life, and ended up
at the University of Erfurt, where he came into contact with the
thoughts of persons such as Gabriel Biel. He also came into contact with teachers who were intent on bringing the fruits of the
Renaissance and the new humanism into education.

One of the results of this new learning was that the recovery
of ancient languages was a part of the age. Not only Greek and
Hebrew, but also theologians like Augustine, who had been obscured, were being rediscovered by an age intent on retrieving the
past. Luther would later write that the Renaissance was like John
the Baptist, preparing the way for the Reformation that followed.
Most notably, Luther benefited from the work of Erasmus and his
translation of the Greek New Testament. This would be influential
in Luther's own work in translating the Bible into German.

Upon his initial graduation from the university Luther went to
study law there, but in 1505 he experienced a moment of crisis
which would change not only his life, but the course of Western
civilization as well. When he was passing through a thick forest
during the height of a fierce thunderstorm, Luther was in mortal
fear for his soul. Because he was sure it was the forces of darkness that had come for him, Luther prayed to St. Anne that if
she delivered him from this moment of terror he would become
a monk.

Unlike most of us, he actually kept his vow after the moment of crisis had passed and entered the local Augustinian order in the city of Erfurt. Even though his family was chagrined, he was a priest by 1507 and, following ordination, celebrated his first Mass. It was in this Mass that we see some evidence of Luther's spiritual struggle for a gracious God. It is hard to know exactly what was in Luther's mind, but his own sense of unworthiness as he was consecrating the host caused him to have what some have called a nervous breakdown. Whatever happened, he faltered at the elevation of the host and had to be helped through the rest of the service.

This one incident was just an example of Luther's search for certitude in divine benevolence. He continued his training to become a theologian and soon was authorized to lecture on the Bible. At this time biblical interpretation took place under the auspices of the authority of the *magisterium* of the church. This was the teaching authority of the church that treated the texts of the Bible in the fourfold manner that emerged with the scholastics. This method broke down various parts of the text and applied a multilayered approach to interpreting them. Incorporating the allegorical, typological, historical, and moral senses of the texts, this method could be very creative in its approach because interpretation was not tied to one particular way of interpreting.

It would become one of the chief issues of the Reformation that it must break through what it considered to be a dogmatic encrusting of the Bible to allow the Word of God free play. Because of the fourfold interpretive scheme imposed on the Bible it seemed that no one could speak outside of the strictures of designated church authority. Luther would be one among many who contested the monopoly of interpretation that had overlaid the text for so long. He felt this resulted in the obstruction of God's word for the world.

Eventually Luther ended up in the university town of Wittenberg, where he became professor and began lecturing on the Bible. Still struggling with the notion of a gracious God, Luther in the midst of his studies received an illumination concerning the justice and mercy of God. The result of this moment was nothing less than the rebirth of Luther's soul and the birth of a new motif in his theology, the concept of justification by faith.

That he received this revelation by his study of Scripture is no small thing. It was upon sustained reflection on Paul's letter to the Romans that Luther would find a huge key to unlock the self-imposed prison of his soul. Because of this episode Luther would change the face of Christianity. He saw the matter as a crisis of doctrine because doctrine had confused the central issue for Luther. What the gospel was and how to set it free from the chains of scholastic theology became a matter of prime importance for Luther.

It was in his lectures on the Bible that we start to see Luther's development of the formal principle of the Reformation, the full and final authority of the Scripture, *sola scriptura*. For Luther, biblical authority should be the touchstone of all faith, but increasingly he would see this authority as disconnected from the teaching authority of the church.

Why was the Bible such an important document for Luther? Because it was the place where the Word of God is found, a word he did not need to fear any longer. In his commentary on Romans Luther says that the Word of God is the whole redemptive activity of God towards sinful humanity. This activity is revealed in Christ and set forth in Scripture and made operative in the hearts of persons by the Holy Spirit. The Word of God is a personal word of address to humankind by God.

As he was working this out in subsequent lectures in his early career Luther relied on the stories of the Bible to flesh out the ideas of faith, righteousness, and the action of a gracious God toward a sinful humanity. As he did so he was led more and more to attack the notion of indulgences within the church. Luther's embrace of a God who justifies one by faith, not works, led him into growing opposition to the practice of indulgences. Offered by the church for the remission of sins—a church in need of money to finance the aspirations of the Renaissance popes—indulgences were a profitable industry for the enterprising seller.

No better hawker of these pardons could be found in Luther's day than Johann Tetzel. While indulgences were not permitted to be sold in Wittenberg, they could be sold in towns on the other side of the river. Tetzel even had a little jingle to sell these to the peasants of Germany: "When in the box the gold does ring, another soul from purgatory does spring." How was a citizen of Wittenberg to resist such a thing? Luther was offended by this negation of salvation by faith and felt that the human relationship with the divine should not be debased by this commerce.

He drafted his famous Ninety-Five Theses, which were intended to be an academic disputation and not really meant for public consumption. Luther had high hopes the church would see its need for reforming itself and return to the gospel truths found in the Word of God. He did not count on the fact that people become anxious when you attack their means of making money. When Luther walked down to the usual place on October 31, 1517, to post articles for discussion he could hardly imagine the firestorm that would erupt.

In the years that followed Luther was called to defend his perspectives in a series of debates, private meetings with various representatives of the church, and conferences in order to see if any resolution could be found. In the early meetings Luther contended the Scriptures were of great importance, but he had not arrived at the point of *sola scriptura*. He still believed that the church fathers, councils, creeds, and papal decrees were necessary authorities for defining the faith.

But in these meetings Luther kept getting pushed into a position that questions the authority of the pope and previous councils of the church. He found himself forced to construct his theology on the full and final authority of the Scriptures. During the years between 1517 and 1521 he was trying to work out the way in which the Bible was the final court of appeal for the Christian.

For Luther this did not mean he felt the need to protect the perfection of the biblical text. In fact, he handles the Bible in a curious fashion. When he refers to the Word of God he means the entire redeeming activity of God, not just the written record of that activity. That he saw the Word as a dynamic narrative becomes clearer when he says that the entire Word of God is invested in Scripture, but it truly comes alive in preaching. The Word becomes ever new by our hearing reception of it. This Word is not a dead letter.

A perfect book was not of interest to him. His interest was to release the Word of God from the layers of encrustations with which scholastic theology had overlaid it. This Word is so important to Luther that he says the Scriptures must themselves speak of the gospel, the true essence of which was not the works of Jesus, but the words. In *A Brief Instruction on What to Look For and Expect in the Gospels* Luther writes:

> Gospel is and should be nothing else than a discourse or story about Christ, just as happens among men when one writes a book about a king or prince, telling what he did, said, and suffered in his day. Such a story can be told in various ways; one spins it out and the other is brief. Thus the gospel is and should be nothing else than a chronicle, a story, a narrative about Christ, telling who he is, what he did, said, and suffered—a subject which one describes briefly, another more fully, one this way, another that way.[49]

And is this gospel that Luther proposes found in or protected by the pages of a perfect text, committed solely to writing? Not at all, for Luther believed the spoken word was more important:

> And the gospel should really not be something written, but a spoken word which brought forth the Scriptures, as Christ himself did not write anything but only spoke. He called his teaching not Scripture, but gospel, meaning good news or a proclamation that is spread not by pen, but by word of mouth.[50]

The Word of God is Christ, but that entails the entire narrative of the Bible. This narrative becomes ever alive in its most pristine form when it comes to us in spoken form, of which the written word of Scripture is a necessary replica. The Word is fullest as event and action of God in the midst of history to fashion and shape the Kingdom of God. In Luther's theology this is a personal word which God perpetually addresses to people through preaching. The Bible is a story of good news to be published orally, which is its most appropriate form. In *Preface to the New Testament* he writes,

> If I had to do without one or the other—either the works or the preaching of Christ—I would rather do without the works than without his preaching. For the works do not help me, but the words give life as he himself says [John 6:63].[51]

It is important to note that for Luther the revelation of the story is central and cannot be extracted from its grounding in the written narrative. This connection meant for him that the Word is self-authenticating. It did not need the authority of the *magisterium,* or any other teaching authority to guarantee its importance for the faith of the Christian. Later, when he is faced with the full implications of his position in the likes of Thomas Müntzer, Luther will find himself being very contradictory as the authority of the state is invoked against those who rely a little too much on autonomy.

His main principle of interpretation was that Christ is the center of Scripture: "For this much is beyond question, that all Scriptures point to Christ alone."[52] Luther at one point uses the imagery that the Scriptures are the cradle that holds the Christ. This can be problematic for us today because by this principle (and others that Luther used, such as the law/gospel dialectic) Luther privileges the Christian message and neglects the integrity of the Hebrew Scriptures to speak of their own understanding of the divine action in the life of humankind.

Those who believe they are protecting the faith by arguing for the inerrancy of the Bible won't find a friend in Luther. His desire to protect the centrality of the gospel narrative meant that he was ready to accept that not all parts of the Scripture were of equal weight or authority. In fact there were some books that Luther felt the Bible did not need because they were not central to the gospel story. He writes about the letter of James: "Therefore, St. James' epistle is really an epistle of straw, compared to these others, for it has nothing of the nature of the gospel about it."[53]

Luther, in ongoing conflict with the church, sought another authority for working out the notion of what the gospel means. For him this meant that we are in right standing with God not through our works, but through our faith in what God has done for humankind in the life, death, and resurrection of Jesus Christ. He tried to anchor himself in that fundamental narrative, but the Scriptures are the written structure behind that moment of God's actions on humankind's behalf. The authority of the Scripture is rooted in the narrative it tells us, not in the form in which it is given to us. What Luther could not anticipate were the different ways in which that story would be interpreted.

After the round of discussions with Luther failed to produce the desired results, the matter of this obscure and profane German monk came to a head in April of 1521. All the political issues of the day had been resolved, but in the ensuing four years Luther had become a hero. Now the combined forces of church and state met in Worms, Germany, to ask for an accounting. This meeting would produce one of the most told stories of Western culture when Luther stood before these officials to answer their charges.

On the day he was brought before the Diet of Worms he was asked if he would recant. After asking for a day to think it over he came back the next day and said upon examination that he would be glad to recant his writings if the emperor or anyone else in the hall could expose his errors against the writings of the prophets and evangelists. This confused those who were prosecuting the case against Luther, so they asked him once more for a yes or no answer. Would he recant? He then purportedly delivered a somewhat cumbersome reply:

> Since your serene majesty and your lordships seek a simple answer, I will give it in this manner, neither horned nor toothed: unless I am convinced by the testimony of the Scriptures, or by clear reason—for I do not trust either in the Pope or in councils alone, since it is well known that they have often erred and contradicted themselves—I am bound by the Scriptures that I have quoted, and my conscience is captive to the Word of God. I cannot and will not retract anything, since it is neither safe nor right to go against conscience.

According to some manuscripts of this event, after this Luther added in German, "I cannot do otherwise; here I stand; God help me. Amen."[54]

Historically, Luther challenged the overall authority of over one thousand years of culture building. The nexus of church and state known as Christendom would never be the same after Worms. And while there were many other forces that would have led to the same thing, history will record Luther as the one who jump-started the process. He refused the assumption that in every instance the church's theology was equal to Christian truth. In this preposterous performance Luther planted the seeds that would bring forth the Protestant church. As far as the unity of the church goes, this was most surely a mixed result.

When Luther and others like Ulrich Zwingli said they wanted to give the Word of God free rein, they always imagined that this freedom would only extend so far. Luther himself was profoundly conservative and was probably horrified at the way his protest was received in Anabaptist circles. But the idea that all were free to interpret the text for themselves, indeed, that everyone was capable through the guidance of the Holy Spirit to interpret the Bible, took Luther by surprise.

Without a structuring authority to channel the reading of the texts peasants started to read in the pages of the Bible thoughts that maybe they had the same right as nobility to lands and game. Others read that the reign of God was not to be found in the way of coercion, but in the way of peace, and still others read in those pages whatever the fertile fields of their imagination and desires yielded. In short, the gates were opened by Luther for revolution and chaos.

Is this the only result, then, for the protestant principle? Is the only way we can understand the authority of the Bible to tie it to a teaching authority? How does the Bible operate in the life of the faithful unless it is tied to an authority that can keep people from running off with any lunatic idea and become the next David Koresh or Jim Jones? Aren't we just setting the stage for the next disaster by not agreeing on how to interpret and read the Scriptures? Maybe Luther made things so much worse because he had the structure that could maintain order, and now we have spiritual anarchy. We will consider these issues as we reflect on Luther and the contemporary context.

Building a Habitation

In the first part of this chapter we explored the ways in which narratives and stories function in religion to legitimate the structures that society has constructed both to maintain order and to answer certain questions of ultimacy. When we are asked to make the ultimate sacrifice of our lives, this is usually put in the context of some story or another. We are situated in these stories, and what we know about ourselves many times emerges from the stories we heard growing up. Sometimes these stories will claim our allegiance in the deepest sense possible, especially if the idea of God is invoked.

We saw how standing behind the structuring power of these

stories is the shadow that asks, "Is this a true story?" Deeper yet, can any story be true, and how would we know if it was? All through this book there has been the assumption that the social construction of reality works through the telling of stories, culturally located narratives that tie us to a certain understanding of the truth. We have also raised the question of whether any truth exists behind the stories we narrate, save for the fragmentary, temporal, and momentary existence we live within.

Of course, in our various states of insecurity we want our stories to have universal status, even our stories of God. We want them to be true for all people at all times because the embrace of my story would mean that I am right. This desire for certitude is one of the unexamined forces that influence our world to a great degree. In some ways an innocent enough desire, it pushes our acceptance and promulgation of social narratives. It is one of the forces that cause us to try to fix a universal foundation that everyone can agree on. But religion is not the only thing that creates this desire.

One of the other forces vying to take the place of religion in the world is economics. This aspect of life has long maintained the appeal of ultimacy in people's lives. The mythology of it has exercised its power from Marx to the hyperactivity of present society that sees so much meaning in economic terms: we check the stock market more often per day than some traditions engage in ritual prayer. We are sent into cathedrals of consummation to buy our identities, status, and a few moments of escape. The acolytes of advertising skillfully manipulate us to want to buy in order to fit some fashion. In the shopping malls we have rituals and liturgies around the exchanging of goods. The pull of this narrative is most powerful among us because it is the most assumed. Most of society sees economic security as the most important pursuit of life.

The reason I mention this is because the church has seemingly left its story for this one. It now seeks to ape the culture by appealing to the needs of today. Not only is this seen in the gyms that become worship space on Sunday or the enhanced child care facilities, but in order not to offend, the church offers its own spin so that we will remain comfortable in the pew. If you are fearful and afraid of a rapidly shifting culture and you can see only the danger, the church will offer you a space where you can come and hear the Word of God, rightly interpreted by duly constituted authorities. And best of all, you can do so with people who think exactly the way you do.

Maybe you are a little frightened by those who are different from you; then we will have congregations that are just the same as you are. No matter what your taste, we will find a way to appeal to you because we have seen how in the world of the market economies the ones who provide the best service win. Peter Berger anticipated this when he wrote:

> The religious traditions, which previously could be authoritatively imposed, now have to be marketed. It must be "sold" to a clientele that is no longer constrained to "buy." The pluralist situation is, above all, a market situation. In it, the religious institutions become marketing agencies and the religious traditions become consumer commodities.[55]

The narrative that everything is economics has assumed the weight of a totalizing structure of reality.

If this is one of the grand narratives of our time, the postmodern is likely to ask the question, Whose story is not being told? Who is being left out? What happens to those on the margins who do not get a say in how this story gets told? These questions are important because stories can be socially embodied narratives that guide our common life together. The main story gives a culture its sense of place and purpose in the world.

This sense in which narratives shape us should come under the deepest suspicion. How can these narratives, which are seen as construals of a socially located community, claim universal status? What happens if we question these stories? If the response is violence, whether physical or emotional, then this serves to indicate the terroristic function of the metanarrative vying for our acceptance.

That Christianity comes under scrutiny should not surprise us given its centuries of power-oriented dealings within diverse societies and cultures. Starting with Constantine the church moved from a destabilizing force of countercultural pacifism to the status quo. It always used its narrative to fashion the divine right of kings, crusades, and inquisitions, and even today to justify the purges and exclusion of those who think differently or see faith as embracing a wider world than the one it lives within. We have not been very truthful about the ways in which we have used God to justify our prejudices and agendas.

In the particular part of the story before us we have been considering whether Luther offers us anything to help us see the grand narrative of Christian faith in ways that do not necessarily lead to oppression of others. This is an especially tall order considering that for Luther it did lead to the oppression of others, Christians and Jews alike. But Luther plays such a pivotal role in the trajectory of Christianity that we cannot dismiss him.

Standing before the powers of his world in the hall at Worms, he found himself before the structures that had been built to protect the right to tell the story of Jesus. Even though the emperor may not have cared much, he was not going to oppose the church. What occurred there is that ultimately Luther appealed to the same story his opponents referred to, but he sought to do so in a far more subversive way (though he did not suspect at the time how subversive that would be). Luther appealed to that story not as a world-building narrative of Christendom, but as the proclamation of good news found in the gospel accounts of Jesus of Nazareth. The fact that both sides appealed to the same narrative of tradition suggests something important for us.

It is not necessarily the story or the narratives themselves that are the problem; rather it is the way in which we respond to and inhabit these stories that constitute the most compelling difficulties. It is this issue of how we live into the story that has so intrigued thinkers such as Alastair McIntyre and Stanley Hauerwas. They have spent considerable time probing the ways in which our responses to narratives speak more about the ability of stories to transform life rather than simply reflect it back to us.

Starting early in his career, Hauerwas talked about faith taking the form of a story. Narrative was seen as the primary grammar of Christian belief, and we know ourselves most truly when we can locate our stories and selves within God's story. Luther saw this too, though he does not use the type of language we might use today. He believed that our reception of the gospel is not a once and for all act, but is a lifetime of continuing reception, which, to put it another way, is learning to become a disciple of Christ. The primary responsibility of the Christian for Luther was a willingness to live into the story of the life, death, and resurrection of Jesus Christ.

While we learn this story from Scripture originally, we are continually being called anew to it by hearing the Word of God preached and the story enacted in the Eucharist. This story situates us in a certain way in the world, revealing our illusions, uncovering our deceptions, questioning our loyalties, and extending the hope and promise of grace. In its simplest form the narrative says that even though we are loved infinitely by the Creator, we turned into our false selves and away from the Creator, and that God embodies Godself to suffer and die in order that we might find forgiveness and reconciliation with God.

The central place that Jesus occupies is crucial for a telling of this story and makes for the distinctive cast of Christian faith. For Luther the center of the story is the story of Jesus Christ, and for those who embrace this story it becomes not only the story of the deepest self-identity but a story that we respond to with gratitude and overflowing love. Through our embrace of this story we find a change in orientation toward the world.

Even though Luther was surprised to see his teachings take such radical form in certain persons and movements such as the Anabaptists, those very movements point to some important implications for how the Christian story is to be lived. Certainly at a minimum when we read the gospel accounts in all their differences we find that Jesus comes to declare to the community that follows him the way of God's reign. We follow this call when we respond to these stories with the desire and intent to inhabit these narratives and allow ourselves to be shaped by them. As we learn how to live our lives in response to these stories, within a community of others, we find selves being reconstituted and transformed by the obedience we give these stories.

As Jesus proclaims the reign of God he does so through the use of powerful stories and sayings that destabilize the structures of political, cultural, religious, and economic authority. Jesus attacks the legitimating structures of his own time in no small part by showing how the living of life according to the conventions of the day leads to an inauthentic self.

We see embodied in Jesus' actions a life lived with the poor and outcast, a life of accepting those labeled as unclean by dominant

society. His was a life of compassion and healing, and the forming of relationships and communities which questioned prevailing
structures and narratives simply by their existence. Moreover,
Jesus seemed to expect that those who heard and responded would
participate in the creation of counternarratives of grace and peace.
Hauerwas writes that "in him we see that living a life of forgiveness and peace is not an impossible ideal, but an opportunity now
present."[56]

This call to community is made with the full recognition of our
failings and faults. As the protagonist of John Irving's book *A
Prayer for Owen Meany* (whose voice in the book is always in
capital letters) puts it:

> IT'S TRUE THAT THE DISCIPLES ARE STUPID—THEY
> NEVER UNDERSTAND WHAT JESUS MEANS, THEY'RE
> A BUNCH OF BUNGLERS, THEY DON'T BELIEVE IN
> GOD AS MUCH AS THEY WANT TO BELIEVE, AND
> THEY EVEN BETRAY JESUS. THE POINT IS, GOD
> DOESN'T LOVE US BECAUSE WE ARE SMART OR
> GOOD. WE'RE STUPID AND WE'RE BAD AND GOD
> LOVES US ANYWAY.[57]

The Christian narrative is a call to be dispossessed. The desire to
possess is one of the greatest manifestations of fear in the world
today. The desire to possess is what leads us to so much violence.
This desire is manifested in personal relationships when we cannot control what we want. Daily newspapers and the existence of
abuse shelters are ample testimony to the gravity that pulls persons into the chaos of violence when they cannot possess another
and control their actions.

We see the dynamic of violence enacted in the desire to possess
material things. Everything from babies snatching toys to nations
going to war over mineral and other resources is a testament to
our inability to inhabit the way of Jesus. In fact it is often here that
we employ our gods to fight for us or give us victory over those
we have demonized because they stand in our way.

But perhaps it is in our desire to possess the truth that we see
the greatest violence being visited upon the earth today. The desire
to be on the right side or to have the one true story of God has
resulted in ethnic and cultural destruction on a global scale. And, it

should be noted, the violence is not done just in the name of master narratives like reason, religion, or commerce. The violence exists within the context of local stories and individual narratives. Tamil separatists, Tutsi and Hutu, Hamas and Hizbollah, the names can be many but the results are the same: the destruction of the other and the refusal to make space for them in the world.

This is especially true in Christianity. Those persons who use Scripture to close themselves off from the grace that embraces the stranger are so intent on being faithful to the authority of the Word they have become blinded to the fact that they live in isolation from the one who gave his life in suffering solidarity for the world. They want a fixed point of identity in a world that is constantly being destabilized by God. It is difficult to see that faith may not be as much about correct doctrine as it is about faithful practice.

This may be difficult to imagine at first. Does not correct belief lead to faithful action? Don't we need to know the truth before we act on it? Isn't this truth we need found in the Bible, rightly interpreted, and tradition, rightly maintained? This is a reasonable assumption; however, there is another side we have missed. Traditions emerged in the shifting and changing of cultures, and they are not fixed. Indeed, the desire to lock down tradition reveals a fear that faith may become embodied anew in the world, and it may not be my group that is controlling it. Perhaps the question then becomes where our most basic identities are rooted. Is it in the authority of traditions or doctrines about biblical authority, or something much deeper, the willingness to love the world the way God does? Can we love the world that much in the face of so much violence?

The question of where we put our ultimate sense of allegiance was brought home to the founder of the radical community Koinonia, Clarence Jordan. Jordan, author of *The Cottonpatch Gospels*, had founded the community in Americus, Georgia, during the era of segregation in the 1950s. He sought to bear witness to the inclusion of God's reign of all people, no matter the color of their skin. He ran up against considerable opposition from the good Christian people of the area, resulting in occasional outbursts of violence directed at him and his community.

One night he got a very late call that one of the fruit stands that the farm ran was going up in flames. Driving out to that roadside stand he saw it engulfed in flames and was so filled with rage he was beside himself. He muttered something to himself along the lines that if he ever found the son of a bitch who did this to his fruit stand he would kill him with his bare hands. Almost immediately came that quiet little voice that responded, "Whose fruit stand is this?" In a moment of revelation he realized that his ministry had become more his than God's and the willingness to use violence to protect it was an indication that there was still much to be converted within him. His ultimate commitments needed some examination. So it is with us.

This is the way we can be when we approach those road signs of faith we find in the Bible. We will fight to protect our truth instead of answering the call to inhabit the stories. Part of this is because while we like to believe in Jesus, we do not believe in his message to us, especially the part about violence, truth, and justice. Perhaps the reason we do not see the life of Jesus as normative is that we realize that the crucifixion of Jesus was the expected end in a world that does not really believe that ultimately everything is God's, even truth.

We see the response of violence in a world ready to destroy all in its path that will not bow down before its wisdom and its cultural narratives. If you do not accept this, then the next time America is involved in an armed conflict make a public statement opposing it. How many Christians supported the ideology of the cold war, justifying the weapons of mass destruction we amassed, unaware of the irony that if the praise of God died out in Russia it would be from the missiles launched by Christians in America? The critique we have been examining is clearly shown in government's willingness to destroy anything that threatens its way of life. In our amnesia we forget to whom we owe our ultimate allegiance, "All social orders and institutions to a greater or lesser extent are built on the lie that we, not God, are the masters of our existence."[58]

For the one who inhabits the narratives of Christianity the crucifixion of Jesus may have been the expected response to his challenge to prevailing structures, but it was not the last word. The resurrection of Jesus gives a word that is a word of promise and hope in the midst of so much pain and suffering. The Christian story offers this word for the promise of transformation.

Ultimately the story of Christian faith is a story of a love that gives itself to the stranger, the foreigner, the other not in our power or control, for their own well-being. The life of Jesus is recorded in the gospels as a life without the deceptions and self-protections that mark most of our lives. This is a life that empowers us to reconstitute ourselves in opposition to all stories that seek the maintenance of power at all costs. This new sense of identity enables us to reinterpret ourselves as persons who exist in the world without the violence that constitutes the primal scar of our self-incurvature.

The story of Jesus' life, death, and resurrection points to the possibility of a community that refuses to situate itself within the prevailing narratives and consequent social structures of the cultures within which they exist. Though these cultures may be the defining nexus of what constitutes their being in the world they are provisionary, fragmentary, and lack the ultimate power to define us. The community of Jesus gathers around a table; its members hear a word, they celebrate baptism, and they should be willing to live their truth in the will to embrace the other in whatever form the other comes to us.

This is where I think Luther provides us with some possibilities to consider. Many today try to locate or even protect faith by putting that faith in doctrines or theories about the Bible. Their desire may be heartfelt and their intentions good, but when we observe the types of community created in the name of these doctrines we see much fear and hatred. This naturally gives rise to questions. As Christians is our most basic identity rooted in authority or the willingness to love the other? Does the self of the other matter more to me than my truth? What means am I willing to use to protect my truth from the other stories and truths in the world?

In his search for a gracious God Luther would not define the Bible's authority in terms that those who followed him used in the development of the Protestant expression of Christianity. He located the authority of the text in the story it brought to us. It was the gospel of God's action towards human beings, given in written form, that transformed Luther. It speaks to the difficulty of human ability to live into these stories that Luther would himself later seek protection for his understanding of reform from the state.

But the fact that for one moment Luther went against the grain of his own cultural narrative and societal power, the fact that he fashioned in his better moments an understanding that the theology of the cross called for solidarity with a world in suffering, points us to another way of seeing the world. For authentic faith is not found in the well-constructed architecture of ecclesial power or well thought out doctrines. It is not even found in having the right thoughts about the Bible. The reality is that the way we inhabit our stories is sometimes as important as the story itself.

Chapter 6

Can We Ever Interpret Another?
Friedrich Schleiermacher and
the Art of Understanding

> Hence the will to be oneself, if it is to be healthy, must entail the will to let
> the other inhabit the self; the other must be a part of who I am as I will to
> be myself.　　　　　　　— MIROSLAV VOLF, *Exclusion and Embrace*

IN DECEMBER OF 1999 over seven thousand people gathered in
Cape Town, South Africa, for the Parliament of the World's Religions. These persons represented an enormous array of diverse
traditions, from animist to Baptist, and constituted an astonishing spiritual and cultural variety. Their goal, as in all meetings of
this group, was to seek understanding in the global community
about the religious life of human beings. It was not the intention
of this conference to create a new religion or diminish what the
website called "the precious uniqueness of any path." They hoped
to demonstrate that the religions of the world can gather in a spirit
of respect and celebrate an openness to difference.

When the opening march took place, there were around twelve
thousand participants who marched through the streets of Cape
Town, past areas like District Six, which the former government
had razed and had then dispersed the population, and on to a
celebration. The sight of so much diversity moving through areas
that were once destroyed because of their very ethnic make-up
was a moving and powerful witness to that which in the human
spirit cannot be erased. Not everyone was celebrating this moment,
however, because along the route there were the usual protests of
those who saw in this conference a betrayal of their faith in God.

For some people this gathering and those like it are interpreted
as a sign of the impending apocalypse, because these are manifestations of the apostate "one world" church supposedly foretold

119

in the Bible. Their reading of the book of Revelation leads them to the belief that one of the signs of the end times will be that the world religions come together to form a global church. So the tension of this moment is played out all over the world. There are those of faith who desire the discussion with others so that they might understand and learn. Then there are those who would just as soon kill the adherents of another religion as enter into dialogue with them. Will there ever be a resolution to these tensions?

Even within both of these perspectives there are problems, struggles, and misunderstandings as persons seek to live out their faithfulness to God. The dance of exclusion and embrace, of difference and sameness leaves us exhausted with how we might honor our own faith and truly respect another's faith. If we could just resolve the problem of religious pluralism, we say, we might have a chance at reducing so much hatred and violence. And yet this remains elusive to us? Why?

One sign of this difficulty was seen in September of 2000 with the release of two statements by the Roman Catholic Church, one a "note" by Cardinal Joseph Ratzinger, and the other, *Dominus Iesus* ("On the Unicity and Salvific Universality of Jesus Christ and the Church"). Published by the Congregation for the Doctrine of the Faith, this document declares that churches that do not have a "valid Episcopate [bishops] and the genuine and integral substance of the Eucharistic mystery are not churches in the proper sense." In fact, the term "church" is not even employed for the Protestant communities; rather the term "ecclesial communities" is used to describe Protestant churches.

Likewise, the official note from Cardinal Ratzinger warns that calling Protestant churches "sister churches" can cause problematic "ambiguities" and lead to confusion. Predictably, these statements were viewed as a blow to ecumenism by some, but they really contained nothing that had not been said before. Within much of Catholicism the claim to Rome's superiority has never been in question, for the "mother" church cannot be seen as "sister" to other churches.

Of more interest for our topic at hand is the reprimand to Catholic theologians who "have argued that all religions may be equally valid ways of salvation." Concerned about what it perceives as the growing relativistic and pluralistic approach to the world's religions among theologians, the declaration argues for the unicity of the Catholic Church and continuity with the church's founder, Jesus Christ.[59]

The response to these documents was one of mixed voices, both within and outside the Catholic Church. Some people declared that a clear statement on these matters was necessary to clear up the confusion. Other voices were dismayed at the statements and expressed concern that they would set the cause of ecumenicity and interreligious dialogue back for some time.

Interestingly enough, right before these pronouncements became public, in August of 2000 the Millennium World Peace Summit was meeting with nearly a thousand representatives from a wide diversity of religions. This meeting, hosted in part by the United Nations, was not without controversy, most notably exhibited in the decision not to invite the Dalai Lama in deference to the Chinese government, but also expressed in the order of proceedings and the speeches of the participants.

Clashes between globalization and particularity resulted in some impassioned exchanges, revealing some of the longstanding difficulties that face the future of interreligious dialogue. Many of the most heated responses came from Hindus in India condemning what they described as the continuing proselytizing by Roman Catholic and Protestant Christians in their country. It was seen as the continuation of the colonial past when imperialistic powers sought to impose their religion, seen by its adherents as being superior, on others.

All of these expressions are part of the tensions experienced today in the shrinking global context. Religion as an expression of the global culture cannot be discussed within the vacuum of its own concerns. Religion is intertwined with such issues as poverty, war, economics, politics, and global competition for resources. To try to sort out all the threads of this discussion is too complex for the purposes of this chapter. However, I do want to think about the intersections of religion and culture I have been trying to describe in this book. This is incredibly difficult to do because of the types of suspicions that we have examined up to this point.

You do not have to identify yourself with postmodernity to realize that we are cast adrift in a cosmos of fragments, traces, pieces of meaning that float on waves of time and constantly change form. In reaction to the Enlightenment's love of and search for the universal, we have the contemporary struggle with the particular. In response to the sameness and homogeneity of McWorld, we have the *jihad* of difference. The productive energies of the world seemingly constitute themselves around novelty and contingency.

This fluidity and privileging of distinctly different categories of interpreting the world is a condition that distinguishes our present time. What is most curious is that in the face of this diversity the postmodern mind argues that the very attempt at understanding another in either individual or corporate expression is a task doomed to failure. If we seek understanding we do so from a perspective that we hope, desire, and want the other to accept. Or at least so runs the suspicion. The assumption is that we cannot be truly content with lasting difference. We want our thoughts to be the same, and your thoughts must be in error because they are different from mine. From the very beginning it seems we violate others in seeking to interpret and understand them.

In its most stringent form the postmodern believes that all interpretation rests on the quest for power. Beneath all selves in conversation and communication rests self-deception or self-negation. To understand has come to signify "to appropriate" or make what is different one's own. One wonders whether we are ever able to interpret experiences, languages, or communities without recourse to something between us that can be shared or mutually explored. Are all such attempts at religious dialogue like the conference in Cape Town merely exercises in religious hypocrisy?

Are we ever able to grasp an authentic understanding of others? What are we to make of those who argue that we should extend our desire for understanding to the nonhuman other? Is it the case that we are forced to wander in the world justly suspicious of all attempts to order the world around languages or categories? These are some of the problems we will reflect upon in this chapter as we think about the role of religious pluralism and how we all might be able to live out our faith commitments in relative peace.

My goal is to briefly sketch out the contemporary lines of the problem with a glance at what has been called the "hermeneutics of suspicion." Essentially this term means that interpreting the world is an act that calls for the utmost care, even suspicion of what we have accepted as true. This term is one we have met before in the context of this book.

From there we turn to Friedrich Schleiermacher, often called the "Father of modern theology," for his monumental work in laying the foundation for liberal theology in the nineteenth century (which still has an impact today). After a brief look at the context of his life we will focus on his hermeneutical perspective and ask if there is something there that might allow us to overcome the suspicion of postmodernity. While this may seem like a fool's errand, to try to distill what are incredibly complex thoughts to understandable and graspable form, the risk seems worth it. My intention is to paint some broad strokes to be filled out and enhanced with further study.

The Hermeneutics of Suspicion

One of the major concerns we have been probing is how an interpretation of anything can ever take place that honors its unique difference. Some of the deepest critiques of recent years have argued that true understanding is close to impossible. Because of the way that society has constructed the world and defined such guardians of civilization as reason and rational discourse all the voices of difference end up outside the gates, muted and silenced.[60]

According to this mind-set all eruptions of uniqueness or difference are leveled by the very way society constructs its ideas of what is reasonable. In fact, the Enlightenment could be seen as one enormous attempt to enthrone a socially constructed "Reason" to exclude the special and the other, especially religion. The goal was to level off all that did not conform to the canons of reason. One needs only look at the way religion was treated by many of the intellectual elites in the seventeenth and eighteenth centuries to see how this was being worked out in some segments of society.

The way this domestication of difference was accomplished was by claiming that our language (which was, after all, our key to knowledge) was reflective of a reality that was really there. All language and hence all thought had direct reference to that which really is. The very notion that we are imbedded in a reality that defines us even as we interpret it did not really occur to many persons. We thought we were reading the world as it is.

Those perspectives and voices that did not fit the categories employed by those who were defining the boundaries of what would become "acceptable" ideas of rationality were excluded from offering their voices to the discussion. This dialogue, or discourse, within society becomes controlled by the ones who set the limits of language. The element of power rears its head in this regard, and certain questions get asked about this perspective.

For example, how does history exclude the interpretation of events which do not advance the historian's interpretation of those events? How does science exclude a hypothesis that does not fit the reigning paradigm that structures knowledge? In short, how does knowledge as power inflict violence towards those perspectives that are marginal or on the periphery? These are the questions we should be asking to ensure that the other can address us beyond the realm of a reason decided upon by the cultural elites.

Carried to its most extreme form, this critique argues that nothing stands beyond our thoughts or language that corresponds to thinking or knowing. No foundation exists that secures the accurate representation of my use of the word "God," for instance. Language and its representations are always in a state of flux, and meaning can never be closed or static; rather it is always dynamic and open, and contextual in nature. Meaning is always elusive, with no ontological anchors.

These ideas are not new to us, for we have encountered them all through this text. It is the notion that self and the world are in a continuous reciprocity with one another, defining and refining our very selves, that gives rise to the concept of "deconstruction." This is a notorious term and can mean many different things, but at its heart it concludes that no fixed or secure meaning stands behind our representations of the world in either thought or language.

This perspective leads to the belief that all attempts to interpret ourselves or the world are productive enterprises that construct reality, both subjective and objective, the way we so desire. To attempt understanding, the argument runs, is to appropriate or bring under control what is different or other. The quest for understanding is itself inevitably a hegemonic and narcissistic endeavor to repress difference and suppress the other, thereby solidifying my construction of reality.

This perspective does have the power to unmask our attempts

to domesticate difference, but the question this chapter is asking is, are all attempts at understanding born from this desire? Perhaps there is another spirit that calls us out into the world, away from our safe constructs of self and world, to truly learn and be transformed by our encounters with another, possible even the Divine Other. Even if we see the validity of the critique, can we think about the issue of religious pluralism in a different way? In order to explore this problem we turn to Friedrich Schleiermacher for a look at how he understood the world in which he lived, and then ask if he might engage us today in responding to the pluralism that marks our age.

A New Theology: Friedrich Schleiermacher

Friedrich Daniel Ernst Schleiermacher stands as a pivotal figure in the ongoing story of modernity. The new world emerging from the revolutions in science and philosophy was re-creating theology and the church, as well as the rest of culture. For many the question was how to respond to the world that Descartes, Newton, Kant, and others were constructing with their acquisition of knowledge.

After the exhaustion of religious and political wars, Europe began making slow progress in overcoming difficult social and natural problems. The appeal to human reason and rational thinking became an attractive path, especially as knowledge was influenced by the practical aspects of scientific inquiry. Empirical and experiential methodology became increasingly important models for the acquisition of knowledge.

The move to empirically based reason had a certain acidic effect on faith systems of the past, however. Not only had the enterprise of science undercut the authority of the church since Galileo, but the empirical principle also made tenuous the basic affirmations of orthodox faith in the minds of many. Enlightenment rationalism not only impacted faith at a theoretical or methodological level; it created a certain set of attitudes in the enlightened mind. This is seen in Laplace's supposed answer to Napoleon when the monarch asked where God was in the scientist's system: "Sir, I have no need of that hypothesis." Suspicion of all claims to authority not universally verifiable resulted in an ethos of challenge for Christianity.

In the face of such rationalistic universality, how could the church appeal to a historically conditioned and revelatory moment? How could a text, like the Bible, that apparently contradicted modern science have any credibility? If humankind, freed from the tyranny of tradition and religion, was able to live a more peaceful and virtuous life, what need would an idea such as original sin serve? When humans questioned their world, they found sufficient answers without resorting to the God "hypothesis."

The full force of the Enlightenment critique would cause Schleiermacher to try to fashion a response that would do justice to both human integrity and Christian faith. He realized that no theology could adequately respond to the Enlightenment on the basis of authority alone, but he also realized that reductionist empiricism ignored other phenomenological and existential dimensions of human existence.

F. D. E. Schleiermacher was born in 1768 in Breslau. He was the descendant of a long line of Reformed ministers; his father, while serving as a Prussian court chaplain, came under the influence of a Moravian community. He experienced a personal renewal such that he sought to educate his son in the Moravian environment. The impact of this would stay with Schleiermacher through his life. Even though he moved away from the theology of the Brethren, he would refer to himself as a "Moravian of the higher order."[61]

He began his theological training at a Moravian seminary in 1785 and first became acquainted with elements of an Enlightenment theology. He also was exposed to the culture of Romanticism by reading Goethe and found himself breaking away from his father. He moved to Halle in 1787 to continue his studies and by 1788 had acquired a significant knowledge of Kant and transcendental philosophy.

In the next few years Schleiermacher experienced numerous personal struggles even in the midst of intellectual growth. He came to see that a theology based on Kant was somewhat sterile, and he explored other options for formulating his beliefs. Part of the reawakening for Schleiermacher came when he was assigned as a tutor in the home of Count Donha of Schlobitten. While there, he experienced an atmosphere of community, even in the midst of difference. He came to value the individual expressions of faith that emerged out of a shared common reality.

He was part of wider societies all his life and sought to learn from them all. In the midst of his life he engaged a breadth of topics and intellectual disciplines that was truly remarkable. The dialectical movement of his life between his religious impulses and his intellectual interests would result in a legacy of achievement that continues to the present day with the many who have been influenced by him.

When he moved to Berlin in 1796 he became involved in the cultural circles of the city, especially the romantic coterie headed by Friedrich Schlegel, who became a close friend. From this association came the publication in 1799 of his most famous book, *On Religion: Speeches to Its Cultured Despisers.* In it he was seeking to address a culture that had engaged in protest against a sterile rationalism by stressing individuality and the uniqueness of the human person.[62]

He knew that all thought is rooted in experience, and theological thought grows out of religious experience, especially the corporate life of religious communities. This forms the origin and touchstone for theology. We cannot divorce ourselves from communities of origin but must return ever anew to continue a conversation. He also realized that we stand at the door of historical consciousness and cannot return to a pristine past unchanged by the experiences we have in the present. How a nineteenth-century theology, immersed in modern thought forms and years removed from its primal beginnings in Palestine, could relate the present to the past became one of the great issues of Schleiermacher's life.

He anticipated the preoccupation of contemporary theology in relating past to present, parts to whole, and reason to faith. He realized that no abstract self apart from the limitations and relativity of history existed. Thus all thought shares this condition, but that does not necessarily entail negative consequences. Final truth eludes our grasp; however, rich and fertile possibilities of understanding exist in the shared life of historical existence.

Schleiermacher was interested in showing his culture an analysis of religion that would appeal to it. He sought to show that we are in relation with a universal ground of experience. In the course of the *Speeches,* he locates this universal aspect in feeling. But he does not equate feelings with emotions. Feeling is something deeper. Through this sense of feeling we are brought to an awareness of indebtedness and dependence on something other than ourselves. In the midst of discontinuity and relativity we find unity, continuity, and the Infinite. Religion is not found as much in thought or action as it is in our felt awareness of dependence on the source of all unity.

Underlying all his thought is the belief that it is God's presence in all things that causes things to be. There is no knowledge of God that is not mediated through finite reality. The reality closest to us is other human beings, and in order for us to receive the life of the World Spirit, we must first, in love and through love, have found humanity. Religion has little in common with a rationalist ethic or a set of propositions written down in a book. It is the expression of what belongs to the highest nature of humankind.

Because religion is social it does not create abstract systems of thought, but communities of faith. Faith creates community because believers are compelled to an expression of their faith. The differences that emerge in history are realizations of the Infinite World Spirit. Religion is always historically conditioned with each religion having its own unique history. The variety is testimony to the vitality of the divine in determining the various circumstances of the world. Both God and humanity interact in the formation of religious life. Structurally understood, religion is determined by its special way of viewing the universe.

Only after he has addressed his "cultured despisers" about the consciousness of dependence, the origin of religion, and its concrete manifestation does he take up the issue of Christian faith. It shares with all manifestations of religion the Infinite seeking to become historically manifest. It differs in its assertion that the union between the World Spirit and the human spirit is most fully revealed in Jesus of Nazareth. In fact, Schleiermacher will argue for the hierarchy of the world's religions and will claim a superiority for Christianity that troubles the modern mind.

In the final part of the fourth speech, Schleiermacher inquires about the organizing principle in the Christian faith that shapes all its teachings and gives its distinctive character. He argues that the recognition of the polar tension between God and the world is the best insight that expresses the Christian perspective:

It is just the intuition of the Universal resistance of finite things to the Unity of the Whole, and of the way Deity treats their resistance. Christianity sees how He reconciles the hostility to Himself, and sets bounds to the ever increasing alienation.... Corruption and redemption, hostility and mediation, are the two indivisibly united fundamental elements of this type of feeling, and by them the whole form of Christianity and the cast of all religious matter contained in it are determined.[63]

Religion was located within human nature and added to the harmonious totality of relationships, yet insofar as all of life shares in the above dialectic, religion could not totally comprise the unity of humankind's existence in a point of harmony. We are constantly striving against harmony between God and world. In the midst of this, Christ appears to overcome the division with a fundamental unity of human self-consciousness with God.

Schleiermacher's development of a general religious foundation on which Christian theology might be erected originated in the feeling of dependence. This feeling of absolute dependence guarantees the universality of the divine self-revelation and ties all manifest religious truth to God. Even in the midst of our alienation from God, one emerges who overcomes the fundamental dialectical tension of sin and redemption, and in whose name a community is constructed.

It was a startling and prophetic effort by Schleiermacher to offer his age a fresh answer to an old question. How is belief or theology even possible in the midst of a culture that increasingly has no need of God? He took a subjective turn inward for an understanding of religious truth. He rejected both supernaturalism and modern reductionism. We can look neither to metaphysics nor morality for the essence of religion. We must look to something that encompasses them both. Faith is discovered in the living relation of God and humankind, and that faith has internal as well as external dimensions.

The book was widely read and established Schleiermacher's reputation in Berlin, but he also realized that he could not follow those whom he wrote for, the circle of Romanticists. After a particularly difficult personal relationship, he departed Berlin for a small pastorate and from there eventually began an academic career in 1804 when he became professor at the University of Halle. He lectured on a wide variety of subjects and furthered developed his views on ethics and hermeneutics.

The early years of the nineteenth century were hard on Germany, and especially on Berlin. Napoleon's involvement in war against Prussia had resulted in the closing of the University of Halle under his direct order. After Halle had been assigned to the newly founded Kingdom of Westphalia, Schleiermacher left and returned to Berlin to begin working on behalf of the Prussian patriotic party. He also became involved with a new university emerging in Berlin.

He argued against state control over the university and envisioned a program of liberal education grounded in the philosophical disciplines. Schleiermacher went on to become professor of theology and dean of the faculty, as well as minister at Trinity Church. In the midst of an intensely active period of scholarly creativity he remained politically active, but when the aristocratic order returned to power after Napoleon's defeat, he was viewed with suspicion.

After conflict with his colleague G. W. F. Hegel over an imprisoned associate, many felt he would be dismissed. His stand against despotism of all kinds was unpopular among the elite of Berlin but proved to be widely popular among the ordinary people. Likewise, his ecumenical attempts drew the ire of conservative clergy who were convinced he was a pantheist.

Ironically, his work on reformulating and thinking through the tradition of the Christian religion, especially as it found expression in his classic work *The Christian Faith,* angered not only the conservatives, but also those such as D. F. Strauss who were more comfortable attacking the older orthodoxy. It seemed like many corners of Germany totally misunderstood what Schleiermacher was seeking to accomplish.

In 1809 Schleiermacher was called to participate in the organization of the University of Berlin. He would spend the rest of his life preaching and teaching there. Numerous works came from him, but the most important was *The Christian Faith.* In this work he picks up some of the themes found in the *Speeches* and systematically works out a Christian theology.[64]

Schleiermacher suggested that finite being is characterized by an unending state of flux. We exist in a fundamental multiplicity in which we define the world and the world defines us. This constitutes the dialectic of knowing and doing. Religion cannot be identified with either of these two, even though they are necessary to it. He conceives a third element of human existence, a third primordial awareness, known as feeling, which points to a deep and abiding awareness of personal unity found in the flux of experience. In this self-consciousness, the deepest intuition is that existence is a gift.

Neither the world nor humanity has the principle of existence in and of themselves. True piety is to know we depend on something that is not dependent upon us. Both self and world are contingent and point beyond themselves to a transcendent *Whence*. Thus the feeling of absolute dependence is not an inference of the existence of something absent, but rather the discovery of a presence or co-determinant.

He takes up again the relationship of Christianity and other religions. While the possibility and actuality of faith is given immanently in humankind's existence, it occurs in historical form. Christianity is distinguished from other faiths by the fact that in it everything is related to the redemption accomplished by Jesus of Nazareth. Redemption implies sin and this dialectical tension points back to the tragic resistance to God by all finite things. Redemption from sin by Jesus forms the definitive central position of Christian faith.

As *The Christian Faith* develops, Schleiermacher draws out the implication of the nature of God from the general God consciousness shared by Christian and non-Christian alike. Insofar as religious awareness points beyond itself to God, religious statements are also statements about God. Theological concepts are reliable only inasmuch as they are reports of the actual state of Christian consciousness in which God is given to us.

But theology also moves from the general religious consciousness to the concrete historical consciousness of the Christian community and its central concern, the redemption accomplished by Jesus of Nazareth. He is not only the historical occasion for the rise of the Christian faith but, more importantly, a living part of the consciousness of his followers. Christ shows that redemption is the completion of creation that brings human beings to fulfillment.

Schleiermacher began his thinking in response to the social, cultural, and psychological milieu in which he found himself. In both the *Speeches* and *The Christian Faith,* he establishes his feeling of absolute dependence as the general religious structure upon which Christianity could rest. The task of theology leads to the practice of developing doctrine from the place of Christian experience, corporate or individual. Theology is formed from the Christian self-consciousness. The implications for this were always thought out in dialectical rigor.

But as Schleiermacher was to explain in his other writings and lectures, dialectical thought is unending. The two contraries can never be resolved by a higher synthesis. However nuanced positions become, individuality is not subsumed by identification, but remains as a goad to further reflection. The goal of logic is not to conclude an argument, but to further it.

In the midst of significant opposition, Schleiermacher ended up touching many lives in various European countries. Students in Copenhagen received him with torchlight processions to mark his visit to them. Perhaps the most moving example of the impact that he had upon his time is found in the historian Leopold von Ranke's account of his funeral. In 1834 Schleiermacher died from an inflammation of the lungs. After his funeral at Trinity Church, Ranke estimated that between twenty thousand and thirty-five thousand people lined the streets of Berlin to bid him farewell. Undoubtedly there were many among the elite who did not mourn as deeply as the crowds who gathered to pay tribute as the funeral carriage made its way through the city.

The Hermeneutics of Understanding

If Schleiermacher could be called the father of modern theology, he could also be seen as the harbinger of the modern discipline of interpretation known as hermeneutics. He sought to address the basis on which truth and meaning is possible, given the limits to the scope of pure reason that Kant had exposed. Beyond this, however, Schleiermacher also embraced the interpretation and understanding of human persons, or, in terms we have been using, the "other" in human life. What we know of Schleiermacher's theory of interpretation comes to us through numerous filters and has been the topic of much study.[65] While running the risks of over-simplification I want to examine Schleiermacher's scheme and use it to raise questions about the postmodern perspective I examined in the first part of this chapter.

Schleiermacher worked out a theory of understanding that was rigorously dialectical and oscillated in a circle between two distinct poles. The best known of these dialectical concepts formed around the notions of grammatical interpretation on the one hand and psychological interpretation on the other. This is difficult to articulate because often Schleiermacher employs subsets of these categories.

On the grammatical side Schleiermacher indicates that to better understand a text (or another person), one must pay close attention to several factors. How are words used, what is their origin, how is language used in the particular discourse of a society? In other words, what are the historical and grammatical factors that form the background for texts, ideas, beliefs, and the identity of persons?

At the opposite end of the pole of interpretation is what is referred to as the divinatory or psychological side. The emphasis here is on making every attempt to understand the one who speaks or writes in his or her particular situation. This would mean that if I truly want to understand another I must seek to know all I can about the one who addresses me.

One of these poles cannot be neglected without unbalancing the act of interpreting. All understanding of another is rooted in concrete diversity of life, where something new and strange has emerged that invites further exploration. As part of this strangeness we find the particularity of an individual or community which differs from the one seeking to understand. Or, to put it into the terms with which I am now concerned, when I encounter the Buddhist I meet another who is different from me in many fundamental ways.

But in the quest for understanding, we may share common things, such as language or culture, which shape us both. As we engage in communicating to one another, new thoughts or ideas may emerge that cause us to become different from the people we were before our interaction. In fact, we may become reconstituted selves in our relationship with one another. To at least leave ourselves open to the possibility of this type of change is important to an authentic grasp of another perspective.

One can even get from Schleiermacher that understanding involves an intuitive side that allows imagination to have a role in grasping the otherness of a person or text. We understand by relating to the one who is communicating to us, even more than by understanding the language that person uses. Of course, the ability to perform this aesthetics of experience arises from my willingness to truly know myself first. The receptivity for knowledge of another emerges from the willingness to truly know oneself. This calls for an unrelenting truth to face one's own motives and agendas in knowing others.

Schleiermacher is always careful to offer a counterbalance which is an artful act. In historical knowledge, speech and text, language and locality, must be carefully examined for an accurate contextual perspective. If I seek to remove my conversation partner from her situation I do violence to her. The sense of a word, the nuance of pronunciation, the original audience addressed, all these and more are crucial for a clearer perspective. The root words, and the historical setting, are crucial for closer apprehension.

Not only do we seek to apprehend what is common, but also that which is different and unique. Understanding involves a deep level of care for discerning another's identity. Nuance, risk, empathy, as well as linguistics and history are important aspects of understanding. If you are an atheist, for instance, and I assume that you use the word "God" to mean the same thing as I do, then already much is lost. If, on the other hand, care is taken to understand your definition of the term, I may find I not only understand you, but I am also an atheist if God is defined in the way you understand.

The freedom of the other to be what they are and not what we wish is one of the primal necessities for this moment. If I impose my will to knowledge on the beliefs or speech of another, I have lost the ability for authentic understanding. Something new may be emerging in the contingencies of life that cause me to be confronted by something different. All possibilities exist in the interpretive dance. All things can change and understanding can enlarge the heart to new realities.

The inner connectedness, the indwelling of Schleiermacher's two means of understanding, indicates that he sees interpretation as an art, the successful execution of which rests upon both the linguistic talent and the talent of the knowledge of individual human beings. Rules cannot encompass or totally inform this approach because particular forms of language are boundless. The relational aspect of interpreting will have to remain open to new possibilities. The parts and wholes stand in relation to one another to form a circle that is never fully closed.

Is this freedom, however, total? Does Schleiermacher represent the notion that every interpretive move is legitimate? He does indicate that there is no master language to which a multiplicity of languages is reducible, which would imply that a multiplicity of futures is possible. Thus he does share with the contemporary world the notion that final or ultimate interpretations will, in fact, be difficult to attain. Understanding will always be partial, provisional, and parochial. In other words, we see through a glass darkly.

However, hermeneutics can be exercised skillfully or unskillfully. Laxness in the art of interpreting proceeds on the assumption that understanding is a matter of course and expresses the whole goal of interpretation negatively by saying that misunderstanding should be avoided. The skillful employment of the dialectical movement proceeds with the assumption that misunderstanding is a matter of course and understanding is to be ardently sought.

In the context of what we have been exploring in this chapter postmodernity argues that quests for understanding are hegemonic and narcissistic attempts to repress difference and suppress the other. Understanding seeks to domesticate difference and order all alien and alternative realities and explanations. If it cannot order them, then they must be pushed to the periphery. If I want to remain open to difference then I must resist the temptation to completely understand the other and so effect a totalizing closure.

But as Hans-Georg Gadamer pointed out: "Schleiermacher's idea of a universal hermeneutics starts from this: that the experience of the alien and the possibility of misunderstanding is universal. . . . In a new and universal sense, alienation is inextricably given with the individuality of the Thou."[66] It is precisely in the encounter with the other that the distinct particularity of another text or life is discovered.

Rather than the immediate imposition of my prior categories, assumptions, thoughts, preunderstandings, I must first listen to the other, respecting her and surrendering my right to interpret. Only in this way can I avoid construing reality for her to conform to. Schleiermacher offered us a perspective 170 years ago that may help us with the issue of religious pluralism. It is only as we allow texts and persons to enter our present understanding as themselves and not some construct of our own devising that any authentic understanding emerges.

Toward Understanding the Religions

We began this chapter with some stories about the ways in which various faith communities are responding to the world as it is presently constituted. These stories represented both inclusivist and exclusivist options for how we understand our faith. Both of these paths carry their own possibilities and problems. Is there a way we can remain faithful to our story and not close ourselves off from other stories?

This can mean that when we come to the issue of religious pluralism we do not have to take the path that interprets another faith in terms of our own. Adherents of many religions have sometimes claimed something to the effect that others are truly Hindu or Christian or Buddhist; they just don't know it. Some Christians, most notably Karl Rahner, have even used the term "anonymous Christian" to speak of those who are in the grace of God, though they may be outside the church. Hinduism has sometimes said that everyone, when all is said and done, is a Hindu. These ideas can represent a form of spiritual colonialism since those not of our faith are subsumed under our faith regardless of their belief.

Another approach, especially popular recently, is to say that ultimately all religions are actually saying the same thing. For understanding to take place we should look for the common core that we can all agree on and work from there to deal with our differences. But this can be another form of seeking control. Who decides what the common core is going to be? How, in the midst of so much diversity, can the notion of a common core be viable? Is the fundamentalist or the Sufi mystic allowed in the core? Trying to narrow things down to a common core violates the richness inherent within traditions, never mind between them.

So, as a Christian, where does this leave me? I believe I live within a true story. I believe that the narrative of God embodying self to meet the world on its own terms is a compelling one that calls for my ultimate allegiance. How do I engage others in the telling of this story and respect theirs? Are there places where we can meet one another that will respect the integrity of one another's faith without betraying our own?

Given what we have said so far, one place to start would be to begin learning about other faiths and religions. While there may be no common core that means everybody is really saying the same thing, there may be resemblances and similarities among religions as well as differences. The Christian may find in the Taoist principle of *wu-wei* the means to understand the way of Jesus in the world in a deeper way. The Buddhist may come to a deeper knowledge of Amida Buddha's grace by learning about Jesus. The willingness to remain open to the other means the freedom to let the other be what she will.

And this is difficult for us. Aren't we meant to go and make disciples of all the world, to proclaim the good news? By all means, but perhaps the best way to do this is to live out of our own faith and not engage in rejection or exclusion of others because they believe differently. This exclusion is a form of violence to the integrity of all others who believe differently.

In the terms that we have been exploring in this chapter, we are called to enter into another person's experience not for imperial conquest, but for understanding and even communion. Those persons stand not only over and against, but beside and with, calling me into question, and, if I have the courage, enabling me to see clearly my own self-deceptions and will to knowledge.

We can bear witness to the truths we believe, but this does not have to entail the rejection of others who believe differently. It does not even mean we have to draw the boundaries of exclusion. If we are skillfully engaging in the art of interpretation, we may find ourselves being changed by what is brought to us by others. We may even discover that we have been wrong about things that are important. This takes courage and cannot be done when we live in a state of fear.

It is this fear, the fear of wanting to protect our faith, to protect the honor of God, that drives much of the world's religious violence and causes so much pain. But if the biblical writer was right when he wrote that perfect love casts out fear (1 John 4:18), then maybe we can see a glimpse of something that shines through the fragmented pieces of our contemporary brokenness. For it is our willingness to love God, no matter what our faith perspective, that allows us to love our neighbors and do them no harm. This is one of the marks of a mature faith and a manifestation of the reign of God. Ultimately, faith is not our possession; it is God's.

But we must go a step further and perhaps inquire about whether the hermeneutical circle we have been reflecting on represents an empty circle that we fill with the realities within which we live, which we want to hear and to read, and which we want to understand. The idolatries to which we often give allegiance are assumed and undetected by us. This is the place where faith can exercise its prophetic function and address the world by calling it to turn away from its collective madness and violence. Faith that engages in the attempt at understanding I have been arguing for does not lose its voice to call into question those forms of belief that result in suffering and pain.

While the desire to understand does not have to represent a totalizing closure of another's difference, it can engage in critique. Some would argue that this is precisely what cannot be done because there is no vantage point from which this can be done that guarantees the validity of the critique. But can we not say at least that faith sets the boundaries for how we live in the world, and there are ways of being in the world that lead away from death and destruction and toward life and peace? For Christians, would this not be a vision of the reign of God?

Perhaps Schleiermacher was closer to something that we still cannot control or even call our own. In the willingness to listen, in the retrieval of symbols and communicative texts are we not met with the truly alien, the ultimately Divine Other? In my willingness to confront myself, to allow you to confront me, to give away any power of absolute interpretation, am I not met with the truly unexpected? The One who loves instead of hates, who reveals Self with narratives of reversal such as we find in the Gospels?

In the hope to know another, whether through reading or hearing, I potentially do enter a realm that all theory cannot grasp and we can only dimly apprehend. It is that which emerges with love and gratitude for the life we live. Certainly, the crowds that lined the streets of Berlin for Schleiermacher's funeral understood something of where he placed himself in the world. Authentic understanding does not have to be right, nor does it need to will to power over others through conversion. Rather it wills to love the world in all its complexity and foolishness, its self-destruction and its beauty, its difference and its familiarity.

Chapter 7

Suffering with God

Dietrich Bonhoeffer and Postmodern Theology

Who is the holy person? The one who is aware of others' suffering.
— KABIR, *The Vision of Kabir*

THE PULITZER PRIZE–WINNING NOVELIST Annie Dillard in her latest work, *For the Time Being*, weaves together various strands of the human story to ask one of the most compelling questions that faces us as human beings. How do we deal with suffering? She begins the book by reflecting on human birth defects. It is a painful topic, not the least because one wonders where God was in the birth of these children. As she continues this strand of thinking throughout the book, the reader is moved not only by the plight of those being described, but the very real anguish that comes through Dillard's pen.

As she continues she works in reflections on the Kaballah and other expressions of Judaism, Teilhard de Chardin, Chinese history, Buddhism, Hinduism, and even Christianity. And this is only a partial list. She explores in a sensitive and probing way the many paths that persons have taken to live with the presence of evil and suffering in the world. She wonders about the many voiceless souls who have died at the hands of the countless atrocities we are capable of committing and asks about the individual, the one. What are those stories buried to us in the sands of history, the ones we never hear? She doubts whether the presence of God counts for much in this world the way we have thought about it traditionally. She interweaves religious accounts of God with real-life instances that seem to betray the confidence that the religious statements indicate. She is not satisfied. The usual ways we have of explaining the presence of evil or justifying the classical omnipotent, omniscient, omni-everything God just don't wash for her. She is on the trail of something unattainable—an explanation that makes some sense.

God is out of the physical loop of the fallen world, Dillard observes, and she says the semipotent God has one hand tied behind his back. She writes:

> God is spirit, spirit expressed infinitely in the universe, who does not give as the world gives. His home is absence, and there he finds us. In the coils of absence we meet him by seeking him. God lifts our souls to their roots in his silence. Natural materials clash and replicate, shaping our fates. We lose the people we love, we lose our vigor, and we lose our lives. Perhaps, and at best, God knows nothing of these temporal accidents, but knows souls only. This God does not direct the universe, he underlies it.... God is the universe's consciousness. The consciousness of divinity is divinity itself. The more we wake to holiness, the more of it we give birth to, the more we introduce, expand, and multiply it on earth, the more God is "on the field."[67]

This is one of the ways that Dillard can come to grips with all the suffering in the world. In her exploration of all the religious expressions of the world found in her book, she tries to find the thing that would be able to unite them, and God as the manifestation of human consciousness is as close as we are going to get. But she is not just content with this. She thinks there is something more solid than this to grasp. But whatever this is comes at the boundaries of our material existence and the place of the divine. God and world are not yet completed, but the more attentive we are to holiness the more the being of God will become manifest in the world.

Dillard probes the concerns of faith in a way that I believe was anticipated by theologian Dietrich Bonhoeffer as he struggled throughout his life with his world. She is seeking a nonreligious account of how God might be found in the world. In the sea of so much pain she wants to know what to make of the notion of God. At one point she refers to Bonhoeffer and explores the notion that we can truly find God only if we immerse ourselves in the world. She seems to indicate that the more we do immerse ourselves in the world the more solid we become, and this is not necessarily a bad thing.

This problem of suffering is one that is universal in human life. In Buddhism it constitutes the fundamental problem of human existence. The first of the Four Noble Truths of Buddhism is that all life is suffering. This is the starting place for the entire religion and the rest of the Noble Truths are laid out in order to deal with and answer the problem of suffering. It is an ultimate concern. The same is true of almost all the other world's religions. And the questions they raise may find no satisfactory answers. From the Job story in the Hebrew Scriptures to the stories of Babylonian culture and even into the religion of Christianity, human beings have been trying to make sense out of that which seems to defy all attempts at understanding.

In what follows I want us to encounter Dietrich Bonhoeffer in order to reflect on how Christianity in the postmodern world might respond to the challenges presented by theodicy. In doing so I want to think about how theology has structured itself in the past and present and look at the ways Bonhoeffer offers us for reformulating our theological perspective. The procedure here will be slightly different in that I want to look at Bonhoeffer's life first and then proceed to the concerns of modern theology.

For This Moment: Bonhoeffer's Life

Waiting on the dock in the oppressive heat of New York in July of 1939, Dietrich Bonhoeffer anticipated the boarding call for the ship that would take him back to Germany. Bonhoeffer had been in New York for less than a month, the result of efforts by Reinhold Niebuhr to secure him a place in America prior to the eruptions of World War II. Niebuhr knew of the arrests, the setbacks, the dismantling of the Confessing Church, the closing of the seminary at Finkenwalde, and the banishment of Bonhoeffer from Berlin. He had arranged for him to lecture in America and stay here as long as the persecution of the Confessing Church in Germany was being executed by Hitler's forces.

Bonhoeffer had come to America confused and uncertain about the course to take with his life, but he had been in America only a few days when he realized that his coming was a mistake. He wrote Niebuhr a letter to tell him he had made a mistake coming to America and he had to return to participate in the sufferings of the German people, in order to help rebuild when the present government was removed. His friends in America came to dissuade him, but Bonhoeffer was resolute; his mind was clear. Back to arrests, more protests, more oppression of pastors and churches who sought to be faithful and resist Hitler. And for Bonhoeffer personally, back to conspiracy and the attempt to assassinate Hitler, back to imprisonment and, ultimately, execution at the hands of the Nazis.[68]

One of the most intriguing figures in recent theology is Dietrich Bonhoeffer. At the beginning of his life it would have seemed unlikely that he would end up in a prison cell, implicated in an assassination attempt. He was born into a family of privilege and accomplishment. His father, a distinguished psychiatrist, encouraged his children to be independent in their thinking, though his own religious inclinations were nominal.

In his schooling, Bonhoeffer studied at Tübingen and the University of Berlin. He was exposed to the leading figures of philosophy and theology, studying the critical philosophy of Immanuel Kant, the liberal theology of Schleiermacher, and the historian Adolf von Harnack, who expressed dismay at his pupil's interest in Karl Barth. It was Karl Barth who provided strong intellectual stimulation for Bonhoeffer, and while Bonhoeffer maintained critical reservations, he did embrace Barth's dialectical theology.

As Bonhoeffer continued his theological training he would respond to Barth's theology with increasing critical rigor, but he still found in him an ally. Bonhoeffer's doctoral dissertation, completed in 1927 at the tender age of twenty-one, was hailed by Barth as a "theological miracle." In it, Bonhoeffer explored the themes of a concrete manifestation of God's community in the world and ways in which Christ is incarnated in the world through the community formed in his name.

In order to explore these themes in a more concrete way, Bonhoeffer became an assistant pastor to a German congregation in Barcelona in 1928. The experience opened his eyes to the realities of parish life, and with the international economic crisis, he began to perceive the trauma of watching certain structures and values break apart. His sermons and writings began making a space for those who were voiceless. As he put it, God's concern has strong focus on the "neglected, the insignificant people, the weak, the unknown, the inferior, the oppressed, the despised."

Bonhoeffer returned to Germany in February 1929, where he began work on his second dissertation, *Act and Being*. In some respects, it was a treatment of the onto-theological tradition, but it also probed a theology that could be divested of self-interests in order that God's word might be made more manifest in concrete manifestations. He expressed suspicion of any theology that located the revelation of God in individualism and subjectivity. He critiqued the Christian Church for being power hungry in arrogating to itself the ability to speak for God through doctrine or institution.

His first visit to America came in 1929 in order to study at Union Theological Seminary in New York. While he missed the theological rigor of his former training, he was pushed by figures such as Eugene W. Lyman and Reinhold Niebuhr to think in ever more concrete ways about the ethical implications of his faith. His experience with the African-American church, both through Abyssinian Baptist Church in Harlem and his friendship with Frank Fisher of Alabama, alerted him to the depth of racism and its impact upon American culture.

Bonhoeffer was to have other contacts in America that would cause him to think about the ways in which culture and faith bind one another in ways that are unhealthy. He strengthened his notion about standing with the oppressed and suffering as a concrete response of Christianity. He also came into contact with Jean Lasserre, founder of the Movement for Reconciliation, who influenced Bonhoeffer in the direction of pacifism.

Bonhoeffer moved back to Germany, meeting with Karl Barth and beginning a career as a professor of theology at the University of Berlin in 1931. He immediately made an impact upon those students who did not go to the classes taught by professors sympathetic to Nazism. His students would form the early core of resistance to the Nazi program. But they would emerge as only a small minority of resistance in Germany, and after a series of defeats at organizing the church to resist the Nazis, Bonhoeffer took a pastorate in London.

Chided by Barth for this move, Bonhoeffer returned to Germany to help lead the resistance of the Confessing Church. Through numerous conferences and meetings, Bonhoeffer sought to uncover the unchristian assumptions behind the "German Christians" who supported Hitler. One of the activities that was to become most important for his life was the establishment of the seminary at Finkenwalde, a type of seminary in exile in Germany.

It was here that Bonhoeffer would work out his thoughts on discipleship that would later find form in the books *Life Together* and *The Cost of Discipleship*. He sought to instill the discipline of a liturgical life, focusing on worship and prayer in a way that struck some as almost monastic. The Gestapo closed the seminary in October of 1937. Events in Germany worsened and Bonhoeffer was faced with a type of internal exile as almost all resistance to the regime dissipated. He eventually took the second trip to America. It was to be a short visit.

He had made a mistake to leave Germany at its darkest time, and he realized that he must go stand with the people of his country in their time of suffering. His boat left in July of 1939, less than two months before the outbreak of war. When he returned, he would be recruited as a member of the resistance to Hitler and his policies. After the attempts on Hitler's life in March of 1943, he would be arrested and imprisoned at Tegal where the collection of writings known as *Letters and Papers from Prison* was written. This led to Bonhoeffer's strongest connection with contemporary theology, as the narrative told of his life ends within the context of Tegal prison leading up to his execution at the hands of the Nazis at Flossenbürg.

It is there that Bonhoeffer wrote some of the phrases that would become so employed, yet so misunderstood by contemporary theology. "Religionless Christianity," "The World Come of Age," "The Powerlessness of God," and "Worldly Christianity" were all phrases that entered the lexicon of theology in the 1960s. This spawned a massive misreading of Bonhoeffer by the "death of God" theologians.

Some people interpret Bonhoeffer as a mark of the end of modernity, leaving behind forever a notion of certainty in theology to strive in the land of exile for answers to the questions of what Christianity is, who Christ really is, for us today. In our age these questions have a sense of urgency that make Bonhoeffer's search for authentic faith timelessly important. When the voices of today contend that our search for signs of a Presence, a trace of rumors of glory, or a whisper from the Other results only in the recognition of Absence, we find in Bonhoeffer a voice that resonates with the search.

What Is Theology for Us Today?

Thus we return to some of the themes found previously in our introduction about theology and its ability to deliver anything other than human projection, and then move to an examination of the prison writings to both critique theology and offer fruitful avenues to explore. We begin, however, with some questions about theology and religion raised by Nietzsche and his heirs.

We discovered in the leveling critique of Nietzsche a fundamental distrust of all religious belief in the sense that any appeal to universal truth is misplaced. In his critique he charges that powerful clerical and ecclesial interests conspire to keep people locked in illusion and deception by the manipulative use of language. By incorporation of language into metaphors and interpretation, the terms of which are defined by the authors, powerful interests conspire to create images of God and religion that will keep the masses bound to a "slave mentality."

We have no firm grasp in reality; all we have are interpretations of interpretations, each built on tools of the Scriptures, which serve as justification for Israel's violence to its neighbors in conquest of the promised land, right up through Paul's desire to destroy a ritual Law he could not keep. Nietzsche is relentless in his attack upon all forms of Christianity that claim to know truth, when in fact it is power they are after.

For those who take Nietzsche's critique to heart all claims to truth must be abandoned and understood as claims to power disguised by the cloak of deception and manipulation. Of course, this perspective finds fertile soil in the ground of late modernity. A culture of suspicion emerges concerning not just religion, or even theology, but all cultural forms of truth claims. Art, politics, economics, all fall under the blade that Nietzsche wields if no one questions the premises of the critique.

The theological implications of this have been felt for some time. As we saw in our last chapter on Schleiermacher, we are caught in a crisis of interpretation. This is not found just in hermeneutics of texts, but of human language and existence. As we saw in the chapter on Luther, one of the major issues for Christianity has been defining the meaning and nature of revelation given in the biblical texts. What was the proper authority with which to interpret the Bible? Whether authority was located within the community of the church or in the individual, the issue was how to understand a foundational reality present in the revelation. The fact of this revelation was not doubted, what was questioned was which authorities defined the contours of Christian identity.

As humankind moved toward the type of autonomy that Bonhoeffer explored through his reading of Wilhelm Dilthey, the critiques of persons such as Kant, Nietzsche, and Freud began revealing problem after problem. As the influence of these critiques increased, theories about the nature of authorities and their respective interpretations of Christian faith shifted.

One of those paths, marked out in the earlier chapter on Schleiermacher, sought the explication of religious beliefs as interpretations of religious experience. When religious beliefs and traditions became grounded in the religious (or Christian) self-consciousness, the authority shifted from an external text and authority to the interior regions of human subjectivity.

Standing at the end of this move, however, were Ludwig Feuerbach and Franz Overbeck, who pointed out that the human subject was as helpless as traditional or textual authority to provide any type of foundational certainty that would be free from the limitations of contingent human existence. And to finish off the project, Nietzsche quite correctly pointed out that the human subject not only manipulated and did violence to others in the name of a truth self-constructed, but so self-deluded are we that we sincerely believe our own self-definitions of truth. The implications of this for theology are particularly crucial.

Presently we live with the collapse of both internal and external authorities. We have struggled with the uncovering that has emerged in recent times. Bonhoeffer anticipated this from his prison cell as he sought to understand a world come of age. He knew that the maturation of the world and its growing autonomy from authoritative and institutional religion would make speaking of God a difficult task. He writes from his prison cell: "How do we speak of God—without religion, i.e., without the temporally conditioned presuppositions of metaphysics, inwardness, and so on? How do we speak (or perhaps we cannot now even 'speak' as we used to) in a 'secular' way about 'God'?"[69] Bonhoeffer wondered how, if language and truth are not anchored in anything other than the vagaries of culture and power, it can say a true word about God. If meaning is always deferred through an ever-increasing chain of interpretation, always overtaken by new meanings and new assumptions that need to be examined for the inherent will to power found there, how can humans speak of God?

In the middle of one of the most diabolical power projects existent on the face of the planet Bonhoeffer tried to anticipate what type of future Christianity might have in the world of Nazis. When he targeted religion, or more precisely, the cultural-religious manifestations of Christianity, for particular attention, he knew that using religion as a cloak of faith could, and often did, result in theological categories far more reflective of human consciousness, both individual and collective, than of an authentic presence of transcendence.

Bonhoeffer's analysis of religion addressed the fact that those anxious souls who used the religion of Christianity in its transcendent clothing to answer the questions of the unknown constructed a religious idol. It was not only the religious conception of God that Bonhoeffer critiqued; he also criticized the stream of theology which used God as the stop-gap, the *deus ex machina,* the working hypothesis of the unanswerable questions of human existence:

> Religious people speak of God when human knowledge (perhaps simply because they are too lazy to think) has come to an end, or when human resources fail—in fact it is always the *deus ex machina* that they bring on the scene, either for the apparent solution of insoluble problems, or as strength in human failure—always, that is to say, exploiting human weakness or human boundaries.[70]

When religiously based metaphysics of being was used in this way it resulted in abstracting the divine into the categories of omnipotence, omniscience, and omnipresence. This type of spatial transcendence corresponded to the mythological constructs of religion in Bonhoeffer's mind and led him to comment that "the God 'beyond' is not the beyond of our cognitive faculties. The transcendence of epistemological theory has nothing to do with the transcendence of God."[71]

Bonhoeffer had been made keenly aware of how philosophical metaphysics as a theological category could obscure the authenticity of biblical faith. Eberhard Bethge writes in his biography of Bonhoeffer:

> Supranatural and mythological formulations obscure the Gospel's direct immediacy, and the exotic nature of the context in which it is presented has nothing to do with the message itself. Instead of this, however, the metaphysically organized Christian religion provided the world with the kind of transcendence that it longed for. God became necessary as the superstructure of being, and religious longing found its goal in a heavenly domain. Thus metaphysics seduces the Christian religion into thinking statically in terms of two spheres and has forced it to give its redemptive nature a one-sided emphasis.[72]

Bonhoeffer understood that when a traditional hermeneutic uses metaphysical clothing to wrap God in a culturally conditioned notion of religion and revelation, God is objectified according to the dimensions of a particular age. And, more, this objectification achieves the status of truth when in reality it is another model.

It was not only the category of metaphysics that concerned Bonhoeffer; he also confronted the dead end of inwardness and subjectivity. This inwardness was not only that of a pietistic individualism where God is entirely a matter of personal concern. No appeal can be made for an authoritative perspective on the basis of human subjectivity. Aware of Feuerbach's critique of religious consciousness, Bonhoeffer knew that a category such as God's omnipotence was not to be seen as an authentic aspect of God's nature, but was our understanding of power extended out into the world.

As modern theologians are acutely aware, the conceptual frameworks of the past lend themselves to certain abstractions. Bonhoeffer's critique of religion (and by implication, theology) gave him an insight possessed by those who, like Nietzsche, interrogate religion. A particular concept or experience of God and a certain way of seeing God's relationship to the world were bound together in much of religious Christianity and were expressed in a particular metaphysical and historically conditioned form. A concept of God was derived from our humanly experienced interaction with the world, and then this concept was absolutized and projected out into the world. One of the results of this was the formation of classical theism.

Bonhoeffer's critique of religious Christianity is a critique of a theology that seeks to attach itself to a foundational certainty, employing the perspectives of transcendence or immanence and claiming for it certain ontological status. Neither offers a neutral, secure standpoint which protects theology from the cultural or linguistic limitations of humankind. The demise of a theology that grounds itself in the external authority of a revelatory text or the internal authority of human religious consciousness still impacts us. Bonhoeffer not only anticipated this; he welcomed it.

We are still struggling with the concerns of modern theology. As we move from the landmarks of a previous age, many theologians are working to ensure theology does not become further marginalized, losing any public voice. In truth, this has already happened, and we should ask ourselves if, perhaps, this is a welcome development.

Francis Schüssler Fiorenza argues that two particular developments mark the contemporary crisis of interpretation and theological formulation:

> On the one hand, there is the universality of interpretation, through which all aspects of human history, knowledge, and experience become subject matters in need of interpretation. This development results in part from the continuing theological task of interpretation itself. On the other hand there is the limitation of interpretation that results from the insight into the limitations of human subjectivity. These two tendencies constitute the crisis of modernity and especially of theology's interpretive task.[73]

The awareness of this interpretive and historical character of theology has become especially acute today. As Schleiermacher's turn to the subject generated a realization of the historicity of human existence and interpretation, a host of postmodern interpreters call attention to the interconnections between knowledge and power. The critiques of various dissenting theologies reveal the suspicion that class, gender, or race interests cannot be transcended in the search for any possible universal human experience which can confirm interpretation. An interpretation of religious experience or biblical texts often reflects the partiality of a person's individual historically and socially conditioned existence rather than a universality of interpretation.

And worse, for those like Nietzsche and his postmodern heirs, theology and Christian truth claims are inherently manipulative power bids over the consciences of human beings. At precisely the point where these claims make their most universal contention, we should stand doubly suspicious for the illusions are most deceptive because more is at stake. If the narratives of Christianity wish to argue for metanarrative status, then the potential for mischief and confusion stands the strongest.

Theological reflection and religious discourse cannot claim any certainty of truth beyond a contextually defined adequacy. No self-validating, autonomous experience of God exists whereby a correlation inherently resides between the human search for meaning and the explicit symbols of Christian faith. Even the word "God" does not refer to an object or an entirely adequate explanation of human existence. Rather, all the notions of God and theology that we work with are the products of human imagination and construction.

Following this perspective, God is not a reality which is a constitutive part of our consciousness, not immediately available in our experience for observation, inspection, and description, and therefore speech about or to God can never be directly referential. How then would we check our concepts or models of God for any sense of accuracy or adequacy? While we may be able to confirm other ordinary objects of perception and experience, we cannot do so with the primary object of theological reflection. This places theological constructions in an entirely different realm than the constructions we employ with ordinary concepts we can revise and check. The concept of God (or even self and world for that matter) can only function as a regulative idea that stands at the limits of experience and delineates our thinking. If this is the case, how can religious beliefs carry authority?

For people who hold them, religious beliefs are authoritative because they are descriptive of reality whether seen or unseen, not because they benefit society by the employment of religious symbols. If it is all a matter of false consciousness, why would we not opt for the autonomy that Bonhoeffer probed from his prison cell? At one point he writes that we must live in the world as if God did not exist. Annie Dillard would find sympathy for such an idea. But this does not entirely address the matter, because in theology we are still trying to find adequate concepts of God that fit our experience of the world.

So the question remains, why one idea or theology and not another? Does theology have a connection to any reality other than that which we ourselves construct? When we bring the baggage of background assumptions, theories of understandings, and the life situations we are in, can theology be anything other than self- or group definition? And more than that, is theology only a self-deluded attempt to wield power and define reality for those who want theologians to do their thinking for them?

On this basis truthfulness in a theological claim resides in the authoritative presence it possesses to offer meaning to persons' lives. Constructive theology works by constructing a conceptual world, a descriptive language, and relating this to the world in which people live, move, and have their being. Thus functional criteria mold and shape how we speak of God and God's relation to the world. While helpful in one way, this raises issues in other areas.

If the question of why one idea of God or a particular "ultimate" frame of reference should be embraced rather than another, do functional criteria offer a sufficient grounding to religious belief? Does every age's construal of God lose force when the experiences and language of that age fade into the coming one, especially when the self-interests that stand behind all theology are exposed?

Does all Christian God-talk, and everything associated with it (prayer, worship, meditation, repentance, obedience) belong to a specific worldview, a specific interpretation of human existence, created by the imagination in one particular stream of human culture to provide orientation in life for those living in that culture?

If so, then the task of theology becomes to interpret the religious myths, symbols, and beliefs in the context of their embodiment in the particular time, place, and cultural location from which they emerged. But this raises related questions that we find perplexing as human beings.

Does this mean that the recognition of our historicity leads to an understanding of humans as creatures of tradition, shaped through language, belief systems, and rituals of distinctive historical positions, but unable to create paradigms and establish priorities in the face of conflicts and changes in context? Is there no space from which we might be able to discern that which transcends self-generated and self-protective theological strategies? It seems to be a commonplace in contemporary theology that recognition of the historical character of human life entails the abandonment or revision of many of the theological and philosophical projects of the modern period. And not just in the modern period, but in all periods that preceded it.

For many today, theology is not necessarily about asserting undeniable truth claims about God or reality, nor is it about finding God in the depths of human subjectivity. Today many theologians believe that the task of theology is to analyze and illumine the fundamental claims about reality and human life that have emerged in specific traditions. In this sense Christian theologians are exercised by searching for understanding the basic correspondence between the human search for meaning and the explicit religious symbols of Christian faith. The problem is that no foundation exists whereby the correspondences can be guaranteed to exist.

This is obscured in the present age because we stand in the room of historical consciousness. We understand that hermeneutics and theories of correspondence are themselves influenced by historical, cultural, and linguistic background assumptions. This means that theologians continually engage in reflection for a contextually defined adequacy. Fiorenza writes, "The background assumptions, life-relation, and concrete interpretations point to the relativity of our self-definitions and the need critically to challenge and revise them."[74]

Bonhoeffer's Promise for Postmodernity

This brings us once more to the difficulty of modern theology. There are no disinterested standpoints, no objective perspectives, no uninvested background assumptions present to us. All theologies embody the distinct interests of the theologian. Considering the projective and creative aspects of contemporary theology, we are faced with several dilemmas, not the least of which are those questions posed earlier in this chapter and the one on Anselm. How do we know whether it is all interpretation right down the line, or whether there are theological projects that connect with the reality of God? If we are at least willing to entertain the notion that God exists, where do we find in theology anything other than projective identification of self-consciousness? Even in the dissenting theological critiques of postmodernity, how can we escape the gravity of self-interests in order to connect with that which is truly Other?

Are we truly caught in the dilemma where all reality is created by interpretation? Worse, are we finally to be led to the truth of Nietzsche, who contends he finds no God—either in history or in nature—but that we experience what has been revered as God, not as "godlike" but as miserable, as absurd, as harmful, not merely as an error but as a crime against life?

The problem for many is that religion and theology represent a flight from the world and its struggles to the illusion of another world. The type of God created by Nietzsche's "slave mentality" serves the need of human illusion and self-deification and, as he would argue, there are nobler uses for the invention of gods than for the self-crucifixion and self-violation of humankind in which Europe over the past two millennia achieved its distinctive mastery. For the harshest critics, theology unknowingly (or knowingly) conspires to legitimate the weak, delusional, and self-crucifying illusions we call God.

But theology is formed within the context of certain communities, and these communities cannot formulate their responses to the world in isolation from these questions. For Christianity, and its interpretive schemes, what is decisive, essential, and even normative to faith? What is paradigmatic to it and what is not? Can Christian theology be anything more than a game of interpretive play among a privileged elite of scholars? Is it only the attempt to construct domains of power to manipulate and deceive persons?

The global pluralism of theology is bringing these issues into focus and calling us to new understandings, and just as Bonhoeffer's instincts concerning the passing of a form of theology (religion) led him to certain conclusions, his instincts concerning a possible future for theology offer us paths that may turn out to be fruitful.

Most scholars who have studied Bonhoeffer have noticed the concreteness that marked his theology. He was strongly opposed to abstractions being used as a substitute for involvement in the world. His disgust for the category of religion was rooted in the idea that religion (or theology) reflects a flight from reality. Contemporary readers may be somewhat disturbed by Bonhoeffer's employment of religion as a negative category; however, in the contextual world he was living in, he had seen the full results of Nietzsche come to fruition. Atrocity was once more being committed under the legitimating force of the Christian religion.

Bonhoeffer's understanding of concreteness and reality was always rooted christologically: Jesus Christ is where God becomes concrete reality, the original reality. This reality is also manifest in Bonhoeffer's ecclesiology expressed in the Christ existing as community. The Christ-person becomes real in the community, and the community becomes real in the other person. Transcendence is removed from metaphysical speculation and related to a concrete reality. This concrete reality does root itself in a particular empirical community and a historical man. Bonhoeffer's understanding of the connections between the particular limitations of empirical reality and the universal dimensions of christology offers us clues in contemporary theological construction. His exploration of theologies that have failed to incarnate God's presence in the world allowed him to see beyond the force of certain critiques.

If theology is about the dialectic between humankind's search for meaning and its religious symbols, then the universality of suffering transcends contextuality. Suffering is transhistorical. The commitment to a transformative praxis in relation to suffering requires us to confront the universality of suffering in human existence. Suffering brings us to the door of human being and cuts across the ideological, social, and economic categories we use to interpret our existence. It stands as a critique of modernity. Those who suffer offer mute testimony before our science, technology, and theories of freedom. Before this witness there is no place of privilege where we can interpret faith for the educated and worldly-wise theologies of this age. Suffering offers its own narrative of human existence.

Bonhoeffer speaks to us today with a voice of solidarity with the suffering. Speaking to the religious constructions we futilely cling to, he reveals the profound difference between the God of abstraction and the suffering God revealed through the narrative of Jesus of Nazareth:

> And we cannot be honest unless we recognize that we have to live in the world *etsi deus non daretur.* And this is just what we do recognize before God! God himself compels us to recognize it. So our coming of age leads us to a true recognition of our situation before God. God would have us know that we must live as men who manage our lives without him. The God who is with us is the God who forsakes us (Mark 15:34). The God who lets us live in the world without the working hypothesis of God is the God before whom we stand continually. Before God and with God we live without God. God lets himself be pushed out of the world on to the cross. He is weak and powerless in the world, and that is precisely the way, the only way, in which he is with us and helps us. Matthew 8:17 makes it quite clear that Christ helps us, not by virtue of his omnipotence, but by virtue of his weakness and suffering.[75]

When Bonhoeffer interrogates religion and theology he raises questions that reveal the unspoken social and political agendas found in any cultural context. When theology fails to raise the question of who benefits from a particular theology, it manifests the difference between the religious and nonreligious interpretation of Christian faith. A religious interpretation springs from the will to power that creates theologies and structures that oppress others. Eberhard Bethge writes:

> "Religious interpretation" is an exegesis of the Gospel of Christ's powerlessness that establishes priests (as the givers

of life) or theologians (as the custodians of truth) as the guardians and rulers of the people of the church's people, creating and perpetuating a situation of dependence. Nothing will be as difficult as overcoming the monarchial and patriarchial structures of hierarchies, theologies, and indeed, dogmas; coming of age contains an element that is alarmingly unreassuring.[76]

Contrast this statement with the nonreligious interpretation which, while it is a hermeneutical category, is also an ethical call to a concrete community of vision, a community whose members exist in distinct relation to the powers of the world. If interpretation is about how people understand the world and God's relationship to it, then Bonhoeffer opens up a path which takes seriously the experience of suffering:

> Here is the decisive difference between Christianity and all religions. Man's religiosity makes him look in his distress to the power of God in the world. God is the *deus ex machina*. The Bible directs man to God's powerlessness and suffering; only the suffering God can help. To that extent we may say the development towards the world coming of age outlined above which has done away with a false conception of God, opens up a way of seeing the God of the Bible who wins power and space in the world by his weakness. This will probably be the starting point of our "secular interpretation."[77]

If we ask who benefits from Bonhoeffer's theology, we find his desire to incarnate God's presence in the world made him sensitive to the universality of suffering and the necessity of Christian faith to embody solidarity with the powerless. Theology does not seek out the powerful. If theology does not acknowledge the suffering of humankind, its primary focus will not incarnate the presence of Christ. If it does, the character of Christianity will be shaped by its identification with the weak and powerless. When the world (or theologians) ask who God is or what our relation to the divine is, Bonhoeffer responds:

> Not in the first place an abstract belief in God, in his omnipotence, etc. That is not a genuine experience of God, but a partial extension of the world. Encounter with Jesus

Christ. The experience that a transformation of all human life is given in the fact that "Jesus is there for others." His "being there for others" is the experience of transcendence. Faith is participation in this being of Jesus (incarnation, cross, and resurrection). Our relation to God is not a "religious" relationship to the highest, most powerful, and best Being imaginable—that is not authentic transcendence—but our relation to God is a new life in "existence for others," through participation in the being of Jesus. The transcendental is not infinite and unattainable tasks, but the neighbor who is within reach in any given situation.[78]

One of the commonplaces in Bonhoeffer studies is a recognition that he connects christology and reality. I would argue that the striking aspect of Bonhoeffer's later work is that empirical reality shapes the dimensions of authentic faith. Theology can devise conceptual schemes of transcendence or other metaphysical categories; but, for Bonhoeffer, faith is in the end an ethical moment. Rather than take flight in theological abstractions or withdrawal into pietism, worldliness and transcendence are brought together in the notions of the suffering Christ and the world come of age:

> I discovered later, and I'm still discovering right up to this moment, that it is only by living completely in this world that one learns to have faith.... By this worldliness I mean living unreservedly in life's duties, problems, successes, and failures... experiences and perplexities. In so doing, we throw ourselves completely into the arms of God, taking seriously not only our own sufferings, but those of God in the world—watching with Christ in Gethsemane.[79]

Bonhoeffer tied his conception of God to the suffering of Jesus. God's power resides in what, for this world, is thought of as weakness. Bonhoeffer was always probing the issue of God's absence and power, and in his captivity he created a matrix of concepts that point away from finely wrought theological constructions and toward a christologically centered reading of the gospel narratives. Rather than being an abstraction of human thought or a self-projection of human desires, Jesus stands as an authentic embodiment of God precisely because he was willing to accept the unexpected and the unanticipated way of powerlessness and suffering. Jesus stands at the seam of reality and interpretation. In the midst of modern theology's struggle to interpret, Christ breaks through the particularities of individuality and confronts us with suffering and weakness. While the contextual positions may change, the reality of suffering spans time and place and calls us to confront the unexpected and unimaginable:

> All that we may rightly expect from God, and ask him for, is to be found in Jesus Christ. The God of Jesus Christ has nothing to do with what God as we imagine him could do and ought to do. If we are to learn what God promises and what he fulfills, we must persevere in quiet meditations on the life, sayings, deeds, sufferings and death of Christ.[80]

But, we might ask, does this not land us on the sword of Nietzsche? Contemporary theologians are likely to ask whether these ideas legitimize victimization. Does not the embrace of powerlessness mean that we acquiesce to the oppressor? This is precisely the point that Nietzsche raises in *The Antichrist* when he says that the ethic of Jesus emerges from his pathological resistance to all contact with reality. Placing all hope on an inner world, a negation of reality, Jesus makes a virtue of necessity. Of course, someone who cannot exercise power, who creates an inner world that is ultimately decadent, preaches that the poor, meek, and blind are more blessed than the rich, strong, and proud.

And by extension we could contend that all of Bonhoeffer's prison writings are the inscription of his own situation. How could it be anything but the case that we must stand beside God in God's hour of suffering? Bonhoeffer writes not of God, but himself. It is his powerlessness and weakness that is projected into the world and created as the image of God. What could be any clearer than the realization that the so-called power of weakness is to be uncovered as yet another delusion of madness and human refusal to face stark reality? This is yet another flight from the world motivated by the destructive illusions of Christianity. Disillusioned by his failure to remove Hitler, and perhaps in doubt about whether the Christian should have been involved in the act of violence, Bonhoeffer does not give voice to the way of God in the world. He gives voice to his own sad predicament.

This critique can be laid at the feet of Bonhoeffer, but Bonhoeffer was safe upon the shores of America in 1939, and nothing was forcing him to go back home other than his sense that he needed to stand with his people. This is not the mark of weakness, but of courage. He believed that immersion in the world, not flight from it, was a necessary condition for truthfulness and an avenue for the entrance of something different and subversive into the world.

The weakness and suffering which authentic faith endures does not necessarily lead to the formation of communities who will not take responsibility for the world or allow the creation of more willing victims of oppression. These communities will instead engage in dialogue with the world to show the structures of power and privilege their own godlessness and oppressive practices. Here a power is brought to bear through weakness. Participation in the powerlessness of God makes evident the illusory power of the godless:

> But what does this life look like, this participation in the powerlessness of God in the world? I will write about that next time, I hope. Just one more point for today. When we speak of God in a "non-religious" way, we must speak of him in such a way that the godlessness of the world is not in some way concealed, but rather revealed, and thus exposed to an unexpected light. The world that has come of age is more godless, and perhaps for that very reason nearer to God than the world before its coming of age.[81]

In these communities we participate in the sufferings of Jesus. As Christ exists for others, we experience divine presence when we exist for others. This ensures we will share in the sufferings of the world, but it does not mean that we are totally at the world's mercy. Rather, the community which takes seriously the reality of the cross finds a strength to offer the distinctiveness of a nonreligious interpretation of Christianity and a critique of culture. When we live in this manner, incarnating the presence of God through Christ, we witness that no one else has power over the community. Thus moral legitimation is peeled from all present cultural and theological expressions of self-aggrandizing power.

These communities are defined not only by worldly solidarity, but also by their cultivation of what Bonhoeffer called "arcane disciplines." The discipline of prayer, meditation, and worship within the community of faith nourish those who live in the world come of age. These disciplines of spiritual formation provide the sustenance for suffering with non-Christians for the common good, and costly discipleship provides the mode of public engagement for that hidden nurture.

As a concrete example of this, and I hesitate to offer it because I believe sacrifice is not an entirely priestly function, it is worth noticing in *Romero,* the movie about the slain archbishop of El Salvador, Oscar Romero, how often the celebration of the Eucharist became the occasion for solidarity with the oppressed or the critical moment of conflict with the principalities and powers. This is a striking example of how the discipline Bonhoeffer discussed does not lead to communities which withdraw from the suffering of the world. In this instance the arcane discipline of worship leads to a solidarity with the voiceless, the suffering, and the powerless which brings a certain power to bear upon the world's suffering. This power is not tied to political agendas or even sophisticated and theoretical theological speculations; rather it is tied to an identification with the life, death, and resurrection of Jesus.

This brings me back to the issue of theological construction. Since we know that our theologies lack foundational certainty or necessary ontological status, we are left with the realization that all theology may be ideology, or even worse, idolatry. Given the projective and contextual nature of theology, how do we adjudicate between constructions of God and world and the relationship between them? Ultimately does not the contemporary critique wash upon the rocks of its own revelations? It too offers its critique in the guise of truth. It too creates the elite whose manipulation will dictate the terms in which existence is to be lived, labeling those who do not agree with their visions as mediocrities. It too seeks the power to interpret under the auspices of uncloaking the hidden will to power found in all attempts to understand.

I believe Bonhoeffer offers us wisdom and discernment because he understood that our constructions of God set the parameters for human response to the possibility of divine presence. If theology is to have a future role in the world it will come through its identification with the suffering. It is here where the questions of human existence are faced in truth and pain. From here theology can move from theory to application. In his critique of religious Christianity Bonhoeffer saw that our theologies are often power-less to create the constructions of alternative ways of seeing reality and living out new visions of human life. Many times this is due to the fact that theology is more about self-projection than discerning the presence of God in the world.

When theology seeks explication between the here and now and the there and then, revision frequently leads to dissolution. Per-haps when a construal of God no longer makes sense it should be dissolved. Bonhoeffer certainly thought so. Theology often fails to disclose the possibilities of divine presence in unanticipated and unexpected avenues.

In the meditation for his godson's baptism Bonhoeffer addressed the need for a nonreligious language with which to express the power of authentic Christianity, and so to utter the word of God that the world will be changed and renewed by it. This may not entail the search for a public theology that serves society. It may not mean asserting definitive and dogmatic statements. But if this language takes seriously the universality of suffering it just may, like Jesus' own language, bring about the presence of God's peace within the world. Today we still need a nonreligious interpretation of Christian faith that creates its own conditions for human deci-sion without manipulative appeals to guilt, sin, or even obedience to God.

This interpretation and its linguistic expression will not secure a space for its own power, being accessible only to the theological specialists. Rather, it will effect transformation and hope. It will identify with the language of Jesus, who calls persons to a new life of vulnerability in the world. It will allow those who are voiceless and oppressed to make known their suffering. It also allows the space for the right to say no to God and will not desert those who believe the way of negation is the necessary path in an age of fragmentation and suffering.

In this I believe Bonhoeffer and Dillard would have found them-selves kindred spirits indeed. She understands something profound about the way of God in the world. The only way the presence of God manifests itself in the world is through those who have the heart to incarnate in their lives and communities the heart of God.

Those incarnations may take many forms, but for those of us who are called to the Christian story it will mean we place ourselves entirely in the world.

Bonhoeffer embraced the way of powerlessness not merely because he was imprisoned. He understood the paradox that power is found in powerlessness, that powerlessness may be the most subversive and destabilizing choice to make in a world in love with its own power. If we open ourselves to the power of the gospel narratives we can learn new languages. These languages will address the limitations of context and self-interests. The closer our theological reflections stay to the narrative disclosure of God's way in the world through Christ, the more they offer a much-needed voice in this world. Indeed, they may work to banish the meaninglessness, to which Dillard gives eloquent witness, that hangs over this culture like a brooding ghost and that none of the theologies of modernity have been able to exorcise.

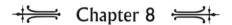

Chapter 8

Tradition as Critique
Karl Barth's Protest of Nazi Ideology

But only he can take mastery of people's freedom who is able to set their
consciences at rest. — FYODOR DOSTOYEVSKY, *The Brothers Karamozov*

I N HIS RECENT BOOK *City of God* E. L. Doctorow relates the
story of a New York City novelist who has come upon the topic
for a possible novel. The book is a fascinating compilation of the
novelist's workbook and the different thoughts, lives, and struggles of the main figures for the novelist's latest project. The text
challenges the reader significantly with its many jumps in consciousness from the historical reality of the theft of a cross from
an Episcopal Church in lower Manhattan, to autobiographical
material of the novelist's own life, to fictional possibilities for a
novel, to philosophical digressions about nature and the meaning of God. You get the point. There are countless permutations
of wildly different, random, yet oddly connected thoughts, reflections, and recordings of people's struggles with God, themselves,
and the problem of evil and suffering. If ever there were a novel
that carried the sense of the postmodern we have talked about in
this book, this is it.

Doctorow is on the trail of a presence, a hint of something that
might provide a clue to the meaning of human existence, something that might even help in our quest with the sufferings of the
world. One of his main characters, The Reverend Thomas Pemberton, an Episcopal priest, tries to tell the reporter and novelist,
Everelist, where to look:

As a secularist, you don't understand—if there is a religious
agency in our lives, it has to appear in the manner of our
times. Not from on high, but a revelation that hides itself
in our culture, it will be on ground-level, on the street, it'll

be coming down the avenue in the traffic, hard to tell apart from anything else. It will be cryptic, discerned over time, piecemeal, to be commonly understood at the end like a law of science.[82]

Pemberton himself is searching for the reality of the divine in the book, and the story of his quest forms one of the major themes. It begins with the theft of a large brass cross from St. Timothy's Episcopal Church, a slightly run-down church in lower Manhattan. In various segments of the book we hear his voice giving expression to his hopes and doubts and the thoughts about the spaces where his life has taken him.

The main place where his life has taken him spiritually is into the desert of a questioning, fierce agnosticism. This is the type of agnosticism that believes deep down in the question, but Pemberton is not so certain of the answers he has received in seminary or his numerous books. Having seen enough of life to be wary of the easy answer, he is rigorous in his agnostic faith. He is tracking something authentic and is not much interested in the gods of the comfort zone, tradition, or the Freudian projection.

The stolen cross turns up in a place called the Synagogue of Evolutionary Judaism, presided over by Rabbi Joshua Gruen and his wife, Sarah Blumenthal. Eventually, after the death of her husband on his quest for a diary of Sarah's father recounting stories of the Holocaust, the task will fall to Sarah and Thomas to try to solve the mystery. Around the core of this story Doctorow weaves narratives, streams of consciousness, midrash on songs, and countless digressions on innumerable topics. The multitude of voices is breathtaking, the number of subjects mentioned, staggering. From Einstein to Augustine, from Wittgenstein to Paul Tillich, Doctorow's riffs on reality comprise a bountiful harvest of topics to consider. But looming large over them all is the topic of the twentieth century, the Holocaust. And in the gravity of this the question becomes "Where do we find God in the face of this?" It is a good question.

Pemberton himself is in a little bit of trouble with the diocese because of the questions he asks and the doubts he has about whether God can be found in the confines of any tradition, especially one that participated in one of the most heinous crimes against humankind in history. Pemberton lives with the tensions of tradition and the reality of God but eventually leaves the church (with some prodding from the diocese), though he still clings resolutely to the belief that the God he looks for exists. At one point he says to Everett:

> But as you will see, all these brilliant theologians end up affirming the traditions they were born into. Even the great Kierkegaard. What do you make of that? I mean, when your rigorous search for God just happens to direct you back to your christening, your bris.... [83]

At one point in his struggles Pemberton comments on the notion of Christianity emerging out of a power struggle. This was a struggle between those who thought of Jesus one way and those who thought of Jesus another way, a power struggle that marked the church and laid the foundations for a future that could only end with something like a Holocaust:

> It was a politically triumphant Jesus created from the conflicts of early Christianity, and it has been a political Jesus ever since, from the time of the emperor Constantine's conversion in the fourth century, through the long history of European Christianity, as we consider the history of the Catholic Church, its Crusades, its Inquisition, its contests and/or alliances with kings and emperor, and with the rise of the Reformation, the history of Christianity's active participation, in all its forms, in the wars among states and rule of populations. It is the story of power. [84]

These are powerful questions from the pen of someone who has taken the time to think about them. Is Christianity the story of power? Can we trust the faith that was forged by whoever had the ear of the emperor? Is the presence or wisdom of God found in a return to our traditions, and if so, how? In a sense these are questions that we must respond to, for they go to the heart of the Christian faith and have a truth in them we must face.

It is the burden of this chapter to explore some of these questions by looking at the theological heritage of Karl Barth and ask whether there may be a minority report that does not understand the church to be built upon power. We saw in the last chapter how

Bonhoeffer thought the future of Christianity would be found in our embrace of powerlessness. In this chapter we shall seek to respond to the critique offered from the mouth of Pemberton and see if the tradition offers us any resources for offering a word to the world that wrestles with so much pain. Following the procedure of the Bonhoeffer chapter, I will first place Barth in his context and then move to consider the contemporary manifestation of the problem; then I will offer a possible response to the issues raised.

NO!

In November of 1934 the theologian Karl Barth made an important decision: he would refuse to give the oath of loyalty to Adolf Hitler in his classes at the University of Bonn, Germany. Hitler had instituted the oath after the death of Hindenberg on August 2. It was mandated of all officials of the state, even those working in university education. Though Barth tried to offer compromises, he was banished from his classroom, his classes were cancelled for the term, and he was exiled from Germany to his home in Switzerland.

This was only the final moment leading to his exile from Germany, for Barth had been in conscious opposition to the National Socialists from the very beginning of the party's formation in the 1920s. Of course at this time Barth found himself in opposition to just about everybody else, including much of the established theological world. Rudolf Bultmann, Adolf von Harnack, Emil Brunner, and Friedrich Gogarten were only some of the names with which he found himself in conflict.

When Hitler was installed as chancellor of Germany early in 1933, Barth and his friend and colleague Eduard Thurneysen established the theological journal *Theologische Existenz Heute* (Theological existence today). In its pages Barth and other colleagues launched attacks against Hitler and those in the church who supported him, the "German Christians." Due to Hitler's very skillful handling of the church, many Christians advocated a synthesis between the National Socialists and the Christian faith. Thus the "German Christians" became recognized as the official church of the Reich.

Barth, in opposition to this, argued that the church had but one true father and that was Jesus Christ, not *Der Führer*. He and other interested parties began their resistance to Hitler and soon formed what has become known as the Confessing Church. Through lectures, sermons, and even letters to Hitler himself, Barth and the others argued on behalf of the gospel of Jesus Christ that it should not be submerged into a quasi-mysticism of blood and soil or identified with any particular branch of the state.

Those who were part of this movement met in Barmen in 1934 to try to work out strategies that would allow the opposing voice a stronger and more faithful witness. While there they drafted a theological statement that Barth had a fairly significant role in writing. These theological statements would form the heart of the Barmen Declaration. This declaration was important for Barth because it declared that the one Lord of the church was Jesus Christ. He said of it:

> Barmen designated Jesus Christ as he is witnessed to us in the Holy Scripture, the one Word of God whom we have to trust and obey in life and death. It rejected as false teaching the doctrine that there could be some source of church proclamation other than from this one Word of God.[85]

Barth had his sights set on natural theology, an approach to theological thinking that worked from the assumption that a connection existed between God and humankind such that ideas or concepts about God and God's relationship with humankind could be "read off" the structures and orders of creation. This is the procedure that informed much of Aquinas's approach, but Barth saw some inherent dangers.

For one thing, human institutions such as the church, or the state, or even the family, could be seen as inherently good and in God's will for the ordered life of human beings. Barth felt this too easily dissolved God into the structures of human life and made talk about God only talk about humans, but with a loud voice.

This antipathy would come to full expression with the pamphlet war between Barth and Emil Brunner, another German theologian. Brunner had written an article entitled *"Yes,"* which dealt with the subject of natural theology, and had argued that some points of contact exist between God and humans that allow for theology to speculate on God's plan and way in the world. He had spoken of the "orders of creation" as one of those structures and suggested that the orders which existed in human life, even the political ones, could be seen as God's will. Barth felt this was fundamentally wrong and wrote the reply, *"No,"* which attacked Brunner's ideas for being dangerous at the time in which they lived. To see the state or the church as inherently ordered by God was a dangerous move in the Germany of 1934.

Eventually, however, for all of Barmen's efforts and those of the Confessing Church, all organized opposition to Hitler and the National Socialists broke down into fragments of differing groups who made various compromises with what was taking place. They were unable to mount effective resistance to the designs of the Nazis and their god, Adolf Hitler. Barth continued to resist from Basel, Switzerland, but he could do little other than offer comfort and encouragement to those who were in the belly of the beast. From that position only isolated voices were able to confess with clarity that Jesus Christ was the one true Lord of the church, and not some figure with a seductive appeal to power. What had led Barth to this point in his life, and why was he seemingly able to see what so many others could not?

Barth's Journey to the Far Country

Karl Barth (1886–1968) was raised the son of a Swiss Reformed pastor. His confirmation seemed to have such an effect on him that he decided to study theology. While he began his studies under his father's eye at Bern, he was to move to Berlin, where he would fall under the spell cast by Adolf von Harnack, the church historian. From there he traveled to Marburg, where he would plunge into the works of Kant and Schleiermacher. It was there that he first met his lifelong friend, Eduard Thurneysen. Barth was trained in the best that liberal theology had to offer at the time, and he entered into the parish, eventually ending up in the small Swiss village of Safenwil.

This parish was small and out of the way, but it was also full of peasants and laborers, and a few families who employed the laborers in their factories. He embraced the causes of the Social Democrat party and in the course of his ministry there irritated the most well-to-do families of his church. He would come into contact with many different expressions of Christianity in this setting, including the socialist critiques of Herrmann Kutter and Leonard Ragaz. He would also be profoundly influenced by the life of Christoph Blumhardt, who represented what can only be called an evangelical, perhaps even pentecostal, expression of Christianity.

These people and the ideas they brought to Barth's life would cause him to start questioning his theological heritage in many ways. But the event that moved him to believe that he needed to start from the ground up was when he heard that many of his former professors had signed the declaration of support for Kaiser Wilhelm's war policy. It devastated Barth and he saw it as the "twilight of the Gods." This struck him as a fundamental failure of his training, and in complete disillusionment he turned away from his theological foundation to return to the writings of the Bible.[86] The result was one of those events that would impact not just the arcane world of theology, but the entire world.

It was said that Barth's *Commentary on Romans* was a bombshell dropped on the fields of European theology, and so it seemed. In it Barth sought to remove any connection or link between God and humankind that was a constituent part of human existence. No inherent link between the two existed save what God and God alone wills, and that is totally out of our power. God is absolutely transcendent and in his words, "Wholly Other." He was reacting to his theological heritage in this journey and especially to the father of liberal theology, Friedrich Schleiermacher.

As he struggled with the new voices and concerns of his life, he was brought once again to reflect on his theological training. He began to realize that this training ill prepared him for life in the parish and its particular trials. He began a critique of this legacy and Schleiermacher would draw the lion's share of his attention. He believed that the fountain of a bad drink flowed somehow from this source, especially when theological concerns became anthropological in nature.

We saw earlier how Friedrich Schleiermacher was also concerned about how Christian faith might speak to his age, and he also thought that it all centered on Jesus of Nazareth. The essence of Christianity was the redemption accomplished through Jesus of Nazareth. This redemption was based on the inherent possibility of humankind to pass from a divided and estranged existence to a higher state of consciousness, one where God was dominant and

not the life of the flesh. Jesus of Nazareth was not only the historical occasion for the rise of the Christian faith, but was also a living
part of the consciousness of his followers. Christ was the means
whereby humans could be oriented to their deepest selves, which
was an overcoming of the antithesis of the finite and infinite and
the recognition that God is all in all.

All this Barth had to reject because it made the relationship
between God and humanity far too close for his liking. In the
commentary on Paul's letter to the church at Rome Barth found a
God who cannot be domesticated by culture, a God who does not
allow God's self to be immediately available to human consciousness. The relationship between God and humankind is one, to put
it in Kierkegaard's words, of an "infinite qualitative distinction."[87]

In Schleiermacher's theology there were relationships which
were constitutive of the connection between God and humanity. In
his understanding of these relationships between the Redeemer and
the redeemed, Schleiermacher believed that the identity of Jesus
Christ was potentially what all human persons could and would
be if they would let their God-consciousness have full reign in their
lives. There was not so much a qualitative as a quantitative distinction between Jesus and the believer. Jesus exercised his God
consciousness to a degree that we have not or may never be likely
to do. But, even if we live in the realm of conflict and separation
from God, we still contain the possibility within us that we could
attain to the level of Jesus.

Barth was captivated early in his career by the gravity of his
nineteenth-century theology. In his earliest works he wonders how
Christ is appropriated by believers, and how Christians can exercise their God consciousness. He always has Jesus as the center of
his musings, but when Barth is met with the origin of the religious
consciousness it is always the shadow of Feuerbach that haunts
him. What actually is present in the life of a believer? Is it truly
God, or perhaps the human written in large letters? Was there a
place he could stand that was not vulnerable to the critiques of
Feuerbach? Do our conceptual thought forms contain only projections of our own design? Or do we make contact with concrete
and objective reality?

It was against Schleiermacher and the theology he spawned that
Barth was reacting because he thought such a theology put us in

control of defining God and not God in control of defining us. Revelation was not dependent on the role of human consciousness; it was addressed by a graceful God to a fallen humanity. All inherent connection between culture and faith was to be rejected as idolatrous. Scripture pushes humankind to struggle and tension, and to encounter with that which is foreign and not natural to us. Barth's protest against all theologies of immanence was made on the basis that God's grace is gracious gift. Revelation is not dependent upon structures of religious consciousness, found in the given relationship of God and human. Rather, the revealing of God is God's affair. What we encounter there is not the best about ourselves, but the truth about ourselves, and Barth thought that was a very different story from the one the theologians were telling.

One aspect of his critique was the belief that knowledge represented a form of power. In this Barth shares space with segments of postmodernity. He came to believe that when Schleiermacher dealt with religion it became reduced to a human phenomenon, explicable on that basis alone. This cannot serve as an adequate place for God's disclosure because Barth was aware of the critiques of the nineteenth century offered by Nietzsche and Feuerbach we mentioned in our opening chapter. Barth understood that there was truth in these critiques that made an anthropologically oriented theology difficult at best. It was certainly not capable of communicating "saving truth."

Where Schleiermacher posited the identity of God and world as the source point for all theological reflection, Barth posited an encounter between two radically opposed beings, a graceful God and a sinful humanity. The natural world, which was a symbol of the spiritual for Schleiermacher, is notably without sacramental or redemptive significance in and of itself for Barth. Any unity comes only with an act of obedient faith.

This assumed connection between God and the world struck Barth as fundamentally wrong. We do not possess power over God to define how and under which terms the "Wholly Other" will reveal God's life to us. Knowledge of God is not to be found in a connection between Deity and the world such that the identification of natural orders such as state, family, or church with the will of God are understood as a given. This brings God into our control and allows us to baptize human institutions with the veneer of sacredness to the extent that we will worship the institution as God. Knowledge of God comes from God as a gracious gift, embodied in the person of Jesus Christ.

Since this was so important to Barth he focused his critique on Schleiermacher's christology. From every approach that Barth took he found in Schleiermacher a Christ that imparts to us a human capability alone. This Christ knows nothing of overcoming the real estrangement between God and us. In other words, Barth believed that Schleiermacher's Christ was the wrong object of theological reflection, a false starting point. The situation is too grave, too serious, for a translation to a higher state; rather a new creation is called for. Barth did not want to allow any room for salvation to be a natural process in the given connection between God and us. The situation was far too grave to warrant the perspective of liberal theology.

After Barth left his crater on the theological world, he was called to become a German university professor. He would serve in various settings, ending up in Bonn before his exile from the country. It was in these years that Barth moved from a theology of crisis to a theology of the Word, which was always primarily the Word of God, Jesus. As he found himself responding to Schleiermacher's legacy, he would come to embrace the Christ of the Chalcedon creed as an adequate expression of the doctrine of Christ.

This comes to the heart of the question with which we began our chapter. How could Barth appeal to a theological understanding that was shaped in the midst of the imperial power of ancient Rome? If Christian doctrine was a matter of who won the ear of the emperor, how can it be seen as anything but a tool of the state to define the contours of Christianity? Is there within any theological appeal something that is able to transcend its particularity and cultural formation, and how would we recognize it? We move to a consideration of these and other issues to ask if theology is forever ideology; we then will return to Barth to see if he, in fact, has a word for us in our time.

Dissonant Sounds: Theology and Political Power

As we have moved through the critique of postmodernity we have done so with an eye toward uncovering the assumptions inherent in all human knowing and the types of issues this brings about. One of the questions that is germane for this chapter deals with the issue of power, specifically political power. In theological terms, what is the relationship between the development of Christian doctrine and political power? Put more bluntly, why should we even trust Christian doctrine if it has been formulated on the basis of who had the upper hand at the time? Can anything other than a power play be evidenced in the intersection of politics and the Christian faith? These are necessary questions to ask concerning theology because the suspicion of how the Christian faith developed is part of postmodernity's landscape.

The reason for questions of this nature arise from consideration of how Christianity moved from the position of being a type of exilic community, existing on the fringes of society of the first centuries of the common era, to becoming the religion of the state. When this move was made, certain changes emerged in the community which would alter the direction of faithful witness down to the present age.

Previous to the year 313 C.E., Christianity was in a precarious position. Outlawed at various times by different rulers, enduring several waves of local and empire-wide persecution, the church had developed a way of being in the world that addressed the present culture in challenging and prophetic ways. Those like Tertullian advocated a stance toward their surroundings that called all worldly wisdom into question with the query, "What has Athens to do with Jerusalem?" The apologists sought to give an account of faith in Christ by critiquing the philosophies of their age. Regardless of the approach taken, Christianity found itself on the defensive.

All this changed when Constantine issued the edict of Milan, a decree of toleration for Christianity. While the accounts differ, the impetus for this shift was Constantine's victory at Milvian over another claimant to the throne of the empire. One account says that Constantine had a vision that showed the cross in the sky, accompanied by the words, "By this sign you will conquer." Whatever may have happened, it is surely the case that with the edict of Milan the position of the church in the Roman empire changed. No longer were Christians ostracized for their faith or persecuted to the point of death; rather, they entered into the agenda of the empire in a new way.

No better example of this can be given than the Council of Nicea, just twelve short years after the edict of Milan. This council of bishops met because of the controversy between Arius and Athanasius concerning the relationship of Jesus to God. Considered to be the first great ecumenical council and the beginning of the orthodox tradition, Nicea represented an interesting picture of how things had changed since the edict of Milan. Just a few years earlier some of the attendees were in peril for their lives because they were leaders of what was then considered to be an atheistic sect. Because they would not participate in the civil ceremonies of the state, they were considered threats to the empire. Because they would not take part in the armed forces or any other social institution that required obedience to foreign gods, they were regarded as subversive.

But now they were gathered together to decide crucial theological issues about the faith, and they had their way paid by the emperor. Not only that, but the emperor was sitting in the assembly and participating in the debates. When the dust had settled and Athanasius's views prevailed, Constantine had had no small part in the outcome of the debate. This did not entirely discourage the supporters of Arius, for they would plead their case with skill to the political authorities, and the emperor who was in the ascendancy. Doctrine was settled by who had the support of the emperor. And the emperor's agenda was not necessarily truth, but unity and peace in the empire. Christianity would serve as the means to unite an empire fragmented by many mystery religions and gods.

This change in status meant that everything was up for grabs, even the doctrines that would one day form the basis for orthodoxy. Everything was different for the church, and while persecution was hardly to be hoped for, the new situation may have done as much harm to the faith of the church as the persecution did. Once the cultural pretensions of the state were baptized with a Christian veneer, the results were mixed to say the least. When Christians held political power they did not hesitate to use it to force conformity to their own beliefs and morals.

And in the captivity to political powers conformity was always exacted to compel adherence to particular doctrines and pronouncements of the church. This history has been one of embarrassment to the church. Even though the church needed to have some discernment about what represented faithful witness to Jesus Christ, the exclusions and history of slaughter and murder carried out in the name of the church make a sorry spectacle. Indeed, the efforts of the church to assure conformity to its doctrines would lead to such a backlash that modernity would seek to deny the church any place at the table of the political process at all.

The removal of the church from the political process and the founding of society on secular principles in the Enlightenment were ample evidence that coercion in matters of faith left a tragic legacy. It also called into doubt how the most central convictions of Christianity became the guiding factor for people's faith. How could you trust something built upon the edifice of political power? Once Christianity let itself be identified with the aims of the state, how could anything be trusted that was a product, not of discerning consensus, but of who had the greatest political power?

Once this move was made the religious legitimation of political structures was complete and the attendant complications were in place. One's personal identity was connected to the fortunes of the empire. In contemporary terms, we are apt to identity ourselves as Americans (or Serbs, Germans, or Koreans) before we see our identity as Christians. How I place myself in the world becomes more a matter of cultural location and less a matter of being in the household of faith. This creates the conditions wherein the causes of the state become the cause of God. Even more insidious, I can now justify any amount of violence toward others who are not mine, who are not like me, who are different, who are infidels. It is the bane of our age.

This is exactly the case that Barth and his colleagues faced in Germany in 1933. Their opponents, the "German Christians," issued a manifesto containing such statements as, "We stand on the basis of positive Christianity. Ours is an affirmative, truly national faith in Christ, in the Germanic spirit of Luther and of heroic piety," and "We want a Protestant church rooted in our own culture.... We want to overcome degenerate phenomena ... by faith in our nation's God-given mission."[88]

This was what was facing Barth and the others at Barmen and in the culture at large. How would persons respond to such a connection of the state with the faith of the church? Barmen was drafted in the following year with an urgent call to "test the spirits." It announced:

> In view of the errors of the "German Christians" of the present Reich Church government which are devastating the Church and are also thereby breaking up the unity of the German Evangelical Church, we confess the following evangelical truths. . . . Jesus Christ as he is attested for us in Holy Scripture, is the one Word of God which we have to hear and which we have to trust and obey in life and death.[89]

Though this was a stirring statement, issued in the face of a particular situation of great danger, it has also been criticized for its failure to disclaim theologically the anti-Semitic racism found in remarks like, "As long as Jews have the right to citizenship . . . there is . . . a danger of bastardization and an obscuring of racial differences."[90]

The question can be asked whether Barth's christological call for theology to be centered upon Christ as the one Word of God results in affirming anti-Semitism in another way. In this exclusion of other words about and from God, such as those found in the Hebrew Scriptures, do we not see the same old racism at work? This may be the case. However, at about this time Barth also preached a sermon entitled, "Jesus Christ Was a Jew," in which he attacked all forms of anti-Semitism.

Even given the criticisms of the Barmen Declaration and the failure of the Confessing Church, it is still instructive for us to take a look at the way that theology can function as something other than a support for the cultural status quo. If this is all that theology does, then it really does not have anything interesting to say. It is open to the criticism that it does not have much to do with truths not produced by human communities limited by their cultural contexts and lack of perspective. In what sense does Christianity have anything interesting to say? Are we only another voice reflecting our prejudices and desires for power in our situation? Moreover, the Christian religion has shown that it will sanctify the incorporation of violence to accomplish its aims of eradicating the other, the different, even the heretical.

That this is still the case can be witnessed on a global scale by those who argue that they are doing God's will by employing violence, either with words or weapons, to exclude others who are different. So we are brought to the door of a perplexing problem that goes to the heart of Christian belief and practice. How is God present in theological formation at all if theology can be understood as the product of social and cultural environments? If theology takes its clues only from the cultural search for meaning, if it seeks to construct worldviews that allow us to cope with the lives we lead or even make us accommodate ourselves to our own cultural context, then in what way can we say that theology offers any authentic reflection of the relationship between God and humankind? If the development of the church occurred under the auspices of imperial power in what way does that impact the subsequent message of the church?

These are complex questions, and I want to suggest that the resources for thinking through some of these issues are found within the tradition of Christianity itself. But before these resources can be used we must first realize that they themselves incorporate the principle of critique within them. Our very most cherished images of God may have to undergo deconstruction so that holy reality may become more manifest. Sometimes our theology is the thing that keeps us from encountering the reality of God.

An example of this can be seen in the biblical text itself, where the traditional images of God face rigorous scrutiny and radical questioning. The book of Job is one place where the symbol of God is brought into deep investigation. The construct of God as the God of retributive justice is called into question by the text through the struggles of Job with his friends. The God who acts according to human understanding is represented by Job's friends who seek to justify God's ways with humans as they interpret Job's suffering. They accuse Job of being a sinner, or perhaps it is not he who has sinned, but his children. Surely something wrong has been done, for God would not punish those who did not deserve it. Job protests this and calls on God to answer him, but for a time no answer is forthcoming.

While the God of religious construal is absent to Job, another reality, less domesticated and controllable, shows up in the narrative to respond. Job and his friends are both confounded by the mystery that makes its appearance and calls them into question. The voice that speaks to them may ultimately be unsatisfying to us as well, but the point is that the God of theological constructs or religious ideation can be very different from the God that becomes real to us. Job's friends had constructed an idol of their own device by appeal to time worn-clichés about reward and punishment.

This is precisely what is taking place today as postmodernity questions the God we have constructed. While we do not live in the time of Nicea or Chalcedon, we must speak to that which seems to us to be an authentic representation of the divine in human life if we are people of faith. Heresy is not really our issue so much as idolatry, the worship of that which is not God. When Barth and the "German Christians" are engaged in their struggle, they are defining God for their culture. Every culture runs the danger of turning God into a graven image. Every society risks fashioning that which is not God into a symbol of ultimacy and worshiping it. As Barth realized, the state will happily allow its image to be worshiped as God and will be happy for the obedience paid to it. Every objectification of God in this way becomes idolatrous, especially when it purports to exhaust the options open to us to rethink the divine.

When we turn our attention to what type of God persons in this culture worship, we do find God defined by certain attributes. God has blessed this nation, chosen this nation, and is present to us in a greater degree than God is present to whatever nation we oppose. Those who oppose us are the evildoers who transgress the will of God by their opposition to us, and they must be defeated. These are the ideas that start to take shape when Christianity ties its fortunes to the empire. What must it have been like for those Christians of the fourth century to find that now they must violate the teachings of Jesus in order to protect the state, for God, supposedly, had mandated a new order?

The suspicions that have been voiced about this type of image, the God who stands as symbol of our own agendas and will to power, are important for us to hear and respond to for we need to search our faith for what is foreign to us. But what resources can we use? The tradition we appeal to is part of the problem, for it is forged in the fires of state control and imperial power. The biblical record contains some internal critique for the self-constructed images of God that we find in our faith, but while the narrative is crucial, we still find that theology is a reflection of more than the narratives. Is there a place where the tradition itself speaks a word of discernment? Can Karl Barth offer us a useful perspective for our dilemma? These are the points of investigation we turn to now.

Against the Tide:
Christianity against the Status Quo

Christopher Rowlands in his book *Radical Christianity* observes that two streams of theology have been present in the Christian tradition. One seeks to ground and legitimate the status quo of its cultural constructs. This path uses tradition as a sacred canopy to place culture under the tent of divine providence and ordering. This is the appeal we saw in the "German Christians" who were using the tradition of Luther and the Reformation as a cloak for their own hatreds and prejudices. Theological undergirding was reflective of a collective and cultural consciousness as later events would rightly show. While the Nazi tent had been pitched to shelter the status quo, many flocked to the shadow it provided in order to justify their actions.

But this is not the only voice that speaks in history, for there are other voices that speak and must be heard. This stream has always flowed against the tide and been more eruptive. It can be seen in the monks and mystics, in the Anabaptists of the Reformation, in the movements such as liberation theology and feminist theology, as well as the other dissenting theologies of today. It can be heard in the words of the Kairos document of South Africa, or seen in the life of Desmond Tutu, who was faithful to the gospel of nonviolence in a violent time. It can even be observed in the life of those like Henri Nouwen, who once said that Christianity was a movement of downward mobility.

One of the distinctive marks of the countercultural stream of Christian tradition is the way in which it uses the foundational documents of the faith to retrieve a different perspective on Jesus. Many times the synoptic gospels and their portrayal of Jesus emerge as the controlling narrative to ground the alternative vision of Christianity. Often the "golden age" historiography is at work, where the age of Jesus and the apostles is set in pristine purity, and reforming the tradition, or the social reality of the church, is a matter of recovering that perfect past in order to renew the present. But the past, while crucial, is never so golden as we like to believe.

The Anabaptists appealed to the past in the 1500s when they established alternative communities to the Catholic and emergent Protestant traditions. Their appeal to the synoptic gospels and the polity of the early church brought them to the position of nonviolence and refusal to conform to the magistrates. Because of their stance they threatened both the other traditions and were subsequently persecuted for their faith. They were swimming against the tide.

But this matter of Christian identity is a difficult one at best. We stand thousands of years removed from the original events and primary documents of Christianity. We have been formed by creedal formulations that defined the very identity of Jesus. We are acutely aware of how these events have constructed the lenses through which we view theological claims and biblical interpretation. And yet for this very reason perhaps it is important that we attend to the other voice that calls Christianity into question, or at least the Christianity that emerges from its accommodation with the imperial order of the Roman empire.

One way of doing this is to explore the alternative visions that have emerged out of the tradition. While we cannot go into an extensive treatment of these, we can take a brief look at one of the contemporary and most controversial forms of this protest against the status quo, the theology of liberation. That this theology should emerge from within such a strong ecclesial structure as Roman Catholicism is testimony to the striking power of protest and solidarity with the poor, which is a tradition deeply rooted in the biblical witness.

It was the life of the poor in Latin America that formed the context for a theological reflection which challenged a tradition that was culturally conceived. Following the changes instituted in the church after the Catholic council Vatican II, the church in Latin America underwent a significant change. The very orientation of the church changed for many priests, nuns, and laity as they no longer understood the church as the lifeboat which persons should cling to; rather the church was understood as the pilgrim community of faith. Many started questioning along the lines of Dietrich Bonhoeffer, who asked from his cell, "Who is Jesus Christ for us today?"

The variety of responses that this questioning generated was testimony to the diversity inherent in any exploration of the meaning of Jesus Christ for human life and existence. Of particular importance here is that the question was not necessarily about the importance of Christianity as a religion or the church as an institution; rather the issue is what difference Jesus Christ makes in a world of pain, poverty, and suffering.

Most often this reflection occurs in communities where the Bible is read and the stories are interpreted on the basis of lived experience. One criticism of liberation movements was that they relied upon certain texts of Scripture to form Christian identity. Thus the story of Exodus becomes a controlling narrative, but not the story of the conquest. Or the story of Ananias and Sapphira in Acts 5 may assume the quality of a direct link between text and the lived reality of landowners who kept more than they needed without sharing with the household of God working in their fields. Of course, this question was not being raised by those who had benefited from the church's blessing of the status quo for hundreds of years and had allowed the structures of oppression to be erected.

The preference that theologians have shown for the teachings of Jesus concerning the reign of God rather than Pauline or Johannine theologies points to circumstances far different for theological reflection than theology done under the auspices of political or social power. From the voice of the other, from the underside of history, from the marginal and disenfranchised of the world, the message of the reign of God preached by Jesus looks rather different from the way it is proclaimed by those who have constructed the dominant tradition. Their critique will always be based on the fact that there are some assumptions that need to be questioned.

From the position of dissenting theology even the traditional understandings of Jesus are called into question. Brazilian theologian Leonardo Boff writes:

> The themes and emphases of a given christology flow from
> what seems relevant to the theologian on the basis of his

or her social standpoint.... In that sense we must maintain that no christology is or can ever be neutral.... Willingly or unwillingly, christological discourse is voiced in a given social setting with all the conflicting interests that pervade it. That holds true as well for theological discourse that claims to be "purely" theological, historical, traditional, ecclesial, and apolitical. Normally such discourse adopts the position of those who hold power in the existing system. If a different kind of christology with its own commitments appears on the scene and confronts the older "apolitical" christology, the latter will soon discover its social locale, forget its "apolitical" nature, and reveal itself as a religious reinforcement of the status quo.[91]

This voice is heard in recent times as the voice of the other Christ, the one ignored or pushed aside by the religion founded in his name. It points to an eschatological hope based on the teachings, life, death, and resurrection of Jesus Christ, and as such it offers a prophetic critique in our world. It does so in the conviction that God indwells the human, and faithfulness will manifest a witness to this.

But is this not more of the same? We have met this before, and so the suspicion can be raised. Do we not see in liberation theology precisely what has been argued previously? Of course their christology is reflective of their own position in the cultural context. Because their views are not in dominance they have fashioned a theology that privileges their position. Once those who formulate this theology achieve power they will in turn force conformity to their doctrine. And, truth be told, there is always the danger that this liberating vision will lose force if it becomes the dominant perspective.

However, this should not cause us to lose sight of the matter at hand. In the development of Christianity structures emerged which produced a domestication of God's revelation in Jesus Christ, and yet in the midst of this a spirit becomes manifest ever anew which is not content with the structures. This spirit is not content with understandings or traditions that have emerged from within Christianity, and usually its attention is centered on Jesus Christ. If liberative movements begin to reflect the privileges of power or neglect of the oppressed, this spirit will find new expressions, and if it can't find them within the community of faith, it will find them outside of it.

This spirit has been tamped down by those who had control of the means of establishing Christianity, but the biblical texts have worked as the means through which the prophetic emerged with a recovery of seeing, a new vision. Often when this vision made its presence felt, the dominant theologies would seek to neutralize and incorporate the opposing viewpoint by subsuming it under the umbrella of the church. One example of this was the way in which the church's insistence on how to interpret Scripture meant that a monopoly on interpreting precluded alternative visions.

And yet the irony is that the development of Christianity carried within its own foundational narratives the seeds of critique that would be available to question the way faith was moving. These seeds of critique, the prophetic witness, would be nurtured and cultivated by many of the movements that arose from within Christianity to challenge the reigning theologies and lived experiences of the community. If the institutional life of the church justified slavery or oppression in the name of a better life that awaited beyond the grave in the realm of heaven, the dissenting voices called us to immerse ourselves in the world and embody God's vision of a new humanity where equality of all persons under God was a guiding principle.

With these types of questions we must admit that this produces enormous ambiguity within Christianity. These questions confront us with the problem of how we are to understand the way of the central figure of the Christian narrative, Jesus Christ. But this figure is not defined for us solely through the biblical accounts, for there is also the matter of tradition. But whose tradition? Can creedal formulations offer us any perspective that might function as a guide to discerning the reality of God for our time?

If we are to be in the world in a contemporary replication of Jesus, we are brought back to a gospel story with certain contours and textures all its own. In these stories Jesus stands as the symbol of nonviolent protest and the alternative vision of God's way with the world. Those who seek a cure for the destructive and mindless forces of violence which are justified and employed by political authorities or media outlets glimpse a different way in the means through which Jesus is present in the world. Things work differently in this vision and all expectations are overturned regarding power:

> You know that those who are supposed to rule over the Gentiles lord it over them, and their great men exercise authority over them. But it shall not be so among you; but whoever would be great among you must be your servant, and whoever would be first among you must be slave of all. For the Son of Man also came not to be served, but to serve, and to give his life as the means of liberation for many. (Matt. 20:25–28)

Traditioning Faith

We began this chapter with the example of Karl Barth in protest against the National Socialists and their virulent strain of ideology which infected Germany and other countries in the middle decades of the last century. Visages of this disease are still present among us in the forms of hatred and fear that become manifest in racism, anti-Semitism, homophobia, and all forms of ethnic cleansing.

We saw that Barth mounted an assault upon a Christianity that had been captured by the state and was used by Hitler to legitimate the oppression of millions of persons. Barth's main impetus for opposition to the National Socialists was not so much political as it was theological. Theologically speaking, he opposed theologies that subsumed the natural world and its institutions into the orders of creation. That state or party or even family could claim to be an inherent manifestation of God on earth was disturbing to Barth. He understood all too well the power of Feuerbach's critique and believed it constituted a dead end for any theology that went down that road of grounding itself in anthropology. He focused on Schleiermacher for specific attention in this move of theology to anthropological concerns. He especially fingered his opponent's christology for particular attention. He called this the great disturbing element in Schleiermacher's theology.[92]

Barth made a connection in his rejection of Schleiermacher between how we know and faith. For Barth, Jesus Christ is known and given to us in faith in such a way that God grants us the ability to truly apprehend holy reality. Because Schleiermacher's christology was built upon an alternative epistemology, Barth felt that Schleiermacher's Christ was fundamentally distorted. To Barth's credit he wondered to the end of his life if perhaps Schleiermacher had not found a different way to speak of the Holy Spirit's work. Still, Barth was keenly aware of the ways in which theology as a product of culture can function as a legitimator of social control and oppression.

We followed this up by raising the question of theology as a cultural manifestation of imperial power and social control. Given the circumstances under which Christianity became the means whereby Constantine sought unity in his empire, we asked whether there was anything in the faith not tainted by the desire for power. Is there anything that seems to point to God and not a projection of purely human constructs? We discovered that within the tradition of Christian faith there is a stream which flows against the tide and offers a radical and prophetic vision of Christian faith.

Of particular interest was the movement of liberation theology because it emerges from within one of the most hierarchical and traditionally oriented institutions in the Christian religion, Roman Catholicism. I argued that even in the midst of the tradition of Christianity something arises which continually brings forward a minority report, a prophetic word against the status quo. This perspective can be found in the Scriptures themselves which contain narratives that question those notions of God or culture that seem reflective of our desire to order the world to suit our desires.

But does this voice speak through other sources? Is there a way in which the tradition of Christian faith can function as tool of critique? It would seem this would be impossible given the circumstances under which it was formed. In this final section we return to Barth to ask the question of how tradition allowed him to be one of the voices of critique against the Christians who were supportive of Hitler. His embrace of a christology formulated under the auspices of imperial power became the tool he used to oppose all Nazi attempts to seduce the church. Even though this opposition may not have been successful, it was nonetheless a faithful witness at a time when such witnesses were few and far between.

Perhaps one of the first things we must do is to consider that the tradition is also present in the stream of radical Christianity we alluded to earlier. Christopher Morse in his very perceptive text *Not Every Spirit: A Dogmatics of Christian Disbelief* makes the point that the appeal to tradition can be a difficult and ambiguous one. He writes concerning the word "tradition" that it can function as a verb or a noun. In the New Testament the meaning of the word "traditioning" is that of delivering something in the sense of handing it on. He cites examples in the biblical text which use this word to cite the passing on of the gospel, conveyed through the word and power that is Jesus Christ, by whom humanity is set free and saved. Morse says we see here what may be called the tradition of freedom.[93]

However, Morse says that there is another sense in which the term "tradition" appears in the New Testament. In the passion narratives of the betrayal of Jesus it is said that Judas "traditioned" Jesus into the hands of sinners, and Pontius Pilate "traditioned" Jesus to crucifixion. Those who criticize the disciples for breaking the tradition are rebuked by Jesus in Matthew 15:6: "So, for the sake of your traditions you make void the word of God."

Morse contends that in addition to the tradition that conveys the gospel of freedom there is another tradition, the one that betrays and crucifies Christ. This tradition can be apostolic and gospel-centered, or it may be a Judas-like betrayal of the gospel. The story of Christianity can be seen as conflict between these traditions: the tradition of freedom and the tradition of betrayal. Both are ancient, long-standing, and have been continuing throughout the history of Christianity.

Postmodernity and voices like Doctorow have raised perceptive questions about the tradition, but it can be argued that what is being called into question is the tradition of betrayal which is uncovered for what it was all along, power masquerading as obedience to God. The countless examples of Christianity as a coercive force, demanding conformity to its views, have only reinforced the belief of many who see it as not really worth attention. Why be interested in a faith that has been the cause of so much pain on the earth (though it is an open question why people allow themselves to be part of political structures that bring pain on the earth and never question their participation in these)? In this sense the critique of Christianity that sees it as a cultural construct of human design, built from the storehouse of our deepest fears,

wishes, hopes, and desires, good and bad, has a truth that cannot
be denied. Inasmuch as the Christian church has conspired with
political power and social convention for a position of dominance
it must stand accountable before the jury of voices that have been
oppressed and killed in its name.

But the tradition of betrayal is not the only word the church has
to utter, nor the only path the church has followed. For another
tradition speaks from within this church and questions whether the
dominant tradition exercises a totalizing control over the community of faith. It is Barth who, for all his faults, points this out in the
midst of one of the most crucial failures of the church. He would
show that sometimes in the midst of the reign of the tradition of
betrayal the tradition of freedom has a word to say, a word that
calls simply everything into question.

Early on in his life and career Barth became aware of the delusions under which the church existed. He saw with clarity what
happens when faith is subsumed under the confines of national
identity. In an address written in 1916 he proclaimed, "We are
Christians? Our nation is a Christian nation? What a wonderful
illusion...what a self-deception."[94] He was at this time in deep
conversation with the tradition he had received through his education and was listening to other voices in his culture that were
offering their own version of matters. As he did so Barth came to
think of theology as trying to catch a "bird in flight." God was
constantly in a state of movement, and nothing we could do would
totally capture God.

Where Barth was centering himself was the event where God
speaks to us in Jesus Christ. But it would take some time and a
long journey from his theological inheritance for Barth to totally
free himself. Yet even in the earliest stages Barth believed that
something ultimate and universal takes place around the gospel of
Jesus Christ. He also felt strongly that while this event of Jesus is
witnessed to and proclaimed in the church it was not to be confined
to it, or even the Christian religion.

Barth works through a perspective that takes him from Schleiermacher to Anselm and ultimately to a very distinctive christology.
That this theology was rooted in the doctrines and perspectives
that were fashioned at the Council of Chalcedon is perhaps one of
the biggest surprises of all. How could tradition have been so em-

braced by someone who was so reactive to the traditions around him? And perhaps even more interesting, why the revisiting of a supposedly dead orthodoxy?

After the first great ecumenical council at Nicea matters became even more complex for the Christian church. Though ultimately the decisions reached at Nicea became the accepted teaching of the church, there were other matters which came from that council that needed to be considered. Specifically, if the theme at Nicea was the life within God and the relation of God to Godself, the issue at Chalcedon was the relationship of God with the human, and what, exactly, one encounters in Jesus of Nazareth.

The tension between God and Jesus of Nazareth was addressed by Chalcedon with the formula of Jesus as truly God, truly human; two natures, but one essence. In this way the significance of Jesus emerges from a particular historical existence; however, this significance cannot be confined to the moment of its historical particularity. The witness of the church is that promise and hope reside in God's work through Jesus for all people, not just those of the first century.

Needless to say there was a great deal of ambiguity about these formulations, and this led to no small disagreement among parties. The community of faith in succeeding generations has exploited the ambiguity of these confessions to justify their theology, so the tradition is still not immune from criticism. But if the disagreement centers on Jesus, and for Barth it most certainly did, then the debate still goes on.

If we believe that Jesus Christ existed as fully human, fully divine, sharing in the contingencies of historical existence, then in the terms under which Barth was living any confessions of Jesus Christ as the one whose ancestry is not from Jews of the lineage of Israel's David are proscribed. Chalcedon functions as judgment not only against the "German Christians," but all other attempts that would dissolve the earthly incarnation into a gnostic religion of national or ethnic identity.

In addition to this, Chalcedon took the step of affirming the true "Emmanuel," God with us. The life of Jesus Christ exists in union with God eternally, sharing the destiny of the divine life and bearing witness in the life, death, and resurrection to God's love and concern for all people. This is especially true for those whose voices have been silenced by power or poverty. The universal dimensions of the Incarnation work as judgment against all theologies that make space for themselves at the expense of the other.

This is one of the reasons why Barth can employ a traditional and orthodox christology as a tool of discernment against the Nazis. The identity of Jesus Christ as truly God and truly human means that any confession of a power manifest in human history that brings evil masquerading as good, or oppression cloaked in the clothes of correct doctrine or dogma, or servitude to the principalities and powers masked as obedience to national duty or any other form of state or economic control, must be regarded with suspicion and rejected as false.

The early church may have fashioned these beliefs under the shadow of the empire, but the implications of their teachings are able to give us a perspective that transcends their birth. They point to something still vital and necessary in the Christian faith. No matter what the cultural context, the centrality of Jesus Christ is crucial to identity of self and the position we find ourselves in. Encounter with this Christ means that we are called into question and challenged to examine our most fervently believed theologies for the products of cultural ideology.

Many charges can be laid at Barth's feet concerning his christology, but in the struggle with the Nazis he saw clearer than many others did. Christopher Morse writes, "But if the Jesus Christ attested in the gospels is not synonymous with any religion, including historical Christianity, but is the identification of both the oppression to be overcome and the power that overcomes it, as Barth argues, then christocentrism has a very different significance."[95]

Postmodernity performs able service in pointing out the cherished communal assumptions that guide our path in the present age. However, it is not the final word. For in the midst of a Christian tradition forged in the context of Roman imperial power and fought over through successive emperors, there were the seeds planted which bear nourishing. Every age is in danger of losing sight of the inherent critique contained within those seeds of Scripture, creeds, and even the theology of the church. Indeed, we live in a time when the temptations to idolatry are extremely strong.

This is the answer to all those who reduce Christianity to a religion or Jesus Christ to an identification with their own goals and agendas. Even the dissenting theologies of liberation stand under this judgment. That Christ lived, died, and resurrected, that the life of God is embodied here, that a hope of those oppressed resides not solely in ideologies, politics, or religion, but in the life of God through Christ is testimony to the freedom of God to confound all our self-contained ideologies and all exclusions of human life.

+≡ Chapter 9 ≡+

Re-membering
Out of the Matrix and Back into the Body

For just as the body is one and has many members, and the members of
the body, though many, are one body, so it is with Christ.

— 1 CORINTHIANS 12:12

Faith is a journey without maps.
— FREDERICK BUECHNER

A NUMBER OF YEARS AGO, a movie came out which played off
the notions of reality that we have been exploring in this
book. It is called *The Truman Show,* and the central idea of the
story was that the main character of the movie, Truman, lived in
a huge and elaborate television set. From the moment of his birth
his life had been captured on camera as part of a television show
named after him. The entire environment, from wife to best friend,
to strangers on the street, were all a part of a huge deception to
keep Truman from realizing that none of his life was real. Millions
of people watched his life every week on their televisions, and he
had no clue that the world he was experiencing was fabricated.

All this was presided over by a director, Christof, who in a
sense was Truman's father figure, creator, and God. Truman was
as much a product of his creation as a television icon. Ultimately
what happens in the movie is that Truman begins to suspect that
something is wrong with the world he lives in. He starts to notice
certain discrepancies and anomalies in his daily life. He begins to
seek the truth of what is happening to him. This comes in the form
of trying to escape the confines that he has been imprisoned in and
seeking the truth from those around him.

He finally finds himself at sea in a storm that has been cued by
Christof, who, because he is a director after all, has the power to do
almost anything in this world he created. Christof uses the storm

192

to try to keep him from finding out the truth and is even willing to let his creation die in his search to leave the ignorance of his true state. Finally, Truman finds himself out on the water (which plays the role of the ocean) when his boat sails to the edge of the world and rips a hole in the sky, which was, after all, nothing more than a set designed by the television people. Truman is devastated by the realization of his breakthrough, both literally and figuratively, to learn that his life has been a total lie. All illusions are stripped away, all life is revealed for what it truly is, a lie. He, like Neo in *The Matrix,* has become an awakened one.

Not as dark or violent a vision as the movie we started out with, *The Truman Show* serves as a suitable parable for what we have been talking about in this book. This is what those masters of suspicion we have mentioned have been trying to tell us. Our lives are largely illusions, built upon the stuff which we ourselves construct. They are illusory in the sense that we believe that the assumptions, truths, ideas, and concepts we live our lives around such as materialism, family, state, nation, politics, war, ethnic identity, religion, maybe even God, are communal truths we should all just accept as reality. Whether or not this is the case is one of the major themes of this book. I am not so sure it is as simple a matter as those who construct our reality wish it to be. For there are many Christofs in the world, each seeking to fashion the world for her or his own purposes and hoping we will never discover the truth.

Out of the Matrix

There are those who stand in the streets of our societal constructions, like Nietzsche's madman, and call us to see that all is an illusion. They are the prophets who are calling us to wake up and ask questions about the world we live in and the lives we lead. This is threatening to us, for none of us like to have our worldview called into question. To touch the very heart of a person's identity can be a dangerous experience, for we all love our illusions and leaving them is painful. Like Christof, we will respond with violence when those who have been living under the umbrella of shared communal assumptions start to question the way of life culture has assigned them.

The headlines of the world's papers are ample testimony to the reality that this violence is woven into the very fabric of our constructing and deconstructing the world. We have our illusions, and reality is really a fine means of crowd control. If you have followed me to this point you have discovered by this time that this book is about the questioning and critique of all social, cultural, and religious orders, especially Christian ones. This has not been done for the reasons of undermining the faith of Christians, but the questions have been asked in order that we might think clearly about what Christian faith might look like in the new millennium.

The thrust of this exploration has been to use the voices of the past to recover our voice and vision. It may seem difficult to imagine those who are as ancient as Augustine and Anselm having much to say to us in the postmodern world. All of the figures we have reflected on in this book have their cultural limitations as well. According to our contemporary understandings they are sexist, racist, violent, authoritarian, naive, and prisoners of their cultural milieus. How, then, could they be of much help to us?

In the first part of this book, we raised the question whether Christianity has a future with its anthropocentrism and particularity. In the world of pluralism can Christianity offer a word that brings healing to God's good creation? Can a Christianity which shares the limitations we have talked about in this book incarnate the presence of God in the face of so much absence? I have argued that one of the ways we may find our path into the future is by understanding our past. This past must be visited often by us to understand where we have come from, for it is only by knowing where we have come from that we can see where we are going.

But the past has become too alien to us. For many people the past becomes the ultimate other. It is dead for some because we are afraid to give it the space to address us. Like the image of God in which a multitude of people on this planet believe, it is static, unchanging, immutable and of little concern. Now think of the past as other. It is that voice which also calls and questions us, asking, "Are you so wise?" Do we actually have a superior position to observe and judge events? Some, given the obvious mistakes of the past, would say yes. So sure they have cast off all illusions and see clearly, they have little use for those whose voices are reflective of other realities.

Others so venerate the past that like all ages they are seduced by the appeal to a "golden age" where purity of life and thought reside. If we can just recover those moments we will have firm anchors to secure ourselves in the storms of postmodernity. If we can just find our way back to Orthodoxy, they believe, we will have firm footing to understand and live out our faith. But this way leads all too often to a veneration of its own set of idols. Whether it is dogma or the biblical text, we often confuse our obedience to God with the forms in which the story comes to us. We seek a pristine past that will serve as a secure foundation for the faith.

Is there a middle way between these two extremes? Can Christian faith move between totally rejecting the past or absolutizing it? When we start thinking about whether Christianity has a future perhaps we ought to start by asking which past brought us to this point. I alluded earlier to the notion that there are two traditions in Christian faith that flow from the same source. In fact there are far more than that, but they basically lead in one of two directions.

One of these streams responds to the world by seeking to become the legitimation of culture and tradition, constructing through doctrine and authority a place for Christianity in order to provide a canopy of sacredness over our cultural constructions. This stream of faith maintains itself by solidifying, perhaps even ossifying, the strands of faith into a rope of authority that they believe will be able to pull the lost from the quagmire of the world into the ship of salvation.

The other stream, inhabited more by the mystics, prophets, visionaries, and counterculturalists, often flows over the banks of the river altogether. It often offers an unsettling and disturbing truth to us. God cannot be captured in our doctrines, decrees, or even our theologies. I believe that if Christianity is to have a future it may well be that we have to drink from this other stream.

Those who seek to call our attention to a past that enables us to see more clearly serve as partial guides to the future and are voices that should be heard. Still, the critique of postmodernity cannot be ignored, though it is only a partial truth. We are meaning-making creatures, and in our constructions of the world we find ourselves to some extent. It is no great secret that religion has sought to be the ultimate builder of reality for us. But too often the buildings have been the habitations of our fears and most loved illusions.

Amid the fragmentation, partialities, and illusions is there anything we can point to that would be foundational or universal? Probably not, if by this we mean something provable, unassailable, and verifiable by scientific and philosophical proofs. But if that means we are to give up the search for the transcendent, the hints of the eternal, or the rumors of glory that break through in spite of everything, then this would be a mistake. I have been engaging you through this book in an exploration of the contours of the postmodern landscape in order to reflect on how the past might inform the present. My argument has been that even in the darkest moments of Christian faith, when power-laden schemes for domination defined our very history, there were lights shining in that darkness.

These lights could come from the very people who would represent for many the solidifying of faith into something dead and inert. And yet something seems to shine through in spite of this baggage. The themes in this book are familiar ones: creation, fall, redemption, christology, salvation, sanctification, theodicy, Trinity, even eschatology have been touched upon in some way in the previous chapters—not as doctrine necessarily, but as themes or motifs, or even movements of the same symphony of faith. In this treatment I have sought to show that Christian tradition, for all its problems with the way people use it, provides enormous resources for understanding ourselves, our identities, and even our most precious illusions.

This is especially true for the postmodern individual. Those who believe that in the world of multiplicity and countless self-identities, whether real or virtual, their ultimate sense of identity is rooted in Jesus Christ can never look at the world or themselves the same way again. The conversions that faith calls us to will always demand that we question our motives and illusions as we construct the world around us. Perhaps we need to reverse course and see the world in new ways. The gospel accounts of Jesus are full of parables of reversal; the first shall become last, the late workers shall get as much as the early ones, the beggars and strangers shall be invited to the banquet to eat and celebrate the inclusion of the master. These stories turn reality upside down for those who hear them and reveal to us that the divine is not captive to the ways we define either the world or God. If nothing else this ought to serve as a clue to exactly what we are dealing with in Christianity.

The narratives of Christian faith call our very lives into question and bring us into full focus. They ask the citizen of all times and places: What are you doing with your life? Where are you investing your heart and mind? Do you look to your money to build the walls of security? Will you build walls of brick and hearts of stone against those who stand outside your constructions of cherished societal truth? The power of those stories of the Bible can be seen in the tensions they elicit not only in their original hearers, but also in their present-day reception in places like El Salvador, Bosnia, or Washington, D.C.

How do I deal with the tension within myself that questions me about the identities I have been shape-shifting into in the post-modern party room? Some of these identities are built by my fears which seek to secure and lock up all I value, especially the very self I have become. Others call me into the world of risks, of losing control of my life, of facing illusions I have employed to build a world I can understand and control, allowing me to manipulate all around me.

Does Augustine still seem so far removed from us that he makes no sense? Do we have to accept the way he formulates the notion of original sin to understand that in every one of us there is a struggle with the shadow? Between the one extreme of seeing Augustine as the one who ruined the gift of sexuality for countless souls and the source of all evil in the world, and the other extreme of seeing him as the one who has spoken more clearly of God than any other, is there another perspective? Perhaps the opportunity exists to recover truths that he offered about the profound self-incurvature that marks human existence without attaching it to a doctrine or dogma. It might be that we can revisit other voices like that of Irenaeus of Lyons to find other visions of humanity in Christian faith. There may be other ways of saying a truth than the ones we are used to hearing.

Augustine's can be the voice of the other, sometimes alien, some-times brother. He is not unacquainted with our experiences of being human and finding ourselves caught in the grips of the forces that send us into self-destructive relationships, lies of a deep sort, and compulsions that we are incapable of recognizing, much less understanding. He may understand us better than we understand ourselves. But a too simple dismissal of him will not allow us the opportunity to explore whether he has a word for us.

Stop and look around you at the world we have constructed. Does Augustine have any insight into why humans have developed so many structures of violence? Either individually or corporately we will try to protect those views and perspectives we have built and embraced that have given us the life we desire. And we will destroy anything in our path to get what we want. Because we have frozen Augustine's insight into certain doctrinal formulations, most people only hear of the doctrine of original sin and not the deep insights about ourselves which rest behind it. This simply becomes untenable in the contemporary world.

This is true of much of Christianity as well. All through the ages we have made the mistake of taking what was timebound, culturally and socially located, and elevating that to the status of the universal and eternal. When the profound insights of reflection on faith become concrete doctrine, the living spirit of faith can be lost. Instead of doctrines serving us as a type of midrash for Christianity, illumining our faith, and being guides into a changing future, they became fixed posts. No longer pillars of fire, they became pillars of salt.

Take for a moment the issue of biblical authority. As we saw earlier, Luther did not tie himself to a particular stream of the Scripture's authority. It was important to him for the narratives it revealed and because as he read it, it illumined his life in such a way that he experienced conversion. He maintained, especially early on, that the authentic Word of God was actually Jesus Christ and not the words on the page.

Yet today many are trying to protect the revelation of Christianity by locating it within the pages of the church's Scripture and assigning abstract and arbitrary doctrines of Scripture in order to maintain authority in their community of faith. In some senses we can be sympathetic with this approach. When embattled communities of faith look around them and interpret the world by the rapidity of change and the obvious moral vacuousness that so mark our age, the temptations for fixed authority are very strong indeed. By tying their communities to a particular view of authority everyone can know the right answer and expect the right questions.

It is understandable that the attempt to tie the faith to the authority of something so concrete as the Bible would be made in the context of this culture. One of the great ironies of this approach, however, is the way in which it buys into the assumptions of modernity about what constitutes proof of the truth. By arguing that the Bible is without error, even in matters such as history and science, they have accepted a particular Enlightenment assumption about the ways in which we know a thing. True things must be historically true and scientifically verifiable for many people, though this is one of the ideas that is most under scrutiny in contemporary thinking.

Scripture claims its own authority not because of the doctrines we assign to it, but because within it we meet a story, or better yet, we meet a host of stories, not just about some people's lives from long ago, but about ours as well. If we enter into these stories, we find there something which encounters us. More often than not we find within the text something which cannot be domesticated by us or fit into our doctrinal formulations. In the midst of the complexities and the complications of our postmodern world, something emerges from our reading and hearing reception of the biblical stories which calls us to pilgrimage from where we presently live.

This is often too frightening for us to deal with because it means that the interpretation of Scripture is not entirely under our control, even though we wish differently. No matter whether we are Baptist, Catholic, Episcopal, Jewish, Islamic, or even Lutheran, we cannot devise a teaching office of the church, synagogue, or mosque that will establish the definitive interpretation of God's story, though today this is where we see the institution of fundamentalist religion exercise its greatest control in the world. This is where the present-day challenge of postmodernity can be helpful as we wonder about the role of the past.

To say that the Bible contains one authoritative interpretation of God's word to us is not only unknown to most of the Christian tradition; it destroys the living character of the Bible as witness to the grace of God. This attempt to root faith in a particular interpretation of the Bible is rooted in our fear that God will speak a new word to us in the matrix of our social space. No matter where we stand God will call us to consider our ideologies and idolatries in spite of ourselves. Does God really not want women to be pastors or preachers? Could hierarchy actually be useful? May not the homosexual be a part of the family of faith? Are we really called to love the sexist or the racist? Is sexual morality an important consideration in living a life of faith? How radical is grace? Questions even more disturbing than these will sometimes confront us with a reading of the biblical text, and sometimes the answers are not as easy as they seem.

Many fear that a type of anarchy of the spirit may arise that will sweep all certainty away and leave us in a land of confusion. One look at the Protestant Reformation and we could be excused for having huge doubts about a faith that allows pluralism. The thought of all believers going off on their own tangent, doing what is right in their own eyes, does give pause. Better to have an interpretation everyone can agree to and guarantee we are all on the same page. The temptation is hard to resist.

But the truth is that depending on which community of faith is doing the interpreting there have been and always will be differing readings of what the Bible says. Luther, for all his struggles with the church, was just enough of a Catholic to be worried about anyone who wasn't. When the peasants of Germany and beyond read the Bible, they saw different things in there than Luther. They questioned the way their society had been built, and this caused revolution. Luther in response to this was not immune from the temptations of order and implored the German nobility to "smite, stab, and slay" the militant peasants who demanded equal access to game, firewood, and water. Of course, the peasants saw things differently in the Bible than Luther and the nobility did. This being God's world, after all, shouldn't all have equal access to the land and resources? Are we finished with this question?

Today we have communities that are not built upon the foundations of the status quo. They read within the pages of Scripture that Jesus expressed solidarity with the poor and disenfranchised, that Mary calls for the humbling of the rich and the exaltation of the poor, and that the reign of God may not come through the mainstream of religious institutions and clerical professionals. Rather this reign of God may emerge through people who have the heart for a new earth and are willing to suffer for it by being peacemakers in the midst of our love affair with violence.

These communities of resistance are global and powerful signs for us that our reception of the Bible is strongly colored by our social and cultural setting. From the Sojourners community in inner-city Washington, D.C., to the liberation communities of Guatemala or Brazil, Christians from the underside find in the Bible an authority that speaks a more powerful word than we are accustomed to hearing.

The authority of the Scriptures does not count on external doctrines of it or on an interpretive grid given it by tradition or teaching authority. The authority of Scripture emerges in those who upon reading it encounter God and suffer conversion from the illusions they live in to a new radical perspective. This perspective calls us to be attentive to the ways in which we have existed in life and unplug from the matrix of our corporate and self-delusions.

This does not mean that scholarship and the study of background, linguistics, social theory, and historical-critical research are not important; these are vital for a wise and discerning perspective. But what it does mean is that ultimately the Christian faith cannot rest on arbitrary doctrines about the Bible if those doctrines serve to isolate us in fear from the God who inspires the lives and stories found there.

This isolation can be seen today in any number of ways. One of these is found in an excessive individualism that sees faith as a matter of total individual concern. Those who occupy this space are legion and usually make statements such as, "I'm spiritual, but not very religious." This reflects our preoccupation with our individual needs. From Robert Bellah and his *Habits of the Heart*, to Robert Putnam's *Bowling Alone: The Collapse and Retrieval of American Community*, this has been territory well covered. It does raise many questions about the role of community in public life, but it also raises the issue of whether we have construed Christianity as a matter of consumer choice. If you don't like the church you are in, just move to another one. Or better still, forget the community altogether because you can find God just as easy on the golf course or the beach or the Internet. And there is some truth to this, for God is always present to us.

I am not intending to engage us in another round of guilt, but this does point to a problem I have touched on. Given the weight of our egocentricity, our total absorption with ourselves, and our blind pursuit of self-interests, how do we hear new truths? We are more likely to stay locked away inside the prisons of our own illusions, hatreds, bigotries, and self-justifications if there is nothing around to challenge us to something different. None of us, left to our own devices, usually possesses the resources to enlarge our hearts to those outside our chosen circle. We choose that circle just so it won't raise uncomfortable questions. We need the existence of communities of difference who will challenge us to see the world in a different way. How we will find them is one of the great challenges of the Christian faith.

Back into the Body

These are the questions we have been asking in this book. What have we built in our attempts at cultural construction? Are we constructing a new Babel to live in so we can become isolated from others? The prophets of our day stand outside our tower and ask if it isn't time to think about deconstructing the skyscrapers of our self- and social isolation. There are Christian communities who refuse to hear this voice in the name of doctrinal purity, but do they have much to offer the world?

Most of us don't even want to consider whether our doctrines of God, Jesus, or the Bible are in fact social legitimation, for we refuse to take seriously the call of God to incarnate the presence of God in the world. We structure communities of faith upon concrete pilings of certainty, never noticing that we have become chained to them and cannot leave when the spirit of God calls us to pilgrimage.

When faith ties itself to the status quo of institutional authority and social control it needs to be interrogated. Most of those who criticize Christianity the strongest are often those who are the most disappointed in it. Perceptive and perhaps filled with the secret longing of wishing that some stories were true, they ask us serious questions. Are there spaces to live in the world that welcome the stranger and offer a word of grace?

We have dealt with some significant voices in this regard. But one story that exhibits the type of truth-telling that sometimes is found in those who are wary of faith comes from the story of Will Campbell, author of *Brother to a Dragonfly*. Campbell tells the story of his life growing up in America's deep South during the days of segregation. He studied to be a minister and became a pastor in the Baptist Church. Touched with a sense of justice and conviction, he worked extremely hard in the civil rights movement in the 1950s and '60s. In the midst of what can only be called a struggle Campbell was rocked with the news of the death of two young seminarians who were working in the civil rights movement. He was good friends with one of these men, Jonathan Daniel. One day he received the news that the two had been shot to death by an Alabama sheriff, Thomas Coleman.

When Campbell heard this news he was with his brother and a friend of theirs, a journalist named P. D. East, who was always questioning Campbell on Christianity. He used to push Campbell to define Christianity in ten words or less. Finally one day in discussion with his friend, Campbell said in response to this question, "We are all bastards but God loves us anyway." That definition seemed to satisfy P. D. East until the night of Jonathan Daniel's death, when he challenged Will Campbell with a question about the student and the sheriff. After establishing that we are all bastards, East asked Campbell, "Which one of these bastards do you think God loves the most? Does He love that little dead bastard Jonathan the most? Or does He love that living bastard Thomas the most?" It was a revolutionary moment for Campbell. He recounts:

> Suddenly everything became clear. Everything. It was a revelation. The glow of the malt which we were well into by then seemed to illumine and intensify it. I walked across the room and opened the blind, staring directly into the glare of the street light. And I began to whimper. But the crying was interspersed with laughter. It was a strange experience. I remember trying to sort out the sadness and the joy. Just what was I crying for and what was I laughing for. Then this too became clear.
>
> I was laughing at myself, at twenty years of a ministry which had become, without my realizing it, a ministry of liberal sophistication. An attempted negation of Jesus, of human

engineering, of riding the coattails of Caesar, of playing on his ballpark, by his rules and with his ball, of looking to government to make and verify and authenticate our morality, of worshipping at the shrine of enlightenment and academia, of making an idol of the Supreme Court, a theology of law and order and of denying not only the Faith I professed to hold but my history and my people—the Thomas Colemans. Loved. And if loved, then forgiven. And if forgiven, reconciled. Yet sitting then in his own cell, the blood of two of his and my brothers on his hands. The thought gave me a shaking chill in a non-air-conditioned room in August.[96]

This was a profoundly conversionary moment in Campbell's life as he came to a new realization of God's grace. Where do we experience these conversionary moments if not in the individuals and communities of difference that will not let us live into our illusions? Sometimes the truth-telling comes from those outside our community.

More importantly, where do we need conversion today? I have mentioned some of them previously. One of them may certainly come from a revisioning of the deep spiritual nature of the world talked about by Aquinas. Because we see the world as an empty vessel for our own desires for wealth and power we are doing great damage to the earth every second. It is not difficult to find examples of poisoning, toxic abuse of the environment.

This has become one of the most important items on the agenda of Christianity, and many theologians such as Sallie McFague, Larry Rasmussen, and Matthew Fox are calling us to be attentive to a planet in peril. Even those who do not share a specific Christian sensitivity are engaging in actions to impede the destruction of the planet. They may not care about Aquinas's notion of the sustaining presence of God in the created order, but they realize that our habitation on this planet rests on fragile grounds. We must change our sense of reality to coexist with the rest of life if we hope to have a future here.

Those persons of faith, specifically Christians in the context of this book, need to cultivate a respect for the earth as the bearer of us all. We constantly make claims on the earth, but in what way would it make claims upon us if it had the voice to do so?

Maybe it does, but we have grown too deaf to hear it. Maybe part of that deafness has come in our refusal to think as seriously or rigorously as Aquinas about the intersection of nature and grace. We have lost a sense of what we should be moving toward, the goal of our lives.

Of course for many this seems like a waste of time. Not seeing that our very survival is at stake, we remain locked in the illusion that this is all being taken care of and there isn't a whole lot we can do about it anyway. But the ways we think about things have consequences. To cultivate a love for the life of this planet is a mark of faithfulness. A careful reading of Aquinas can help us to recover the theological grounds for mutuality between ourselves and the environment. Though God is the other who addresses us, this One is also the sustaining presence of all life. Misuse of the planet is a sign of spiritual blindness.

This blindness has led us into another wilderness and another place where the past offers space for a more discerning perspective. Even though the demise of the cold war seemingly moved us to safer ground, the nuclear problem is still with us. We have in our countries enough nuclear tonnage to destroy the earth. Nations are developing these weapons every day. And yet few Christians have made the connection between the existence of these weapons and the presence of evil in our lives.

When the biblical narratives allude to the presence of something in this world that seeks to threaten the good creation of God, we sometimes ignore what that might mean for the corporate life of humankind. In the biblical accounts of Satan he is portrayed as the one who deceives those who are susceptible into believing they are doing well when they choose against God's intentions. How much more seductive can it be, then, to believe that our weapons will save us? We have listened far too long to the voice that whispers into our ears, "Surely if you build these devices you will be safe. No one will dare attack you and take your power if you have these threats to the stability of the earth in your possession."

Where do voices like this come from? Have we embraced the ultimate deception—that we must create, build, and deploy weapons that will destroy the creation of God and every living thing if we are to be protected from "them"? We worship at the altar of the negation of God in the service of our illusions. Perhaps it is time we got in the boat and set sail to the edge of the world to hear the voice that calls us to another reality. Or maybe we need to unplug from that matrix to think about the way we have allowed culture to establish our allegiances and identities.

Fyodor Dostoyevsky challenged Christianity with this question of what it really serves in the story of the Grand Inquisitor in *The Brothers Karamozov*. Rendered in surreal fashion and narrated by an atheist, Ivan, to a believer, his brother Alyosha, the story has Jesus returning to earth during the Spanish Inquisition. After Jesus heals people and draws a crowd, the Grand Inquisitor has him arrested and put in prison.

While Jesus is there, the Inquisitor comes to him to interrogate him and subjects him to a monologue based upon the temptation narratives found in the gospels of Mark and Luke. Commenting on the last temptation when Satan takes Jesus to the mountain and shows him all the kingdoms, political structures, and earthly power in a moment of time, he tells Jesus:

> Perhaps you want to hear it from me, then listen: we are not with you, but with him . . . since we took from him that which you in your indignation rejected, that final gift offered to you, when he showed you all the kingdoms of the world: we took from him Rome and the sword of Caesar. . . . Had you accepted that third counsel of the mighty Spirit, you would have supplied everything that man seeks in the world, that is: someone to bow before, someone to entrust one's conscience to, and a way of at last uniting everyone into an undisputed, general and consensual ant-heap, for the need of universal union is the third and final torment of human beings.[97]

Do we see ourselves in this story? Have we been so seduced by power that we no longer see clearly? Content with whatever government we find ourselves under, do we acquiesce to it in the name of Paul's supposed command to be obedient to the government found in Romans 13:1–7? There are many today in the Christian community who believe that Christians should be involved in gaining political power to further their goals, but this can be the greatest idolatry and illusion of all. More often than not political structures will consign the realm of faith to the internal world of the believer and seek to seduce the church with the promise of power and influence. It will not listen when the church has a word of dissent to its power or pretensions.

This is the concern Bonhoeffer and Barth faced in all its malignant force. It is easy for us to lose sight of the fact that their culture formed the basis for what seemed normal and natural at the time. So few people really questioned what was happening during the years between the world wars when Hitler played on the fears and hopes of Germany. When the National Socialist Party tied Christianity to the aspirations of the state, far too few raised any sound of protest. This can only be accounted as one of the greatest failures of Christianity in its history. Even though the pope and other Christian communities have offered repentance and pleas of forgiveness for the Holocaust, this is not enough. Maybe nothing is or will be.

Barth and Bonhoeffer offer us two very different responses to the great horror of the twentieth century, a horror Christianity has just begun to address. We saw how Barth was able to use the formulations of early church creeds as a tool of discernment against the pretensions of the Nazi state. This use of doctrine would seem to have promise for the future of Christianity, not to legitimate ourselves in the world, but to consider what truly shapes us in it. This does not entail an unthoughtful and slavish appropriation of the past, but a critical and careful employment of our tradition to continually ask ourselves where our allegiances rest. No one who calls Jesus Lord should engage in the oppression of any other human being or justify violence in the name of God.

Bonhoeffer also offers us a way into response to the Holocaust. Taking the way of powerlessness, Bonhoeffer calls us to put away all those fine theological constructions that lead us away from the suffering of the world. He offers us the realization that Christianity cannot survive as a tool of the principalities and powers to shape and fashion this world for their own purposes. In embracing the suffering of God we find something emerging in the world that was previously absent, a power that confounds the world. It does not play in Caesar's ballpark, under Caesar's rules, but does continually engage the world in questioning the realities it has fashioned and called truth.

We could prevent the recurrence of this sad moment in the history of the world if we became more attentive to the idolatries

we unwittingly embrace. Perhaps the place to start would be to
ask the question whether or not the role of Christian faith is to
accommodate the projects of culture-building. Maybe the role of
Christianity post-Holocaust is to wander the earth, without secure
habitation, recovering its prophetic voice and pastoral heart for all
of God's creation.

Perhaps we should become exiles in the world that we have
constructed, for if we were truly faithful we would probably find
ourselves as strangers and aliens in a far land. To believe that
Christians should not root their identity in nation, state, or ethnic
origin, to maintain that no government on the face of the planet
deserves our unqualified allegiance, to think that the way of peace
is blessed; all this puts us on the other side of the fence from society.
To suggest that the gospel reveals God's destabilizing way in the
world can be the ultimate threat to a world that loves its order.

We fear this because it would mean that Christianity might
break out of its own delusions and Babylonian captivity to culture
and become unsettling in the world. Think about how threatened
we feel when communities within Christianity start to transgress
the boundaries of cultural construction. When those like Oscar Romero, Gustavo Gutiérrez, Henri Nouwen, Dorothy Day,
Desmond Tutu, Martin Luther King, Jr., Catherine of Siena,
St. Francis, even St. Paul, or the multitude of other prophetic voices
of our tradition have stepped outside the lines of our accepted realities and called us into question, we have usually responded with
derision and martyrdom. We do not like hearing that other word,
even when it comes from within our own community. But we are
one body, and this is the body we belong to in the world.

But this word, unsettling as it is, brings gifts with it as well. It
brings the wisdom of discernment. This word of God, from God
found in the mouths of these others, slips through our communal
defenses to compel us to pilgrimage in a strange land, the one
now called postmodern, but tomorrow probably called something
else. This land may be a place we never knew existed because we
were settled in our own secure homes. We enjoyed the comfort of
our own creations. But now we see the fragility of that which we
called home, and we realize that we cannot rest there. We become
pilgrims in need of grace.

In this land we learn that faith may take different forms than the ones we are familiar with. The journey of faith may mean standing outside my culture and calling it to attend to the world in a different way. It may mean cultivating an understanding of other people in such a way that does not violate the integrity of who they are or close me off from the word they may have for me. This may ask of us a more sensitive understanding of the world than we presently possess. For the faces of the world are vastly different and demand of us much. It is easier for us to ignore them than to seek to understand them.

The reason we ignore them is because far too often they are the voices of the suffering. The suffering exist in far greater numbers than the nonsuffering, and sometimes the demands are too much for us to bear, because we, each of us, carry our own particular load of pain. The magnitude of it overwhelms us and sucks us into the vortex of hopelessness. We see it on a global scale in São Paulo, Johannesburg, Jakarta, Kashmir, Jerusalem, or countless other places where humankind lives. It is etched in the geography of our cities with the dividing lines between the rich and poor.

But it is also found in the deepest part of our lives and touches the most fundamental parts of our soul. In the movie *Magnolia* the various characters of the opening part of the movie are portrayed as each living lives of intense and sometimes hidden pain, alienation, and suffering. As the movie progresses the stories of the characters start to connect with one another in one huge mass of pain. Fueled by the self-deceptions and illusions that are so woven into the fabric of our lives, they disintegrate before the viewer. From suicide attempts to deathbed confessions of regret for lives of deceit, selfishness, and fear, the long-buried truths of their lives come boiling to the surface to create the worst kind of pain, the true realization of how life was really lived. No longer secure in the comfort of their masks, their delusions, their deceptions, many of these characters confront the most painful thing a person can encounter, their true selves, stripped of all lies and falsehood.

The only redeeming aspect to this collective self-destruction is one of the characters talking about forgiveness. But it is shallow and empty because it never really comes to grips with our inability to truly forgive either ourselves or one another. The suffering remains for many with no real healing taking place.

What will be able to speak to this suffering? In this world it

will not be a church or community that trusts in its own philosophical or theological sophistication. It will not be found within
a community of persons who live as mirror images of the culture
or society around them, worshiping at the altars of governmen-
tal power. It will not be found in the groups of those who seek a
return to doctrinal purity and unquestioning obedience. No, this
is not the space where the word of grace for a broken world will
be found.

This whole text has been about asking the question where it
may be found. I believe we cannot ignore the resources of the
past in our search for it. I am sure some readers of this text have
probably been thinking that this is a futile exercise. They would
point to my own projections and illusions and argue that I am
imposing on the past the grid of my own desires to make things
my own. The critique that I have been colonizing the past for my
own purposes is one that cannot be ignored.

In this attempt at retrieval have I bent those so far removed
from me to my purposes and not let them have an authentic word?
This may in fact be true, but before this judgment is made I would
invite you to also return to those considered in this book, read their
writings, study the history of their times, and reflect on whether
or not they have anything to offer us in this present context.

These reflections I have offered have been made in the realization that no one can truly capture the totality of another person's
life. I am only suggesting that when we think about these lives the
dead weight of tradition or doctrine is not the only spirit to approach them with. Nor is the dismissive attitude that points to their
faults, failings, and cultural limitations an excuse to ignore what
they might have to tell us of that which transcends time. We need
only remember that later generations will find in us prejudices,
blind spots, and weaknesses of which we are presently unaware.
Would we want to be summarily dismissed for the failings that
future understandings of reality will find among us?

The past can serve as our guide into the future, but it can also
be a critique of the way in which we become so lost in the constructions of the age. In conversation with our heritage, bringing
to it our problems and questions, we can sometimes find that there
exists a continuity between past and present that links us all together. It is this notion that I am not a stranger to those who have

gone before me or will come after me that has driven this book. I believe the continual discussion with our tradition does offer a way to the healing of the world's suffering. Perhaps it can even enlarge our hearts and increase our compassion.

This way is found in those who resist the lure of the postmodern carnival to climb aboard the ride of constantly shifting identities, ever changing with the tides of commerce, personal desire, and life in cyberspace. It will be found in those communities of resistance that read stories in the Bible that cause them to question the way of the world. They will be the holy fools who pull the veil off our collective madness of infatuation with violence and our justification of it with, "The world is thus." They will suggest that the world can be made anew.

The way of faith for the future will be found in those who realize that the critiques of the past, present, and future ages offer a word to both secular and religious pretensions to universal and unassailable truth. It will be found in those with the heart and courage enough to stand with other communities of pilgrims and call the world to the way of reconciliation with God and one another. These communities, formed around the reality of the biblical narratives, will not rely on the abstractions of the past, but will draw from it wisdom and understanding. In their desire to incarnate the presence of God in the world they will engage in Bonhoeffer's "arcane disciplines" of prayer, meditation, and worship in the community of faith. In doing so they will gather around a table to be fed anew by the spirit of God found in Eucharist.

These communities, by participating in the powerlessness of God, will reveal to the world what it already knows: this life is ridden with tragedy, but this is not the last word. As we live into the life, sayings, deeds, sufferings, death, and resurrection of Jesus Christ we will lose our lives. We will lose those lives that shape-shift at the whim of culture or social pressure, living naively in the constructions of our world without question. We will lose the innocence of those who don't know, because we will know. We will know that we can no longer betray, oppress, or neglect those who emerge from the shadows of our grand illusions to make their own claims on us.

What we will find are lives that have unplugged from the matrix of unknowing, that have become truthful lives, no longer lived in deceit or delusion. We will find lives that can offer forgiveness because we know we are forgiven. This will not be a cheap grace, for the awakening that comes with true knowledge of ourselves before God is never easy. But realizing that we are accepted and embraced by that which lies at the boundary of all conceivable thought and will not let us go, we will find our most fundamental and truest selves. It is from here that we will be able to prophesy the words of grace and healing that a tired and exhausted world hopes to hear. Even more, it is here that the body of Christ will become incarnate in the world to live freely, unconstrained by the prior claims of social and personal illusion and unplugged from the matrix of false realities.

Notes

Chapter 1: Unplugging from the Matrix

1. James Davidson Hunter, *Culture Wars: The Struggle to Define America* (Chicago: University of Chicago Press, 1987). For an introduction to the postmodern context see Frederic Jameson, *Postmodernism, or the Cultural Logic of Late Capitalism* (Durham, N.C.: Duke University Press, 1991); Steven Conner, *An Introduction to Theories of the Contemporary* (Oxford: Blackwell, 1989); Zygmunt Bauman, *Intimations of Postmodernity* (London: Routledge, 1992); Hans Berten, *The Idea of the Postmodern: A History* (London: Routledge, 1995); Joseph Natoli, *A Primer to Postmodernity* (Oxford: Blackwell, 1997); Albert Borgmann, *Crossing the Postmodern Divide* (Chicago: University of Chicago Press, 1992); Linda Hutcheon, *The Politics of Postmodernism* (London: Routledge, 1989); Walter Truett Anderson, *Reality Isn't What It Used to Be: Theatrical Politics, Ready-to Wear Religion, Global Myths, Primitive Chic and Other Wonders of the Postmodern World* (San Francisco: Harper & Row, 1990); Kenneth Gergen, *The Saturated Self: Dilemmas of Identity in Contemporary Life* (New York: Basic Books, 1991); David Harvey, *The Condition of Postmodernity: An Enquiry into the Origins of Cultural Change* (Oxford: Blackwell, 1989); Steven Best and Douglas Kellner, *Postmodern Theory: Critical Interrogations* (New York: Guilford, 1991); Jean-François Lyotard, *The Postmodern Condition: A Report on Knowledge* (Minneapolis: University of Minnesota Press, 1984). For works dealing specifically with theological concerns, this is just a small list. One place to begin might be the SUNY Press series on postmodern theology edited by David Ray Griffin. Fortress Press also has a series, Guides to Theological Inquiry, which deals with postmodern themes. One of the best-known names in a particular area of theology is Mark C. Taylor, whose work *Erring: A Postmodern A/theology* (Chicago: University of Chicago Press, 1984), influenced many young theologians over the last decade. For someone on the opposite end of the spectrum see John Millbank's *Theology and Social Theory: Beyond Secular Reason* (Oxford: Blackwell, 1990). Other well-known theologians working this territory include Gordon Kaufman, *In Face of Mystery: A Constructive Theology* (Cambridge, Mass: Harvard University Press, 1993), and Sallie McFague, whose books *Models of God* and *The Body of God* (Minneapolis: Fortress Press, 1983 and 1993, respectively) have been influential.

2. Anderson, *Reality Isn't What It Used to Be,* 75.

3. See Allan Megill, *Prophets of Extremity: Nietzsche, Heidegger, Foucault, Derrida* (Berkeley and Los Angeles: University of California Press, 1985).

4. Sigmund Freud, *The Future of an Illusion,* trans. and ed. James Strachey (New York: W. W. Norton, 1961), 42.

5. Berger writes about this in his works, two of which have been well read in

the area of religion and social theory. One of these is entitled *The Sacred Canopy: Elements of a Sociological Theory of Religion* (New York: Anchor Books, 1967). The other is *A Rumor of Angels: Modern Society and the Rediscovery of the Supernatural* (New York: Anchor Books, 1969).

6. Richard Rorty, "Pragmatism and Philosophy," in *After Philosophy: End or Transformation?* ed. Kenneth Baynes, James Bohman, and Thomas McCarthy (Cambridge, Mass.: MIT Press, 1987), 60.

7. David Tracy, "Theology and the Many Faces of Postmodernity," *Theology Today* 51, no. 1 (April 1994): 104–14.

8. Jean-François Lyotard, *The Postmodern Condition: A Report on Knowledge, Theory and History of Literature,* trans. Geoff Bennington and Brian Massimi (Minneapolis: University of Minnesota Press, 1984), xxiv.

9. Kenneth J. Gergen, *The Saturated Self: Dilemmas of Identity in Contemporary Life* (New York: Basic Books, 1991), 7.

10. Paul Lakeland, *Postmodernity* (Minneapolis: Fortress Press, 1998), 85.

Chapter 2: Searching for Myself

11. Giovanni Pico della Mirandola, *Oration on the Dignity of Man,* trans. A. Robert Caponigri (Chicago: Henry Regnery, 1965), 7–8.

12. Walter Truett Anderson, *The Future of the Self* (New York: J. P. Tarcher, 1997).

13. See, for example, Robert E. Ornstein, ed., *The Psychology of Consciousness* (San Francisco: W. H. Freeman, 1972).

14. Ludwig Wittgenstein, *Tractatus Logico-philosophicus* (German and English, London: Routledge & Kegan Paul, 1961), 4.002.

15. Augustine, *The Confessions,* trans. Maria Boulding (New York: New City Press, 1996), 4.12. From this point on all the quotations of this source will be referenced by the numerical distinction. For other works on Augustine the reader is invited to consider some of the following: Garry Wills, *St. Augustine* (New York: Lipper/Viking, 1999), is part of the Penguin series of biographies. It is highly readable and accessible to the general reader. Some of the classic texts in interpreting Augustine are Peter Brown's *Augustine of Hippo* (Berkeley: University of California Press), or Etienne Gilson's work *The Christian Philosophy of Saint Augustine,* trans. L. E. M. Lynch (New York: Random House, 1960). Another work of a more biographical nature is Henry Chadwick's *Augustine* (Oxford and New York: Oxford University Press, 1986). For more recent studies on Augustine and the self, consult Charles Taylor's *Sources of the Self: The Making of the Modern Identity* (Cambridge, Mass.: Harvard University Press, 1989). Also, a recent book by Sandra Lee Dixon is *Augustine: The Scattered and Gathered Self* (St. Louis: Chalice Press, 1999).

16. *Confessions,* respectively: 8.8.19; 8.8.20; 8.9.21.

17. Ibid., 8.10.23.

18. Ibid., 8.10.26.

19. Ibid., 11.29.39.

20. Ibid., 9.1.

21. Ibid., 8.10.22.

22. Ibid., 10.23.33.

23. Ibid., 1.1.1.

Chapter 3: Thinking about the Unthinkable

24. In fact any search will turn up many references to the interest in Anselm, some of the most interesting of which are R. W. Southern's biography *Saint Anselm: A Portrait in a Landscape* (Cambridge: Cambridge University Press, 1990); John Hick and Arthur C. McGill, eds., *The Many-Faced Argument: Recent Studies on the Ontological Argument for the Existence of God* (New York: Macmillan, 1967); Charles Hartshorne, *Anselm's Discovery: A Re-Examination of the Ontological Proof for God's Existence* (LaSalle, Ill.: Open Court, 1965); Robert Brecher, *Anselm's Argument: The Logic of Divine Existence* (Aldershot, Hants., England: Gower, 1985); G. R. Evans, *Anselm and Talking about God* (Oxford: Clarendon Press, 1978); Karl Barth, *Anselm: Fides quarens intellectum,* trans. Sam W. Robertson (Richmond: John Knox Press, 1960).

25. Bertrand Russell in P. A. Schilpp, *The Philosophy of Bertrand Russell* (Evanston: Northwestern University Press, 1944), 10.

26. Kant suggested that something other than the simple attainment of being was at stake. There was also the matter of this being attaining existence solely by means of its pure essence. From a historical perspective, the term "ontology" itself appears six hundred years after Anselm.

27. Jean-Luc Marion, "Is the Ontological Argument Ontological? The Argument according to Anselm and Its Metaphysical Interpretation according to Kant," *Journal of the History of Philosophy* 30 (April 1992): 201–18. Marion is only one of the many who read Anselm differently than those who followed Kant's interpretation. See also Colin Grant, "Anselm's Argument Today," in *Journal of American Academy of Religion* 57, no. 4 (1989): 791–805.

28. Ibid., 208. In chapter 15 of the *Proslogion* the theme of the highest possible thought reaches its final determination. "Ergo Domine, non solum es quo majus cogitari nequit, sed es quiddam majus quam cogitari possit"—"O Lord, not only are You that than which a greater cannot be thought, but You are also something greater than can be thought."

29. Southern, *Saint Anselm,* 449.

30. The result was a small but significant book on Anselm entitled *Anselm: Fides quaerens intellectum: Anselms Beweis der Existenz Gottes in Zusammenhang seines theologischen Programms,* English trans.: *Anselm: Fides quaerens intellectum,* trans. Sam W. Robertson (Richmond: John Knox Press, 1960). For many years the accepted interpretation of this book and its significance for Barth studies was influenced by Barth's own statements on its importance, one of which was found in the second preface for the book: "Only a comparatively few commentators, for example Hans Urs von Balthasar, have realized that my interest in Anselm was never a side issue for me or ... realized how much it has influenced me or been absorbed into my own line of thinking. Most of them have completely failed to see that in this book on Anselm I am working with a vital key, if not the key, to an understanding of that whole process of thought that has impressed me more and more in my Church Dogmatics as the only proper one to theology." This has been challenged by Bruce L. McCormack in his recently published *Karl Barth's Critically Realistic Dialectical Theology: Its Genesis and Development, 1909–1936* (New York: Oxford University Press, 1995). Building on the work of a new generation of German scholarship, he argues that inter-

pretation of Anselm's influence on Barth has been unduly influenced by Hans Urs von Balthasar's paradigm of Barth shifting from dialectics to analogy. Mc-Cormack sees the shifts in Barth's theology being more subtle and organic than a sudden reversal of method. However, Barth himself does indicate that Anselm was crucial for his thinking about theology, and while it may not have resulted in the change indicated by von Balthasar, it was a significant aspect of Barth's future work.

31. *Anselm: Fides quarens intellectum,* trans. Robertson, 68.

32. John Thiel, *Nonfoundationalism* (Minneapolis: Fortress Press, 1994), 96.

Chapter 4: Creation Calling

33. Matthew Fox, *The Coming of the Cosmic Christ* (San Francisco: Harper, 1988), 13.

34. Ibid., 16.

35. *Raleigh News and Observer,* July 5, 2000.

36. Neil Postman, *Technopoly: The Surrender of Culture to Technology* (New York: Vantage, 1993), 74.

37. Thomas Aquinas, *Summa Theologica,* trans. Fathers of the Dominican Province (Westminster, Md.: Christian Classics, 1981), I.92.1–3.

38. Ibid., I.44.4.

39. Ibid., I.1.8.

40. Ibid. I.44.4.

41. Thomas Franklin O'Meara, O.P., *Thomas Aquinas, Theologian* (Notre Dame and London: University of Notre Dame Press, 1997), 75. This book should be the starting place for anyone interested in the theological shape of Aquinas's work. I have made generous use of O'Meara's insights. The reader will also find fine treatments of Aquinas in Brian Davies, *The Thought of Thomas Aquinas* (Oxford: Clarendon Press, 1992), and Jean-Pierre Torrell, O.P., *Saint Thomas Aquinas,* vol. 1, *The Person and His Work,* trans. Robert Royal (Washington, D.C.: Catholic University of America Press, 1996).

42. *Summa Theologica,* I.45.6. Matthew Fox has written a book about Aquinas that argues along many of the same lines I am using. His interpretation of this passage is a little different and instead of the image of a craftsman, he uses the image of an artist. The book, *Sheer Joy: Conversations with Thomas Aquinas on Creation Spirituality* (San Francisco: HarperCollins, 1992), is an interesting exercise in appropriating Aquinas for contemporary reflection.

43. *Summa Theologica,* II, II, 8.1 and 2.

44. *Summa Theologica,* I.13.17 and I.4.3.3.

45. *Summa Theologica,* I.8.1.

46. Peter Gay, *The Way of the (Modern) World: Or, Why It's Tempting to Live As If God Doesn't Exist* (Grand Rapids, Mich.: Eerdmans, 1999). See especially his second chapter, 79–120, from which I benefited greatly in thinking through this chapter.

47. Lesslie Newbigin, *Foolishness to the Greeks: The Gospel and Western Culture* (Grand Rapids, Mich.: Eerdmans, 1986), 79; quoted in ibid., 93.

Chapter 5: Living into Our Story

48. In what follows I have relied mostly on the unpublished lecture notes I received in a Luther seminar taken in graduate school at Drew University and taught by the late Bard Thompson. However, there are numerous books on Luther that offer much of the same information. The best known has to be Roland Bainton, *Here I Stand: A Life of Martin Luther* (Nashville: Abingdon Press, 1950). Another work of more recent origin is Heiko A. Oberman, *Luther: Man between God and the Devil,* trans. Eileen Walliser-Schwarzbart (New York: Image Books, 1992). There are many more.

49. Martin Luther, *Luther's Works,* vol. 35. *Word and Sacrament I,* ed. E. Theodore Bachmann (Philadelphia: Fortress Press, 1976), 117–18.

50. Ibid., 123.

51. Ibid., 362.

52. Ibid., 132.

53. Ibid., 362. See also Luther's remarks on pages 395–97.

54. Bainton, *Here I Stand,* 144.

55. Peter Berger, *The Sacred Canopy: Elements of a Sociological Theory of Religion* (Garden City, N.Y.: Anchor/Doubleday, 1969), 138.

56. Stanley Hauerwas, *The Peaceable Kingdom* (Notre Dame, Ind.: University of Notre Dame Press, 1983), 85. This is one of Hauerwas's early books. He has written, edited, and contributed to a number of other books which explore the role of narrative in shaping life.

57. John Irving, *A Prayer for Owen Meany* (New York: Ballantine Books, 1989), 310.

58. Hauerwas, *The Peaceable Kingdom,* 142.

Chapter 6: Can We Ever Interpret Another?

59. Accounts of the Vatican's position were in papers all across the world, but I am drawing specifically from *The Christian Century* 117, no. 25 (September 13–20): 2000.

60. For some of the best known of these critiques see Michel Foucault's writings, most notably, *Madness and Civilization: A History of Insanity in the Age of Reason,* trans. Richard Howard (New York: Vintage Books, 1973); *The Order of Things: An Archeology of the Human Sciences* (New York: Vintage Books, 1973); *The Archaeology of Knowledge and the Discourse on Language,* trans. A. M. Sheridan Smith (New York: Pantheon Books, 1972). One could also read Didier Eribon's *Michel Foucault,* trans. Betsy Wing (Cambridge: Harvard University Press, 1991). Also the works of Jacques Derrida have contributed much to this perspective, and one place to start is his "The Ends of Man" in *Margins of Philosophy,* trans. Alan Bass (Chicago: University of Chicago Press, 1982). For an interesting treatment of these themes consult David Toole's work, *Waiting for Godot in Sarajevo* (Boulder, Colo.: Westview Press, 1998).

61. In much of what follows I drew from one of the standard works of Schleiermacher studies, Martin Redeker's *Schleiermacher: Life and Thought,* trans. John Wallhausser (Philadelphia: Fortress Press, 1973). There are other works the reader is invited to consult, all of which go into some depth about Schleiermacher's life and thought, including Robert Williams, *Schleiermacher*

the Theologian (Philadelphia: Fortress Press, 1978), and Richard R. Niebuhr, *Schleiermacher on Christ and Religion* (New York: Scribner and Sons, 1964).

62. In what follows I have given a synopsis of the book. There are two different translations of this work, the most recent by Richard Crouter, published by Cambridge University Press in 1992.

63. Ibid., 241.

64. Once again I have summarized parts of the original text: F. D. E. Schleiermacher, *The Christian Faith*, ed. H. R. Mackintosh and J. S. Stewart (orig. published 1830; Edinburgh: T. & T. Clark, 1928). I used the edition published by Fortress Press, 1976.

65. This has been one of the most studied areas of Schleiermacher, and there are numerous persons today who have contributed much scholarly work to an examination of his hermeneutical theory. The text most often used in this study is Schleiermacher's *Hermeneutics, the Handwritten Manuscripts*, ed. Heinz Kimmerle, trans. James Duke and Jack Forstman (Atlanta: Scholars Press, 1977, 1986). The interpretation of Schleiermacher's hermeneutics by those such as Paul Ricoeur, Hans-Georg Gadamer, and Richard Palmer has greatly influenced their reception in the contemporary world. Laying the charge of "psychologizing" at Schleiermacher's door, they contributed to the notion that he overly concentrated on discerning the author's intentions or mental processes and divorced thought from language. Of particular concern to many was his notion that one goal of interpreting was to understand an author's discourse better than the author understood it. One of the benefits of recent scholarship is that the assessment of Schleiermacher has become a little more complete.

66. Hans-Georg Gadamer, *Truth and Method*, trans. Joel Weinsheimer and Donald G. Marshall (New York: Crossroad, 1989), 179.

Chapter 7: Suffering with God

67. Annie Dillard, *For the Time Being* (New York: Alfred Knopf, 1999), 139–40.

68. The most definitive biography of Bonhoeffer's life was written by his former student and lifelong friend Eberhard Bethge. It has just been published in a new edition by Fortress Press: Eberhard Bethge, *Dietrich Bonhoeffer: A Biography*, rev. and ed. Victoria Barnett (Minneapolis: Fortress Press, 2000). The synopsis of his life comes from this source.

69. Dietrich Bonhoeffer, *Letters and Papers from Prison*, 4th ed., trans. Reginald Fuller, rev. by Frank Clark et al., additional trans. John Bowden for the enlarged edition (New York: Macmillan, 1975), 280–81.

70. Ibid., 281.

71. Ibid., 282.

72. Bethge, *Dietrich Bonhoeffer*, 873.

73. Francis Schüssler Fiorenza, "The Crisis of Hermeneutics and Christian Theology," in *Theology at the End of Modernity*, ed. Shelia Greeve Davaney (Philadelphia: Trinity Press International, 1991), 122.

74. Ibid., 131.

75. *Letters and Papers from Prison*, 360–61.

76. Bethge, *Dietrich Bonhoeffer*, 877.

77. *Letters and Papers from Prison*, 360–61.

78. Ibid., 381.
79. Ibid., 369–70.
80. Ibid., 391.
81. Ibid., 362.

Chapter 8: Tradition as Critique

82. E. L. Doctorow. *The City of God* (New York: Random House, 2000), 254.
83. Ibid., 34.
84. Ibid., 71.
85. Eberhard Busch, *Karl Barth: His Life from Letters and Autobiographical Texts,* trans. John Bowden (Philadelphia: Fortress Press, 1976), 247.
86. Ibid., 81.
87. Karl Barth, *The Epistle to the Romans,* trans. Edwyn C. Hoskyns (London: Oxford University Press, 1953), 10.
88. Peter Matheson, ed., *The Third Reich and the Christian Churches* (Grand Rapids, Mich.: Eerdmans, 1981), 4–6.
89. Clifford Green, ed., *Karl Barth: Theologian of Freedom* (London: Collins, 1989), 148.
90. Matheson, *The Third Reich,* 6.
91. Leonardo Boff, *Jesus Christ Liberator: A Critical Christology for Our Time,* trans. Patrick Hughes (Maryknoll, N.Y.: Orbis Books, 1978), 265.
92. See, for instance, Barth's remarks on Schleiermacher found in his *Protestant Thought: From Rousseau to Ritschl,* trans. Brian Cozers (New York: Simon and Schuster, 1969), 312, 344, 352.
93. Christopher Morse, *Not Every Spirit: A Dogmatics of Christian Disbelief* (Valley Forge, Pa.: Trinity Press International, 1994), 47.
94. Karl Barth, *The Word of God and the Word of Man,* trans. Douglas Horton (Boston: Pilgrim Press, 1928), 20.
95. Morse, *Not Every Spirit,* 30.

Chapter 9: Re-membering

96. Will Campbell, *Brother to a Dragonfly* (New York: Seabury Press, 1977), 222.
97. Fyodor Dostoyevsky, *The Brothers Karamozov,* trans. David McDuff (New York: Penguin Press, 1993), 296.

Index